Attention Deficit Hyperactivity Disorder (ADHD):
Research, Practice and Opinion

ADHD: Research, Practice and Opinion

PAUL COOPER PH.D.,
Cambridge University

and

KATHERINE BILTON ED.D.,
Educational Consultant, Tucson, Arizona, USA

W

WHURR PUBLISHERS
LONDON

British Library Cataloguing in Publication Data
A catalogue record for this book is available from the British Library.

ISBN 1 86156 108 3

Printed and bound in the UK by Athenaeum Press Ltd, Gateshead, Tyne & Wear.

Acknowledgements

·.

This book would not have been possible without the work and support of Dr Ved Varma.

Thanks also to Peggy Nunn for her unfailing and good humoured secretarial support

Royalties from the sale of this book will go to the Ronan ADHD Trust, a registered charity which provides support for young ADHD suffers.

Contents

The Contributors   ix

Part I   **1**

Understanding ADHD

Chapter 1   **3**

Making Sense of ADHD
Paul Cooper

Chapter 2   **14**

A Mother's Story – Beyond the Debate:
Living with the Reality of ADHD
'Ann Douglas'

Chapter 3   **28**

A Brother's Story – Through the Eye of the Storm
'Paul Douglas'

Chapter 4   **33**

Struggles with an Inebriated Horse: The Pain of Having ADHD
'Joseph Frank'

Part II   **41**

Supporting People with ADHD

Chapter 5   **43**

A Multi-Modal Approach to the Assessment
and Management of ADHD
Robert E. Detweiler, Andrew P. Hicks and Mack R. Hicks

Chapter 6   60

The Role of Medication in a Multi-Modal Approach
to the Management of ADHD
Geoff Kewley

Chapter 7   76

ADHD – A Different Viewpoint I: Dietary Factors
Joan Kinder

Chapter 8   111

ADHD – A Different Viewpoint II: Holistic and Other Approaches
Joan Kinder

Chapter 9   138

ADHD and Effective Learning: Principles and
Practical Approaches
Paul Cooper

Chapter 10   158

Cognitive Approaches to the Education and
Training of Children with ADHD
Égide Royer

Chapter 11   170

ADHD in the Classroom: A Teacher's Account
Jane Lovey

Part III   185

ADHD in Practice

Chapter 12   187

How Professionals Perceive ADHD
Lesley Hughes

Chapter 13   203

Teachers' Classroom Strategies for Dealing with
Students with ADHD: An Empirical Study
Samuel Daniel and Paul Cooper

Chapter 14   223

ADHD From the Inside: An Empirical Study of
Young People's Perceptions of the Experience of ADHD
Paul Cooper and Trevor Shea

Index   246

The Contributors

Paul Cooper is Lecturer in Education at the University of Cambridge.

Katherine Bilton is an independent educational consultant living and working in the USA.

Samuel Daniel teaches on the island of Anguilla.

'Ann Douglas' is the mother of two sons, one of whom has been diagnosed with ADHD.

'Paul Douglas' is the brother of an ADHD sufferer and was an undergraduate student at the time when he contributed to this volume.

Robert E. Detweiler is former headmaster of the Centre Academy in London.

'Joseph Frank' was a mature student at an English University and an ADHD sufferer.

Andrew P. Hicks is a Clinical Neuropsychologist and founder and Clinical Director of the Centre Academy in London.

Mack R. Hicks is a Clinical Neuropsychologist and founder and Director of the Centre Academy in London.

Lesley Hughes is a Lecturer in Health Studies at the University of Bradford.

Geoff Kewley is a Consultant Paediatrician and Director of the Learning and Assessment Centre, Crawley, Sussex.

Joan Kinder is a Consultant Paediatrician at Eastbourne General Hospital, Sussex.

Jane Lovey is a Research Associate at the University of Cambridge.

Égide Royer is Professor of Special Education at the University of Laval, Québec, Canada

Trevor Shea is a doctoral student at the University of Cambridge and a citizen of Canada.

Part I
Understanding ADHD

Chapter 1
Making Sense of ADHD

PAUL COOPER

This chapter explores the nature of attention deficit hyperactivity disorder (ADHD). The exploration begins with a description of the conventional medical approach to understanding ADHD and proceeds with an account of some of the scientific research that informs current conceptualizations of ADHD. The remainder of the chapter seeks to place this information in its broader social and cultural context by drawing attention to some of the ways in which ADHD is experienced daily by individuals with the condition.

The nature of ADHD

ADHD can be defined as a diagnosis of the American Psychiatric Association (1994) encompassing behavioural symptoms of inattention, impulsiveness and hyperactivity that significantly interfere with affected individuals' family and peer relationships as well as their educational and occupational functioning. The APA diagnosis divides ADHD into three subtypes: (1) the mainly hyperactive/impulsive subtype; (2) the mainly inattentive subtype; and (3) the combined subtype of hyperactive/impulsive/inattentive. Internationally, prevalence rates are conservatively estimated at between 3% and 6% among children from a wide variety of cultures and geographical regions, with boys outnumbering girls by 3:1 (Tannock, 1998). For many people, ADHD is a lifelong condition that places sufferers at high risk of such diverse problems as social isolation, motor accidents and psychological problems (Tannock, 1998). People with ADHD are often seen as incompetent, disorganized, aggressive, lazy, disruptive, untrustworthy, neglectful, selfish, accident prone, antisocial or asocial. Research suggests that children with ADHD are more likely than most to fail in school academically, in spite of the fact that they tend to score in the average to above average range on standardized ability tests (Hinshaw, 1994; Barkley, 1990). In the UK they are also more likely than most to be excluded from school for behavioural reasons (Hayden, 1997). Adults with a history of ADHD (or ADHD-type symptoms) are at greater risk than most of experiencing marital break-down (Hinshaw, 1994) and imprisonment (Farrington, 1990). Having said this, there are widely (even wildly) varying estimates claiming that between 30% and 70% of children and juveniles diagnosed with ADHD 'grow out' of the condition (Hinshaw, 1994). Some of the variation in these statistics can be accounted for by the fact that ADHD was considered a childhood disorder for many years, with the result that affected adults tended to be diagnosed with alternative 'adult' disorders, such as depression.

Although ADHD is a distinct clinical condition it is common for it to co-occur with one or more other emotional, behavioural or learning problems, such as Conduct Disorder, Oppositional Defiant Disorder, Anxiety Disorder and dyslexia. Although these 'co-morbid' conditions are often aetiologically distinct from ADHD, they may interact with the ADHD to create a distinctive set of problems (Tannock, 1998)

Theories of causation

There is a common view among authorities on ADHD (e.g. Tannock, 1998; Hinshaw, 1994), which is expressed succinctly by Barkley (1997: 29), that:

> the precise causes of ADHD are unknown at the present time, if by cause one means the direct, necessary, and sufficient events that immediately precede and directly lead to the creation of this behaviour pattern in children.

Having said this, ADHD has been for many years a focus for a consider-able amount of high-quality research, which has appeared in interna-tionally respected, peer-reviewed journals. A significant amount of this research has aimed at isolating the cause or causes of the condition. Tannock (1998), in a recent and authoritative review of international research on ADHD, identifies three major areas of theoretical explo-ration of this subject: cognitive research, neurobiological research and genetic research. What follows is a brief review of each of these areas.

Cognitive research

Cognitive research has increasingly focused on impulsiveness as the central feature of ADHD, and the possibility that a dysfunctional response inhibition system is the neuropsychological mechanism, located in the frontal lobes of the brain, underlying this problem. This means that children with ADHD are characterized by these researchers as experiencing significantly greater problems than most in inhibiting or delaying a behavioural response. The nature of the dysfunction in this system is described alternatively in terms of:

• underactivity, whereby the inhibitory control system has a tendency

not to become activated, whereas the behavioural activation system is
fully active;

or

- extreme slowness of the inhibitory control system, whereby the
individual responds to the impulse to act before the inhibitory system
has been fully activated.

Barkley (1997) proposes a different model, which suggests that neuro-
logically based problems of response inhibition lead directly to
problems in four major 'executive functions' of the brain that are essential for effective self-regulation. The first of Barkley's executive functions
is working memory, impairment of which makes it difficult for individuals to retain and manipulate information for purposes of appraisal and
planning. The second function is that of internalized speech. It is
suggested that self-control is exerted through a process of self-talk,
during which possible consequences and implications of impulses are
weighed up and internally 'discussed'. The third executive function is
that of motivational appraisal. This system, Barkley suggests, enables us
to make decisions by providing us with information about the emotional
associations generated by an impulse and the extent to which the
impulse is likely to produce outcomes we find desirable. The final executive function is that of reconstitution, or behavioural synthesis. The role
of this function is to enable us to plan new and appropriate behaviours
as an outcome of deconstructing and analysing past behaviours.

Another cognitive theory suggests that problems with inhibiting
responses are situation-specific and characterized chiefly by individuals'
'aversion to delay'. This severe impatience has been defined as an attitudinal characteristic (Sonuga-Barke et al., 1992) and more recently
described as arising from dysfunctions in temporal processing systems
(Sonuga-Barke et al., 1996). An important difference between these two
explanations for 'aversion to delay' is that the former attitudinal explanation contrasts with other, neurobiologically rooted, explanations by
implying the possibility of a much greater role for socialization in the
development of the problem. The temporal dysfunction explanation, on
the other hand, conforms to the more usual neurobiological accounts.

A different theory, of causation, prominent in the work of Dutch
researchers, is a 'cognitive-energetic' model of ADHD (Sergeant, 1995;
Van der Meere, 1996). This approach places the emphasis on dysfunctions of the so-called 'energetic' or 'state' mechanisms, which are
hypothesized to influence the speed and accuracy with which the brain
activates the response processes that deal with sensory stimuli.

It should be stressed that these models apply almost exclusively to
the hyperactive/impulsive and combined subtypes of ADHD. The mainly
inattentive subtype is believed to be caused by impairments in individuals' speed of information processing and their ability to focus or select
the object for their attention. This contrasts with the impulsive/

hyperactive and combined subtypes, which are believed to be under-pinned by more fundamental problems that cause the regulatory functions to fail (Barkley, 1997).

Neuroimaging research

Although there is a variety of cognitive theories of ADHD, most of these theories are based on the assumption that the cognitive dysfunctions are underpinned by neurological problems (Tannock, 1998). The basis for this assumption can be traced through a long line of research dating from the early years of the twentieth century, which repeatedly indicates close similarities between the symptoms of ADHD and those produced by injuries to the frontal lobes and, in particular, the prefrontal cortex of the brain (Barkley, 1997; Hinshaw, 1994). Other research has suggested a link between neurological damage affecting this part of the brain as a result of toxin exposure and ADHD-type symptoms (Barkley, 1997). Authorities suggest that whereas recent research has added support to the neurological aspects of ADHD, such research is far from conclusive, and has been at times inconsistent in its findings. Barkley (1997: 32) expresses the need for caution in this regard when he states that:

> far more research is needed before we can be as sanguine about the biological nature of ADHD as we might like to be.

This view is supported by other authorities (such as Tannock, 1998; British Psychological Society, 1996; Hinshaw, 1994). It is also important to point out that research on ADHD that has employed modern neuroimaging techniques, such as computerized transaxial tomography (CT), magnetic resonance imaging (MRI) and electroencephalography (EEG), has been limited. For example Tannock (1998) reports that there were only 14 published MRI studies of ADHD, involving a total of 378 children with ADHD and 295 normal peers. Eleven of the 14 studies were investigations based on studies of samples generated in one of only three main studies.

With the above qualifications in mind, experts conclude, on the basis of existing neuroimaging research, that individuals with ADHD sometimes exhibit abnormalities in the development of certain brain regions. In particular these studies show that individuals with ADHD tend to have smaller structures in those regions of the brain, particularly the striatal regions, which control movement and behaviour (Tannock, 1998; Barkley, 1997). These findings, however, like EEG studies, leave us with a great many unanswered questions. The main problem is that the studies do not show a direct link between the brain abnormalities and ADHD. What they do indicate is that these abnormalities have been found to commonly co-occur with ADHD. Barkley (1997) is able to identify only one study which begins to suggest a causal link. This study, by Castellanos et al. (1996) of 57 boys with ADHD and 55 boys without

ADHD (aged between five and 18) found a direct relationship between the size of some of the brain regions investigated and degree of ADHD-related impairment. This was demonstrated by correlating the variation in size with variations in performance on a laboratory test of response inhibition. This is an important finding, but one study of 57 boys with ADHD does not amount to solid generalizable proof of a hypothesis. The neurological basis for ADHD, therefore, remains an interesting and promising hypothesis that is as yet unconfirmed.

As Barkley (1997) notes, the neuroimaging studies find no evidence of brain damage. The characteristics identified, therefore, are thought to be the product of abnormal neurological development of unknown cause. One of the richest areas that has been and continues to be explored for such causes is that of genetics.

Genetic research

There are two major approaches to establishing whether or not a condition has a genetic component. The first examines the frequency with which a condition occurs among family members. The second involves the study of twins. Tannock (1998) reports that there is strong evidence from studies that have been carried out over the past 30 years that ADHD is more common in the biological relatives of children with ADHD than it is in the biological relatives of children who do not have ADHD. The problem with these studies is that it is difficult to control for environmental factors that family members often share and that may influence the development of ADHD-type behaviours. This problem is addressed through twin and adoption studies, which have repeatedly shown a much greater incidence of ADHD among identical (monozygotic) twins than among non-identical (dizygotic) twins. Similarly, studies that compare the incidence of ADHD among children and parents who are biologically related with that of children and parents where the child is adopted have tended to support the heredity argument (Tannock, 1998).

These findings are given further weight by molecular genetic research that has identified certain genes as being implicated in the etiology of ADHD and ADHD-type symptoms. In particular there is evidence that genes in the dopamine system are implicated in ADHD (Tannock, 1998). Dopamine is a neurotransmitter which is found in systems of the brain concerned with, among other things, the regulation of movement (Thompson, 1993).

The biopsychosocial perspective

As the foregoing review illustrates, ADHD is likely to involve an intricate interplay between complex human systems. The above evidence suggests that the individual with ADHD responds to the world in ways that are different from the general population. The consistency and pervasiveness of these behaviours is taken to imply that individuals with ADHD experience the world differently; that is, they have different ways of processing and responding to the external world at the level of their cognitive processes. The apparent level of resistance of these patterns of response to external influence, in the form of normal behavioural correction of the type practised by successful teachers and parents, is taken to imply deeper structural underpinnings to these cognitive problems. This leads researchers to the brain and an exploration of the neurological structures that regulate cognitive functions. The evidence for the relationship between neurological abnormalities and ADHD is difficult to interpret (Tannock, 1998) but there is a small amount of reliable evidence to support an association between neurological abnor-malities and ADHD. Interestingly, the neurological abnormalities can be related to some of the cognitive theories of ADHD. The fact that the neurological evidence most commonly appears to implicate abnormal brain development rather than brain injury justifies the increasing interest in familial and chemical genetic studies of ADHD. Again, these studies appear promising in that both familial and chemical studies suggest that ADHD can be transmitted from one generation to another.

The above account illustrates that one of the shared limitations of the dominant research approaches to ADHD is their tendency to focus the search for explanations of the condition on within-person factors. That is to say that all of the approaches described above assume that a major reason why individuals with ADHD behave as they do is located within the individual who bears the ADHD diagnosis. There is a peculiar, if predictable, circularity to this state of affairs, which can be expressed in terms of the following propositions:

- ADHD is a medical diagnosis;
- clearly, medical diagnoses are always applied to individuals;
- therefore, ADHD must best be understood through an exploration of the characteristics of individuals.

Writers of texts on ADHD remind us, ad nauseam, that it is the British physician George Still's paper in the *Lancet* (Still, 1902), nearly 100 years ago, that marks the beginning of the modern era of ADHD. Over the years the diagnosis has been refined considerably, with extensive changes being made to theories of its nature and etiology. What we now know as ADHD has been known over the years by many different names. Since the 1960s alone it has been successively termed minimal brain damage, hyperactive child syndrome and attention deficit disorder (Barkley, 1990).

Throughout this period, however, there has been an at times fierce debate about the legitimacy of the fundamental validity of medical concepts of this kind. Critiques from different disciplines and cultures have argued that explanations for emotional and behavioural problems, such as ADHD, which place strong emphasis on 'within child' (biological) factors, are merely convenient labels that are used to cover up the true, social causes of these problems. This view is articulated by Slee (1995: 74) when he writes:

> The monism of locating the nature of disruption in the neurological infrastructure of the child is myopic and convenient. As complex sites of interaction on a range of levels, classrooms provide opportunity for dyfunction across a number of fronts [. . .] the search for institutional dysfunction is ignored by the diagnostician's probes. ADDs [sic] simply refines and extends the individualising and depoliticizing of disruption in schools.

Slee has a point. To automatically assume that an individual's behavioural problems are a product of characteristics within the individual would be very misguided. Such assumptions would inevitably lead to a misdiagnosis of the nature of problems in many instances. In turn, such misdiagnosis would disadvantage individuals whose behaviour was the product of unsympathetic or harmful environmental conditions. On the other hand, in the face of a growing body of evidence in support of the contention that there are systematic differences of a neuropsychological nature between persons with ADHD and persons who do not have ADHD, it would seem ill-advised to automatically dismiss the validity of the ADHD diagnosis in all cases.

Unfortunately, there has been and continues to be a destructive tendency which encourages an unhelpful polarization of views of ADHD (Cooper, 1997). In particular there is a tendency to see ADHD as a set of problems that are induced by biological factors *or* as problems that are generated by the environment. This crude nature-versus-nurture argument contributes virtually nothing either to our understanding of ADHD or our understanding of emotional and behavioural problems in general. It does, however, tell us a lot about the tribalism of competing disciplines and professions (see Chapter 12).

This situation is compounded by the fact that researchers, including many of those whose work was considered earlier in this chapter, have tended to focus their research on single factors in the etiology of ADHD, such as neurological structures or cognitive processes or the genetic pathways (Tannock, 1998). This is in spite of the fact that many of these same researchers would claim to view ADHD as a biopsychosocial problem (for example Barkley, 1990; 1997) – that is, a problem that has a biological element to it, but that interacts with psychosocial factors in the individual's social, cultural and physical environment. Clearly, once we recognize this consensus view we find that simplistic nature versus nurture arguments are untenable.

Interestingly, we have to look outside the realms of ADHD research for a model that will help us to understand the way in which biopsychosocial factors might interact. Frith (1992) offers a model of developmental disorders (for example, autism) that describes biological causes leading to cognitive deficits, which then lead to behavioural manifestations (such as the behavioural symptoms of autism). The extent, and indeed to some degree the nature, of the behavioural manifestations are influenced by a set of social and psychological factors, namely experience, maturation, compensation and motivation. Thus the extent to which neurological problems result in behavioural and social dysfunction will be influenced by the individual's learning and experience, which may, for example, give the individual skills which enable him or her to compensate for cognitive deficits, or provide the individual with a high or low degree of motivation, which in turn will affect his or her ability to cope. Clearly, the severity of the initial biological problem will vary, as will the nature of the individual's experience and environment. Thus in some cases biology will be more dominant than environment in the etiology of the disorder whereas, in others, environment will be more dominant than biology. Given that biology is heavily implicated in most prominent theories of the nature of ADHD, although its precise function is still being debated, it seems only sensible to take the biopsychosocial perspective and recognize that in a given case it will always be very difficult to tease out the biological and psychosocial strands.

With regard to experiential aspects of ADHD, there has been research that has identified patterns of parental behaviour that have been related directly to childhood ADHD. For example, Barkley (1990) in a review of research on this topic, refers to studies that show that children with ADHD tend to experience a high level of interpersonal conflict with their parents. Furthermore, the mothers of children with ADHD have been found to be more commanding and negative towards their children than the parents of children who do not have ADHD. Barkley cites further evidence which shows that children with ADHD tend to experience more commanding and negative responses from adults and children from outside the family (such as teachers and peers) and that, when children with ADHD are placed on medication, the mothers' levels of disapproval and frequency of commands decrease. He concludes from this that it is the child's ADHD that precedes the parents' negative behaviour rather than the other way around. This is the basis for the important claim that bad parenting or ineffective teaching do not in themselves cause ADHD. What does seem to be the case, however, is that the kinds of interactions that children with ADHD experience do have an effect on the way in which their ADHD manifests itself, and in some cases the extent to which it is seriously or not-so-seriously debilitating or disruptive.

Recently published research by Nigg and Hinshaw (1998), which examines the relationship between parents' personality traits and childhood ADHD, provides interesting findings that may bring us closer to an understanding of the way in which the biological, psychological and social factors interact. Principally, their carefully designed study found an association between specific parental characteristics and the nature and manifestations of children's problems. Children with ADHD were found to be more likely to have a mother with marked anxiety symptoms or one who had experienced a recent major depressive episode than children not diagnosed with ADHD. Children who exhibited ADHD co-occurring with conduct disorder and oppositional defiant disorder had fathers who scored lower on measures of 'agreeableness' and higher on measures of 'neuroticism' (on a personality inventory) than fathers in the comparison group. Thus, this study indicates that the extent to which a child with ADHD exhibits seriously antisocial behaviour is influenced by the characteristics of parents.

Clearly, the evidence just presented might be interpreted through a biomedical/genetic model and it might be suggested that the children inherit antisocial characteristics from their parents. This suggestion, however, has to be taken alongside the well-established research tradition that places considerable emphasis on psychosocial factors as being chiefly implicated in the etiology of anxiety disorders, with some – though at present limited – evidence of heritability (Mills, 1996). Where oppositional defiant disorder is concerned, Blau (1996) reports that environmental explanations are the most persuasive. Common to both oppositional defiant disorder and anxiety disorders is the implication that dysfunctions in the parent–child bonding process are significant factors in creating difficulties, causing affected children to find themselves trapped at the stage of infant dependency, sometimes into their adolescence and beyond.

The need for an holistic approach to ADHD

As the foregoing indicates, ADHD is a complex phenomenon that can be understood in different ways. The emphasis of much of this chapter has been on the role of biomedical and psychological research in shaping our understanding. These are important perspectives that will continue to develop as more research is carried out. As has been noted already, it is hoped that these different approaches to research will move beyond the current tendency to restrict studies to the exploration of single factors and concentrate attention on interactions between different factors.

In addition to the understandings that can come from sometimes abstract and reductionist research, however, it is important that we do not lose sight of the human dimension. It is very easy for professionals and academics to become lost in the mire of argument and to forget that the concepts being discussed relate directly to the lives of living people. For this reason we need to include within our holistic approach to understanding ADHD a willingness to listen to the voices of those who, in one way or another, live with the daily reality of what some people call ADHD. It is not necessarily the case that these voices are more important, in terms of their contribution to our understanding of ADHD, than the research perspectives already mentioned. What is clear is that these voices have things to tell us that are not made available to us through conventional scientific research channels. Perhaps more than anything these voices bring images of living, breathing people to us, and so remind us that whatever value there is in a concept such as ADHD, it is best judged on the basis of the extent to which it has the potential to contribute to positive human growth.

This book

This book offers an exploration of ADHD. The exploration is guided by the recognition that ADHD is multi-dimensional. The book is presented in full recognition of the fact that there are many different and important perspectives on this subject. These differing perspectives are not always as compatible with one another as we would wish. For this reason during the course of this book the reader may well encounter apparently contradictory views. Where this is so, the authors are simply reflecting the range and complexity of views of ADHD.

The intention of the book is to present an honest appraisal of some of the key issues that are at the heart of the ADHD debate. The book, therefore, considers issues of professional practice in terms of the assessment, diagnosis and management of ADHD, from both medical and educational perspectives. Many of these chapters are written by practitioners, each of whom has his or her own perspective rooted in daily practice and opinions. Other chapters relating to these themes are more concerned with presenting current research and theory in an attempt to indicate possible directions for current and future practice. Central to this book, however, are the voices of individuals who have first-hand experience of ADHD – not as a professional interest, but as a central aspect of their personal lives. The most unique contributions to this book are those that are written as first-hand accounts of the personal experience of living with ADHD.

The book is presented, then, as a collection of writings dealing at different times with professional practice, personal opinion and systematic research in relation to ADHD. The book is rooted in the conviction that these different sources of knowledge are each vital to a rounded understanding of the nature of ADHD and the challenges it presents. No one of these perspectives is alone more valuable than each of the others, and each perspective is equally indispensable. The aim of this book is not to convince the reader that a single view of ADHD is the most valid, but rather, to provide information and insights that thoughtful and critical readers will use to inform their own thinking about this complex issue.

References

American Psychiatric Association (APA) (1994) Diagnostic and Statistical Manual of Mental Disorders (4 edn). Washington DC: APA.

Barkley R (1990) ADHD: A Handbook for Diagnosis and Treatment. New York: Guilford.

Barkley R (1997) ADHD and the Nature of Self Control. New York: Guilford.

Blau B (1996) Oppositional defiant disorder. In G Blau, T Gullotta (eds) Adolescent Dysfunctional Behavior. Thousand Oaks CA, London and New Delhi: Sage.

British Psychological Society (BPS) (1996) ADHD: A Psychological Response to an Evolving Concept. Leicester: BPS.

Castellanos F, Giedd J, Marsh W, Hamburger S, Vaituzis A, Dickstein D, Sarfatti S, Vauss Y, Snell J, Lange N, Kaysen D, Krain A, Ritchie G, Rajapakse J, Rapoport J (1996) Quantitative brain magnetic resonance imaging in attention deficit hyperactivity disorder. Archives of General Psychiatry 53: 607–16.

Cooper P (1997) Biology, behaviour and education: ADHD and the bio-psycho-social perspective. Educational and Child Psychology 14(1): 31–8.

Farrington D (1990) Implications of criminal career research for the prevention of offending. The Journal of Adolescence 13: 93–113.

Frith U (1992) Cognitive development and cognitive deficit. The Psychologist 5: 13–19.

Hayden C (1997) Exclusion from primary school: children in need and children with special educational need. Emotional and Behavioural Difficulties 2(3): 36–44.

Hinshaw S (1994) Attention Deficits and Hyperactivity in Children. London, New York, New Delhi: Sage.

Mills H (1996) Anxiety disorders. In G Blau, T Gullotta (eds) Adolescent Dysfunctional Behavior. Thousand Oaks CA, London, New Delhi: Sage.

Nigg J, Hinshaw S (1998) Parent personality traits and psychopathology associated with antisocial behaviors in childhood ADHD. Journal of Child Psychology and Psychiatry 39(2): 145–59.

Sergeant J (1995) Hyperkinetic disorder revisited. In J Sergeant (ed.) Eunythydis: European Approaches to Hyperkinetic Disorder. Amsterdam: Sergeant.

Slee R (1995) Changing Theories and Practices of Discipline. London: Falmer.

Sonuga-Barke E, Taylor E, Hepenstall E (1992) Hyperactivity and delay aversion II: the effects of self versus externally imposed stimulus presentation periods on memory. Journal of Child Psychology and Psychiatry 33: 399–409.

Sonuga-Barke E, Williams E, Hall M, Saxton T (1996) Hyperactivity and delay aversion III: the effects on cognitive style of imposing delay after errors. Journal of Child Psychology and Psychiatry 37: 189–94.

Still G (1902) Some abnormal psychical conditions in children. The Lancet 1: 1008–12, 1077–82, 1163–8.

Tannock R (1998) ADHD: advances in cognitive, neurobiological and genetic research. Journal of Child Psychology and Psychiatry 39(1): 65–99.

Thompson R (1993) The Brain: A Neuroscience Primer (2 edn). New York: Freeman.

Van der Meere J (1996) The role of attention. In S Sandberg (ed.) Monographs in Child and Adolescent Psychiatry: Hyperactivity Disorders of Childhood. Cambridge: Cambridge University Press.

Chapter 2
A Mother's Story – Beyond the Debate: Living with the Reality of ADHD

'ANNE DOUGLAS'

While many professionals and non-professionals alike continue to debate the existence of ADHD – and thus hold sufferers and their families to ransom – vital recognition and understanding of the reality of the condition and its disabling effects are further hindered.

There are a lot of myths and a great deal of misinformation surrounding ADHD and its management, often perpetuated by the media and those in positions of authority. Sadly, this is often the only 'information' they have and this prevents many sufferers from obtaining appropriate assessment and treatment. ADHD – or whatever one wishes to call it – is a very real condition. I now realize that I have lived with it for much of my life – as a daughter, sister, mother and aunt, although it is my experience as a mother that has enabled me to fully appreciate the reality of this grossly misunderstood and handicapping condition from all perspectives.

It is, I suppose, only human nature to take everything at face value. The more obvious symptoms of ADHD, all too clear to the sceptical and judgemental eye, encourage trite and simplistic explanation. Indeed, in the past, I too was guilty of forming opinions without an awareness of deeper issues. However, the worry and pain of watching one's loved child struggle with the effects of untreated ADHD has shown me that there is often more behind many seemingly everyday situations than meets the eye.

By chance some years ago, an unexpected turn of events led me to become involved in helping children, their parents and professionals in unravelling the facts and traumas of ADHD. My personal experience of the condition and that of so many others has given me great insight and objectivity in appreciating the encompassing problems of ADHD, while maintaining a balanced stance.

Tom: the early years

The first of my two sons, Tom, came into the world angry and demanding from the start. He was a very fretful baby, crying most of the time, day and night. He was unrelaxed and nothing seemed to soothe or pacify him. Life soon became one round of racing against the clock to get essential chores done to the constant accompaniment of screaming. It soon became obvious that his behaviour – even at so young an age – was different from that of other babies I knew and it never seemed to change as he began to mature. Unlike most other children, he never seemed to enjoy being cuddled. We began to feel we were on a treadmill, our lives dictated to by this small being who never seemed satisfied with anything. Health checks showed nothing obviously abnormal and a wealth of helpful suggestions from friends and relations only served to demoralize us further as we had usually tried everything – and nothing worked. When other babies were cooing and gurgling in their cots or prams, he would become more and more frustrated and indignant at being there, showing fleeting interest in the toys or outside distractions. Attempts at consoling him were unsuccessful. Even when he had our attention, it was never right or enough. It became clear that he seemed to have a very low tolerance for frustration, stress and boredom, with a short attention span. Very few things appealed to him and we endlessly tried to think of something new to amuse him. Once he could crawl, he wanted to walk and when he was walking he wanted to run – but at full speed all the time. When thwarted there were major tantrums. He struggled and screamed if it was necessary to put him into a pram or pushchair and couldn't bear to be restricted. How well I recall my embarrassment and desperate struggles to contain my hyperactive child in public places – dismay and judgement reflected in the faces of those around me. Shopping trips were a nightmare as he constantly raced around and disappeared from sight as he resisted attempts at putting him in reins. He wanted instant gratification and was rapidly and relentlessly into everything, despite consistent attempts to stop or distract him. He never seemed to learn from his mistakes and no amount of reproval made any difference. It began to seem that he really didn't care about anything except himself and it was impossible to do anything other than try to control his behaviour rather than enjoy him. Well-meaning friends tried to comfort me, remarking that it was 'what boys are like', he was 'just a handful', he 'would grow out of it' and so on. Social visits were a nightmare as he constantly touched everything and demanded attention, was never satisfied with new toys or new people and was always dashing around at lightning speed with no sense of danger. Bumps and bruises became the norm as he often fell and hurt himself, howling with rage if anyone tried to intervene. One simply had to have eyes everywhere and could never relax for a moment or enjoy normal everyday activities. The days always began as soon as he was awake and we never had a chance to collect ourselves before the onslaught of demands began once again. He could never amuse himself for more than a few moments and even the most interesting toys failed to capture his attention for long. He demanded to be played with all the time and required a high level of persistent stimulation. It was a matter of trying to keep several steps ahead all the time to try to avoid having to resort to crisis management of his insatiable demands.

He obviously had amazingly high energy levels. Before visiting anyone it was necessary to take him for a long walk to burn off some of the excess energy in the hope that it would make him a little calmer. It never seemed to make any difference. I recall one such day, when he was four years old. Whereas many of his peers were still in pushchairs, he took a three-mile walk in the snow in his stride and was less tired than his father who took him! Needless to say, with each day the same as the one before, week in week out, I was perpetually exhausted and had little opportunity to think or recharge my batteries or to get away from the relentless strain. It was necessary to be at least 100% fit and well to have the physical and emotional energy to cope with my loved child, who seemed increasingly like a runaway train. I began to dread being unwell as no one was prepared to look after or babysit for him because he was so exhausting and a liability.

Just hyperactive!

I particularly remember a lengthy wait at my doctor's surgery, when my then 18-month-old son incessantly raced round the waiting room oblivious to my desperate attempts to keep him calm and occupied. I mentioned that he was a very active, difficult and defiant child, faintly hoping for some understanding and support. However, the doctor's casual remark that he was 'just hyperactive' failed to appreciate the significance of this extreme behaviour and he offered no further suggestion. I came away feeling further demoralized. Life continued to become more and more stressful as Tom increasingly seemed to be impervious to any form of discipline, did not learn from his mistakes, was possessive and overcompetitive, unable to share, volatile and quarrelled with friends. His only love was sport but even that always ended in rage or tantrums when things didn't go right. When he did find something that interested him he would become over-focused, intense and insist on a game being played endlessly. Cooperation was just not possible as, with him, it was all or nothing.

By this time, I was experiencing a sinking feeling that we could not enjoy our own child, added to growing demoralization and exhaustion, and I began to doubt my ability as a parent. All the usual disciplining strategies failed to have any effect on our son and he always seemed to want something more.

A playmate

The arrival of his brother a few years later, who appeared to develop and behave more appropriately, increased our growing sense of worry about

Tom's behaviour. By this time, it was also apparent that our 'whirlwind' was standing out as different from his peer group. His demanding and difficult-to-satisfy personality continued to make both his and our friend-ships/relationships fraught. Indeed, I became increasingly isolated and lonely, wondering where I was going wrong. I felt in need of support and some respite and that there was never a let-up or a moment of peace and quiet. I felt deprived of adult company and imprisoned by my unrewarding and exhausting daily existence. However, it was obvious that my participation in toddler clubs, coffee mornings and so forth would mean constant supervision of Tom to prevent him hurling toys at or disrupting other children and conversation would be impossible. Indeed, even attempts at telephone conversations at home were fraught with trauma as he repeatedly interrupted even the briefest call.

I read all the child development and parenting books I could get my hands on, desperately try to find better ways of managing and loving Tom, but our relationship was becoming very stressed as he constantly confronted and defied and was resistant to any attempts to improve the situation, no matter how hard one tried. Although I always seized any opportunity to praise Tom for 'good' behaviour or endeavours, these rarely occurred and could never be built on when they did. Each everyday day task was an uphill struggle. Family mealtimes became an endurance exercise as he strenuously resisted certain foods, regularly causing friction with his continuous verbal and physical defiance and non-conformity, always hypersensitive to others' conversation, noises, actions or movements. He would only use a specific mug, cup, plate or spoon, etc. and became quite hysterical if he could not do this. He would only sit on a particular chair and threw enormous tantrums if this was not possible. He was unable to concentrate on watching television unless such things as ornaments on the periphery of his vision were removed. One Christmas a bunch of balloons was unsuspectingly hung above the television and upset him very much. There were – and still are – certain items and colours of clothing that he refused to wear, in partic-ular shirts/ties or polo-necked sweaters. As he grew older, he began carelessly cutting labels out of his clothes as he could not tolerate them against his skin. I had not appreciated the extent of the obsessions until both boys were awaiting their photograph to be taken just before a family christening. Tom, aged four, had been unwillingly dressed in a loose, casual T-shirt with a collar and buttons. He became increasingly difficult and in one swift and intolerant action, ripped at the collar wrenching off the buttons, complete with chunks of the material!

Frustration bred more frustration but I increasingly blamed myself for the way he was, feeling I must be a bad mother, despite being told I was very tolerant, warm and caring. I was unable to reach my child and yet was always there for him, trying to understand his needs. I began to realize that he didn't seem to have a conscience and nothing stirred feelings of compassion, yet he was not an aggressive child, except when under stress. Rather, he was very easily frustrated with low tolerance and lacking in sensitivity to others. He was increasingly single-minded. He would never accept the restrictions of the word 'no'. However, his growing oppositionality meant that it was a frequently used word in his own vocabulary.

Playgroup and junior school years

At playgroup I was told that Tom was there for the 'social side' and was very active, rarely engaging in any task or completing it. At school, he was sociable but gave up easily when things were difficult. From an early age it was felt he had the potential to do better and was just lazy, disorganised, forgetful and easily distracted. He was always easily upset and angry but there were never tears – only tantrums. His reaction to events and situations at home and school was increasingly hypersensitive and life was like walking on eggshells.

I was encouraged to believe that Tom would gradually grow out of the behaviour and conform as he matured and settled down. While our friends were able to relax and enjoy their weekends and family holidays, for us they were becoming a regular nightmare. Having exhausted all the activity options at home, the only way to survive weekends was to arrange regular, stimulating outings to save our sanity. Needless to say, these were marked by tantrums and insatiable demands with little enjoyment for anybody. As Tom burned off some of his hyperactivity, we were left feeling drained and in a vicious circle. No matter what sort of outings and holidays might have been appropriate for his brother or us, it was essential to seek something that would primarily provide entertainment for Tom. Every holiday had memories of confrontations and the inability to relax as we tried to find a happy medium and address the needs of everyone. No one could really understand why we seemed to return from holidays as stressed as we were before we went but there were so many places we just could not contemplate. (At the age of 17, Tom refused to take part in family holidays any more and we were faced with yet another dilemma. He insisted on staying at home, while refusing to co-operate in any arrangements for his well being and responsibility for the house while we were away. Hence, our need to have a break was always significantly tempered – for me anyway – with worry about his activities and welfare both in and out of the house in our absence.)

As the boys grew up, their attempts at playing together were always marked by quarrels and cries, as Tom was possessive of toys and over-competitive in games. He always had to have his own way and dominated events and it was always necessary to intervene to try to regain a sense of fair play. Even as teenagers, one was very reluctant to leave them alone together for too long in order to go out. Tom's intolerance and impulsivity meant that invariably there would be a major confrontation with worrying consequences. Friends thought us overprotective when we were loathe to leave the boys alone together as they grew older but we found ourselves in a catch 22 situation – they were too old for babysitters but Tom was too immature and unpredictable to behave responsibly. Any social life was very difficult.

Secondary school/further education

By puberty, things were rapidly getting worse as relationships both at home and school were very strained. Life was one round of arguments and tantrums from morning to night – only with more damaging effects. Tom also seemed to gain enjoyment from goading people, mostly close family members, never knowing when to stop and not satisfied until he had pushed them to the limits. The harder one tried to ignore this, the more he would try to do it. We were at our wits' end and desperate to know where to turn for help, while feeling too ashamed to expose our apparent inability to bring up our child appropriately. Every parents' evening told stories of poor compliance, shoddy and incomplete work, class clowning, no homework, incessant talking, and how he would be easily distracted and distract others. At that time, a tutor told me that he felt Tom was 'different' from his peers. When I remarked that I felt that Tom didn't seem to understand cause and effect, his somewhat patronizing retort was that 'at 13 years of age of course he does'. No amount of encouragement, incentive, praise or reward made any difference as he would say 'I don't want a reward because I won't do it anyway'. It became hard to believe that his actions weren't deliberately intended to annoy. Varying degrees of reward/punishment failed to motivate him to improve his ways. Far from having the desired effect, Tom often seemed to view punishment as a challenge to beat. Teachers clearly looked to us as parents to improve the situation and obviously questioned our discipline. When he came out of the restrictions of a school day, he would unleash all his frustrations and pent up energy at home. Increasingly, we realized that Tom had little perception of how his verbally and physically impulsive behaviour affected others. He was extremely volatile and easily roused to anger when things didn't go his way but, once forgotten, he failed to appreciate the effect his reactions had on those around him. It has proved fruitless trying to rationalize or reason with him as he has a tendency to see everything in black or white and have the last word. His GCSE results were, of course, disappointing, but it was with mutual relief that he managed to achieve a few pass grades on a second attempt and go on to further education. However, the lack of structure and demands on him for deadlines for assignments, further reading/research meant that he struggled to maintain effort or interest. Although finally scraping a further qualification, clearly studying had been a burden and had no interest for him.

Increasing problems

I had never admitted Tom's problems to anyone. Relationships with the extended family have been fraught with tension and embarrassment with overt and implied criticism from some members that we were just not being firm enough with Tom – with little understanding of our despair and distress. Loving grandparents have been denied the joy of that special and unique relationship with a grandchild. Tom does not know what he has been missing. Of course, the relentless strain and worry was taking its toll on me as life was just a downward spiral of arguments, lack of co-operation and defiance with little to share and enjoy. I knew that I had tried everything imaginable and more and couldn't give up, but that his brother was different and so were other children. Having another child – to whom we were the same parents – who appeared to act in an age-appropriate manner helped to keep a sense of perspective, although it didn't help the nagging worry and sadness at all Tom was missing.

Increasingly, the moment Tom appeared, we would all unconsciously become tense, waiting for the inevitable arguments and demands to begin, feeling defeated before we started. Regularly, we felt the discomfort of guilt at the relief that flowed over us when he went out – knowing that we were nevertheless concerned about his welfare. He has always resisted the courtesy of telling us where he is going or of respecting any 'house rules' that we have tried to implement and comes back when it suits him – angry and indignant at our intrusion into what he sees as his privacy. It has never been possible to hold a conversation unless it was one of the few subjects that caught his interest and even then, if one said the wrong thing, he would erupt and storm off. His impulsivity and intolerance often leads him to misinterpret our caring words and actions, which he readily perceives as patronizing. Mornings, in particular, were – and still remain – a problem and one interacts with Tom at one's peril. He is invariably particularly ill-humoured, predictably unpredictable, volatile and definitely best avoided! He has shown little interest in other people's lives, 'switching off' because he found them boring. Increasingly, his poor self-control meant that he developed an impulsive repertoire of bad language, which he uses when thwarted, and he is frequently adept at aversive techniques to discourage interactions for which he has no time. His relationships tend to be shallow and fleeting.

He does not know the joy of finding companionship in another or of feeling loved and feels no need to show it. He does not seem to have the ability to care deeply about anything and resents attempts to encourage motivation or what he perceives as any interference in his life. He is a master of manipulation, which invariably gets him his own way and is very plausible. Relationships and jobs have no more than passing attraction for him. He lives life on the surface, needing constant stimulation and occupation and remains more immature than his peers in all situations. Yet underneath it all, I sense there is someone longing to be more 'normal' and find his direction in life. When he does feel a transient need to communicate – always on his terms – one can see the lost soul behind all the layers of chaos. Never is it so important to be there – listening, talking, sharing and loving – before the moment is lost again and the mutual frustration of the status quo returns.

He is unable to manage money – it has no meaning to him and metaphorically slips through his fingers in a moment – impulsively spending and running up debts that he cannot repay as he cannot maintain motivation or interest in anything for long. He lives in the 'here and now' with no thought for the future. Although he requires a high level of stimulation and activity, his interests remain insular and he dislikes change. No attempt at loving support makes the slightest difference as he spurns everything, putting off until 'another time', continuing to dictate the terms of others' existence, unable and unwilling to take responsibility for anything – unless it suits him – and his own worst enemy.

He leaves a trail of chaos in the home as he is thinking of the next thing he wants to do before he has executed the previous task. Hence, things dropped are left where they fall, he ploughs through his meals at breakneck speed scattering and spilling food; tops are left off tubes, bottles, jars, tins; his hasty and impulsive actions often result in broken and damaged items; his bedroom has to be seen to be believed, where all his possessions – clean or otherwise – cover the floor and every available surface, together with food remains, dirty crockery and cutlery, important documents, muddy football boots, etc. The disorganization and chaos is unimaginable but the layers just keep growing and he regularly invites friends to sit in there or occasionally throw a mattress down on top of it all and stay the night! Such is the chaos of his disorganized mind with its poor concentration, short-term memory problems and impulsivity. Needless to say, possessions are regularly lost or mislaid and he finds it very difficult to keep to time. He quickly loses interest in activities. No attempt can encourage him to hold on to the moment. Such is his impulsivity and haphazard existence that anything that takes time is dismissed and the easiest route is taken to achieve what is necessary. Shopping is too time-consuming and boring and he has little interest in clothes. Hence, he soon discovered that helping himself to his brother's and even some of his father's clothes satisfied his immediate needs – the resultant discord carelessly ignored and disregarded as he proceeds to lose or spoil many of them and repeat the process. For many years, we have endlessly had to evolve new techniques to combat his impulsive tendencies to help himself to food and others' possessions in the home, often to the significant detriment of the family. His inability to consider the consequences of his actions has driven us all to lock and hide such things away – only to discover that, being thwarted, made him all the more determined to track them down. No amount of retribution has any effect. His impulsiveness adds to his tendency to ignore the rights of other family members or friends, and he is oblivious to the concept of give and take or sharing. He simply does not seem able to care as he has had what he needed and for him the moment has gone. Impulsively he 'borrows' money from family members without their agreement because he needs to go out somewhere to stave off the endless boredom he feels. His oppositionality – and having probably genuinely forgotten in many cases that he has borrowed or taken anything – means that no amount of coaxing or cajoling encourages its return. Fortunately, he has always managed to retain a sense of law and order outside the home. He is often drawn to similarly immature friends with a weak and easy-going disposition but whom he can dominate.

A mother's despair

As I see Tom's life story unfolding on paper, I am filled with an even greater sense of worry and fear for his future. His greatest strength is plausibility and superficial confidence and, despite everything, he has a basically gentle temperament. Despite his problems, he can impress people with his charm and unorthodox ways. He is a talented sportsman, although motivation lets him down, and he will take on anything verbally – hence he has been transiently successful in any sales/marketing jobs he has undertaken. However, he cannot see beyond the moment and resists all attempts to guide him towards a more stable future. He is fiercely independent in his everyday existence but it is difficult to see an appropriate progression towards real independence, maturity and responsibility.

An answer at last?

In my quest to understand and help him, I have left no stone unturned, nor turned my back on him, although I have been truly stretched. It gradually became clear to me, for example through my reading, that he may be suffering from ADHD when he was in his mid-teens, although there was then scant recognition and acceptance of the condition amongst professionals. At that time, I desperately tried to obtain help for Tom but by then he was so oppositional and refused to co-operate in any attempts to address his problems, which he felt were more ours than his. I was advised that my only hope was that he would gradually see the need to receive help himself. In the meantime, I have felt quite impotent and have had to watch his life deteriorating predictably in all spheres, while the lives of his brother and his friends unfold appropriately. I shall always mourn Tom's deprivation of a normal and happy childhood and that of my role as a caring mother. His brother feels his own childhood has been blighted by the endless arguments and stress, as each member of the family has tried to find ways to cope with the inevitable dysfunction that living with ADHD has caused. He also feels the loss of an appropriate relationship with an older brother. There is no doubt that his own needs and achievements have been overshadowed by the constant demands and disruption from his brother. Sadly, he was often subjected to a flow-on effect of the tension and irritability such stresses caused.

Hope – the end of the road?

Six months ago, Tom finally acknowledged he had a problem and turned to me for help. His entry into the working environment had made him realize that he was finding difficulty coping as his concentration was so poor. He recalled that he had struggled at school because of this. He recognized that he could not maintain interest in anything for long and quickly became bored and aimless, constantly needing stimulation, and he also recognized how this was affecting his life. However, we could not enlist the support of our GP. He, in common not only with colleagues in his large practice but many of his GP peers across the country, fails to appreciate the reality of such problems and thus refused to refer Tom for assessment because he did not acknowledge either the existence of ADHD or the necessity of its appropriate management.

Too little, too late

Tom was officially diagnosed with ADHD and complications at the age of almost 25 – although I had realized that this was his problem for many years through copious reading and talking to those who know. However, I had no illusions about the problems associated with a late diagnosis of this common but complicated condition. Sadly, the very nature of the condition, combined with the predictable co-existence of complications acquired over the years, has meant that he could not co-operate with treatment and gave up all too easily. This was undoubtedly compounded by the fact that, even when diagnosed, his GP refused to prescribe what he inaccurately perceived to be the dangerous medication recommended, without understanding its necessity. To our concern and dismay he also saw fit to undermine specialist advice by allowing his own personal bias and obvious lack of knowledge of ADHD to confuse and demotivate our son, who had taken such a huge step in finally confronting his own problems. Tom has a lot going for him but only comprehensive effective treatment – albeit far too late – will give him any chance to channel it to best effect. His life has clearly already been damaged by the handicap of untreated ADHD. We have come so near and yet so far. While some may be able to enjoy benefits of having an adult offspring living at home, Tom continues to create as much, if not more, chaos and havoc on a daily basis both physically and emotionally as he did when he was a child. He continues to live his life at home as he always has – expecting to take what he needs and do as he pleases, unwilling to help or co-operate in anything. For him life stands still.

The reality of ADHD

This is the reality of the torment of ADHD – to the sufferer, his family and those involved with him. It is no respector of intelligence levels (in Tom's case he has been deemed to be above average). In my work I have counselled many hundreds of parents from all over the country and abroad who relate similar experiences to my own – indeed the similarity of patterns of behaviour and clusters of symptoms and overall problems is quite uncanny. This is despite the fact that no two people will present with ADHD in exactly the same way. I have gained a wealth of knowledge about the condition and its variable manifestations from international research and conferences, as well as its undoubted effects on all those it afflicts. This and my personal experience of living with the condition has enabled me to encourage and support an understanding of the reality of ADHD to a wide variety of professionals and non-professionals alike.

I cannot help but wish that I could have my time again and make up for lost years; to have been able to seek the help of an early diagnosis and treatment for Tom's ADHD so he had the chance of a happier child-hood and a positive future; to know then what I see so clearly with hindsight are the reasons for his trying and worrying ways; to have been able to ensure he could feel the love we have for him. We all deserved a more normal family life. In common with others like us, we are acutely aware that we have sometimes not managed Tom in the most appro-priate way as we have become exhausted, demoralized and defeated in our efforts and life has become a vicious circle. It has not been for want of trying. We are only human and always tried to do our best in difficult circumstances.

The debate

Sadly, however, there are many who still seek to debate or deny the very existence of ADHD, let alone its management. They seem determined that all childhood behaviour problems are rooted in parenting or environment. They prefer to challenge copious research data, and are unwilling to acknowledge and believe that such a condition could and does exist. They do not know the despair, personal, social and academic failure that dogs untreated sufferers of ADHD.

Many professionals assume that parents' accounts of their children's behaviour must, by default, be biased or coloured by variables such as depression and that evidence of the latter be seen as the prime cause of a child's problems. Many mothers, especially, will demonstrate depression, anxiety and stress as a direct response to the distress of living with a child with ADHD. It cannot be overstated that, in such circumstances, parents themselves need a considerable amount of support and understanding – not blame. Let us not lose sight of the fact that parenting provides ample opportunity for a wide range of useful and important physical and emotional skills to be deployed. Contrary to belief, it is my experience that most parents dealing with the ongoing problems of a child with ADHD are, in fact, more likely to be objective rather than subjective in their evaluation of their child across a number of situations. Indeed, they invariably expend more time and energy showing more unswerving love and support than many others. It is arrogance for any professional to consider that he or she knows more about a child than its parents do.

Those who seek to debate the issues of ADHD can merely do so from a hypothetical angle. What right does anyone who does not have first-hand experience and knowledge have to be sceptical and dismissive? Those who are do not know what they are debating. Debate and scepticism in ADHD serves only to hinder, demoralize, insult and further defeat. It also encourages the perpetuation of myth and misinformation. Poor concentration may just seem at face value to be no more than a passing nuisance. It must be appreciated that trying to live one's life with any degree of appropriateness/normality when one is unable to concentrate on anything for any length of time has devastating effects. True ADHD is not an excuse for poor parenting – often there are other children in a family who have no such problems. True ADHD is not pathologizing naughty children – one would of course encourage an experienced assessment to ensure that an accurate diagnosis is made and that there are no other reasons for the manifestation of such symptoms.

Understanding ADHD

Untreated ADHD is a living nightmare for sufferers and their families. It prevents a happy childhood and blights a future. It gives rise to family dysfunction as each member struggles to cope with the stress and distress of such a pervasive and relentless disorder. Parents of children continuously manifesting the range of symptoms that significantly interfere with their everyday life are only too aware that their child has a problem and usually tirelessly try to seek help – often without success. In doing so, they invariably become well informed but are often further demoralized and frustrated by unsupportive and negative attitudes to their plight by professionals to whom they turn for help. Many of these professionals clearly know nothing of the condition and do not wish to discover the facts, apparently content to ignore and dismiss genuine cries for appropriate and essential help.

Lack of insight and knowledge of the nature of ADHD, its cause and appropriate management can be very detrimental to a child and family. Children with ADHD tend to attract negative labels that have a devastating effect on their self-esteem. ADHD is a hidden handicap but should be viewed in a positive way. Many such children have positive traits that can easily be overlooked. There are many areas in which they can excel and the challenge is to manage the child to encourage this potential. ADHD is not all bad news. It should be noted that there are many successful people with ADHD who, because of their high energy drives and enthusiasm, have succeeded despite their disability. The future is positive if the condition is managed appropriately, but it does need to be identified, treated and understood as early as possible to try to prevent the destructive difficulties it can cause. Children with ADHD are not 'problem' children but children who have a problem. They are often in crisis and confusion. There is considerable stress on their families who are often at their wit's end. They are markedly different from their peers at all stages. No semblance of normality is possible in everyday and family life. Their condition makes it difficult for them to control their behaviour. Their disability is complicated by negative responses from others, who do not know how to cope with the children or their own frustrations as a result. Children with ADHD experience repeated failure in many aspects of their lives. Early experienced assessment and diagnosis is important to avoid continuing stress and setbacks for years. Once understood and managed, the future is likely to be greatly improved.

ADHD does not just mean poor concentration, hyperactivity and impulsiveness but difficulties with self-control and regulation of important elements of behaviour, especially those that involve rules, instructions or requests. These children are less likely to respond to discipline, incentives and rewards that influence other children. A child with ADHD cannot be consistent and is prone to behave like a much younger child. The temperaments of children with ADHD are very different from those of other children as they have poor behavioural control, they experience great difficulty in some situations and are vulnerable to life's stresses. It is critical to appreciate this fact.

The ADHD temperament is inclined to be demanding, impatient, easily frustrated, domineering, aggressive and oppositional, especially with the mother. The attention deficit disorder (ADD) temperament tends to be shy, sensitive and passive, but both types can be disorganized and unmotivated with poor decision-making and self-esteem. It is vital for those who are sceptical and biased to realize that there is thought to be an underlying brain dysfunction causing such behaviours in those with ADHD; to realize that such a cause is also likely to be responsible for the variability of symptoms in individuals and inconsistency of behaviour on a daily basis. One would not choose to go through life being constantly blamed, accused, rejected and criticized for one's daily behaviour. It is impossible to implement behaviour modification with a severely hyperactive and oppositional child who cannot concentrate.

Those who debate and postulate what they naively consider to be helpful hypotheses miss the point in ADHD. Questioning and dissecting each other's theories over the heads of those who actually suffer from the condition wastes valuable time and helps nobody. Such time should be better spent understanding the reality of the condition. Ask any parent of a genuine sufferer. There are plenty of them. Listen to what they tell you and believe it. The identification of the condition with its essential management can only be of benefit to the sufferer.

The future

Society, professions and other disciplines need to acknowledge the existence of ADHD rather than challenge it. Those who should be offering appropriate help have become paralysed and polarized by their moral dilemma. They should understand the anguish and frustration and disabling effects of those who suffer and their families so that they can focus on the part they need to play in co-operating in its overall management. Only then will ADHD be truly recognized for what it really is and effectively treated. Childhood, family life and a positive future surely deserve it.

Chapter 3
A Brother's Story –
Through the Eye of the
Storm

'PAUL DOUGLAS'

I would not consider my childhood a normal one. It was significantly altered by the behaviour of my brother, Tom, and the reaction of my parents to his problematic adolescence. I look back on the memories of my earlier days with a great sadness, not just from the viewpoint that I suffered because of the animosity in the family home, but because my parents and my brother will find it hard to remember the good times that we did all share together, albeit few and far between. Instead, only the never-ending arguments, the tears of despair and the punishments forced on my parents in a desperate attempt to restrain my brother from causing yet more unhappiness to us all.

I first remember becoming aware of my brother's behaviour when I was around the age of eight or nine, my brother being three years my senior, and from that point on, relationships in my family began to deteriorate. I recall witnessing many upsetting arguments between Tom and my parents and also between my mother and father, both at their wits' end and taking out on each other the frustrations of yet another demoralizing battle.

I still cringe when I cast my mind back to weekday mornings before school, when my father had already left for work and my mother was left to face a torrent of abuse, mental and sometimes physical, from my brother. The arguments would continue in the car on the way to school, my mother's face a picture of emotions and her mind in no state to concentrate on a day's work. There was never a kiss nor a goodbye from my brother as he raced away from the car once at school. We were all upset and distressed and Tom shunned and forfeited the loving hugs I was to know. Many times I would look back to see my mother reapply her make up to disguise the many tears that were shed on those dreaded school mornings.

The evenings were no better. The frustrations of my brother's school days were all too evident. Once again my mother would bear the brunt of his foul temper. He would be happy initially, kicking a football around the garden, burning off the excess energy, until he became bored with this routine and then required a new game of some kind to amuse him. I would be quite happy to sit in front of the television and relax for a couple of hours before dinner was served but Tom appeared to be unable to enjoy the undemanding children's entertainment and stay seated for more than ten minutes. This resulted in his becoming embroiled in yet another war of words with my mother for many different reasons, perhaps because he was hungry and wanted his dinner then and there. If his meal was still being prepared, then he found it unreasonable that my mother should not allow him a snack that would have obviously ruined his appetite. It always seemed to me to be the most trivial of things that appeared the most important to him and if he did not get his own way then all hell was let loose.

My father would return home punctually every evening when dinner would be served. My mother was so much in need of support that she immediately wanted him to talk with my brother and make sure that he understood that explicit language and rudeness would not be tolerated – not that it made any difference to Tom. My father always preferred to keep a low profile and resented this. Mealtimes therefore became increasingly tense affairs as my brother would become sulky and insolent. The only contribution he ever made to a discussion was designed to provoke an argument. He refused to sit next to my mother and the slightest thing irritated him, such as the noise of someone else eating. He would never be able to remain seated once he had eaten his meal, ignoring my parent's requests for him to be seated while everyone else finished.

This type of behaviour went on every day for about eight or nine years and grew worse by the day. My parents would go out of their way to try to create a calm atmosphere in the home and their form of discipline was no different from that of my friends' parents. As a result of the bitter animosity that my brother felt for my parents, I found myself becoming caught in the crossfire on a frequent basis. The arguments would become more serious and as I became older I would try to diffuse the situation as the family atmosphere became intolerable to live in. The result of my endeavours only seemed to be to make matters worse as I was accused of sticking up for my parents by my brother and he appeared to adopt an aggressive stance against us all.

The strain on the family was becoming increasingly evident as my brother grew older. By the time he was fifteen he was of a similar height to my father and this, coupled with his aggression, made him a physical threat, especially to my mother. It was as though he was aware of this factor and he pushed my parents to the limit. He did not care about authority. He would do as he pleased, whether it was steal money from my parents or threaten to physically harm one of them if they did not conform to his unreasonable demands.

There was little that I could do to prevent these actions. At times he was reasonably calm and would confide in me about various matters that obviously played on his mind, such as his difficulty in making friends at school. I would use these rare opportunities to persuade him that he should not treat our parents as he did, but he never listened to me.

He resented what I would consider to be the good relationship that I had with my parents. As a result he pushed himself further and further away from the people that cared for him the most. I knew that if I had any problems with schoolwork, for example, I could talk to my parents and they would guide me as best they could. My brother would bottle everything up and seek no help whatsoever. This only fuelled his resentment for my parents as I was seen to gain all the attention and his own schoolwork suffered while I gained credit for various achievements.

This combination of factors prevented any kind of normal relationship between my brother and myself. Unlike other brothers who sometimes fight and argue, which I suppose is the norm, we would be constantly at loggerheads. This resulted in many attempts by me to stay out of his way, such as staying at school for an extra hour or returning to a friend's house so that my brother would not goad me into either fighting or arguing with him. He would just hang around me making the most bizarre and juvenile noises or he would sing songs (which his own imagination had created) while I would try to watch television. He never listened to my requests for him to be silent or just be normal – in fact this would make the situation worse. Ignoring him did not help as he would not relent until he gained that all-important reaction from me. I would then ignore him for as long as possible or at least until the volume of his music nearly raised the roof of the house. I then had no choice but to ask him, or rather scream at him, to turn it down. His pathetic mannerisms were just the tip of the iceberg for me. I could just about cope with the way he treated me but, as the arguments with my parents increased, both in hostility and possibly in volume, I was nearly at breaking point. My attempts to complete any school or college work in the evening were thwarted by disturbance of some kind every night. This became a way of life in my household. Many times Tom would provoke my parents beyond belief with his ill temper and foul mouth. When he realized that they were past breaking point, he would lock himself in the bathroom for hours at a time to escape recrimination.

It was clear, when I was 16 and he was 19, that our lives were going in very different directions. I was at college studying for a place at university, while my brother, also at college, showed not the least bit of interest in bettering himself. Instead he spent most of his time drinking and gambling in public houses, with money that my parents had given him for college. When he did attend seminars he would be either drunk or uninterested in his course. I hardly ever saw him sit down and work. If he did have a deadline to meet he would become short-tempered as he hurriedly copied a friend's work, blaming everyone but himself for his lack of organization.

The gambling took its toll on the whole family as he would steal from any one of us to fuel his addiction. The arguments with my parents turned to more serious matters when letter after letter appeared from the bank demanding repayment of his loans.

The disregard that he showed for our possessions was a worrying trait of my brother's and his lack of remorse equally so. He would help himself to anything that he fancied from my bedroom, taking my favourite clothes, personal stereo or anything else that he could get his hands on. This was reflected in his money management – or should I say the lack of it? He never seemed to consider the repercussions of his actions – it was as though he had no conscience. He would borrow from friends, neighbours or whoever he could find to lend him some money. The problem with this was that he had no way of repaying and no remorse when his friends felt aggrieved and cheated. People turned their backs on him when they found out that he was unreliable and this became a part of his everyday life. His lack of maturity in dealing with the real world was his downfall – a boy living in a man's world – and he failed to acknowledge his own duties in repaying to society what he had taken so eagerly.

His lack of maturity spoiled my chances of entertaining friends, and later girlfriends, at home as I was always on edge when he was about. I would try to organize a time to see friends when I knew he would be out. The friends that were brave enough to visit me were subjected to a barrage of childlike questioning from my brother that was designed to annoy me. He would hang around and disturb what time I did have with my friends. This resulted in my brother being thought of as peculiar among my circles of friends, leading to a dislike for him. His own friends have always been totally dominated by his intoxicating character. As a result he gets his own way in any argument he has with them. Nowadays he seems to argue as much with his friends as he does with his own family.

My current relationship with him is without doubt much improved. Hopefully this will continue as we grow older. It is as though Tom is starting to realize that the lives of others around him are moving on and he is being left behind. There are still moments of ill temper that evidently show his dissatisfaction and unhappiness. Our relationship is stronger than it has ever been. Instead of feeling bitter at the way he treated his close family, I look back at his life and hope that he can form a genuinely good relationship with not only my parents, but hopefully settle down and experience a normal family life with his own partner and offspring.

There will never be anyone closer to me than my brother. We have shared the same saddening experience and will try as best we can to forget the endless arguing, the fights and ill feeling that reigned supreme throughout much of our childhood. We still argue, but not with the same ferocity, and certainly not about the same issues that seemed so important to him a few years ago. I consider our friendship to be much stronger than any I have with my closest friends. We both acknowledge the fact that we will always be there for each other.

It is only since my departure to university, which unfortunately corresponded with the failure of his own course, that we have begun to see eye-to-eye on a regular basis.

The timing was particularly cruel and seemed to happen when he was at his lowest ebb. He had no money,but huge debts, few qualifications, few close friends that he could depend on and a quite awful relationship with his own family. He saw my success in stark contrast to his own failure and at first blamed my parents for aiding me and not him. It is only now that he is in his twenties that he realizes that our parents were always there to do whatever they could for us. He is, at last, albeit slowly, attempting to improve his current situation, but it is a long and lonely road to travel.

Chapter 4
Struggles with an Inebriated Horse: The Pain of Having ADHD

'JOSEPH FRANK'

Editor's preface to Joseph's narrative

This chapter is devoted to the personal account of a young man who was diagnosed with ADHD. He wrote the following account some time shortly before he committed suicide at the age of 24. As his narrative indicates, ADHD became an extremely important part of his life and was central to his image of himself. In this and in other documents that he left he cites ADHD as a major contributing factor to what he saw as his personal failure in life and thus as one of the reasons why he chose to end his life. It would be alarmist as well as inaccurate to suggest that ADHD is commonly associated with suicide, but there is evidence to suggest that ADHD sufferers are more prone to suicide attempts and death by suicide than the normal population, with up to 10% of sufferers attempting suicide over a three-year period, 5% dying as a result of suicide or other non-accidental causes (Barkley, 1990). This compares to a suicide rate of 12.3 per 100 000 in the 15–24 age range of the general population (Blau, 1996). Joseph's story, therefore, is not typical, but it is significant. Joseph's account makes constant references to his feelings of worthlessness, his sense of powerlessness and his belief that he will not be able to succeed in what is essentially a hostile world. These thoughts and feelings, when experienced to an extreme degree, are commonly implicated in suicide (Blau, 1996). Joseph relates these feelings closely to his experience of ADHD. Such problems are, in turn, also commonly experienced by between 33% and 50% of individuals with ADHD (Barkley, 1990).

Joseph was an interesting, intelligent and lively young man whom I was fortunate enough to meet on a few occasions in the 18 months before his death. He came from a prosperous background with high-achieving parents and siblings. He was painfully aware of his own failure to reach the high standards set by his family. He had attended a prestigious public school but had failed to achieve any examination passes by the time he left at age 16, being branded as lazy and unmotivated. He had then drifted through a number of jobs before taking A levels at a Further Education College, and finally gaining a place to read for a bachelor's degree at a prestigious British university, where competition for places, particularly at undergraduate level, is very fierce. Joseph was rightly proud of this achievement, not least because it finally showed everyone who took the time to notice that he was not the failure and waster that many others (including himself sometimes) believed him to be. He got through his first year, though not as well as he would have liked. He found it difficult to settle in his second year and left during the first term, with the agreement of the university that he could return in the following academic year to retake his second year.

It is possible that Joseph's disappointment at meeting this setback in his university career had a more powerful impact on him than he indicated at the time or in his voluminous writings during this period. It is clear from the document presented here that he experienced a sense of fatigue and loss of motivation in certain aspects of his life. It is also suggested that there were long-standing problems in his family relationships. In the midst of all this was the experience of ADHD and the way in which his life was made utterly miserable, not only by the condition itself but, more importantly, by the way in which the condition was (in his view) consistently misunderstood and misinterpreted by just about everyone.

Joseph's narrative is a combination of personal reflection, advice to fellow sufferers and polemic against those in power who, in his mind, should know better. It is an intensely personal and deeply felt piece of writing. It deserves to be read for these reason alone. It also deserves to be read because it represents a voice that is not commonly heard in books and publications about ADHD.

Joseph was very keen that this document be published, leaving clear written instructions that this be done after his death, with the proviso that any financial reward that was accrued by its publication be donated to a charitable trust for the support of adult sufferers from ADHD. It is presented largely as he wrote it, with only minor alterations. Where alterations have been made this has been done for one of two reasons, either (1) to improve clarity and coherence, or (2) to protect the anonymity of Joseph and his family. Joseph Frank is a fictitious name.

Joseph's narrative

The primary objective here is to portray a life through my eyes. I should say from the outset that my life has been dominated by the feeling of depression that has been broken by occasional spurts of happiness. The depression came in bouts, rarely lasting for more than a few hours, and as I got older, it has to be said, they were more and more peppered with happiness. I know that everyone goes through times of sadness and depression but only as I grew older did I begin to understand that for me the depression was a consistent feature of my life, occasionally lifting, but always returning. Indeed, I can say that since the age of 18 the moments of happiness have increased. Yet as time passes, my limitations become more apparent and the moments of happiness begin to seem hollow. I understand that people will form their own impression: my depression and unhappiness may not be apparent to an outside observer. However, from my own experience I know how easy it is to form diverse and sometimes contradictory conclusions. Suffice it to say only I know how unhappy I am at the moment; and the extent of my problem.

It seems that every time I have tried to explain the problem of ADHD and its manifestation people have responded with a dismissive comment like: 'ah sure we all get that'. I have, therefore, given up bothering to even try to explain the condition. I know this is a defeatist reaction but I also know that I just don't have the emotional energy or stamina to carry on banging my head against a brick wall. Basically, when people say 'we all get that', what they really mean is: 'you're a fucking hypochondriac! Stop making excuses and blaming others for the way your life is turning out!' Indeed I don't feel too optimistic about the plight of any ADHD sufferer trying to convince anyone but the most educated or supportive professional or friend.

I often wonder why some conditions are accepted and others not. For example MS is accepted universally because its physical symptoms are clear and obvious. Similarly AIDS is accepted because it is very much a cause–effect condition with inevitable premature death being the effect. Yet ADHD probably affects more of the population than these two conditions put together. One problem may be that ADHD has no obvious physical symptoms. It is also hard to diagnose and is often seen as a cop-out for parents and sufferers. It's only when I think of all the undiagnosed sufferers out there that I think how lucky I really am. Then by the same token when I look at myself I see how irreparably damaged I am. Which is the bummer of these two deals? Personally I'd rather know why I fuck up so regularly.

I remember as a child attending a country school by where my parents lived. The principal there was, in my opinion, a religious fanatic of the worst kind and saw me as some kind of evil distraction cast upon him by the devil. Indeed I used to think that the devil was in him because of the hard time he gave me. Not that I was completely undeserving of this. I was the bane of any classroom: wild, impulsive, easily distracted, attention-seeking, very emotional and generally highly volatile. For me, learning certain subjects was virtually impossible. Although I did often think myself to be as thick as pigshit, I was never fully convinced of this, as there was, I felt, something bright about me.

I knew about hyperactivity from a young age as people often referred to me as such. The family GP, when I was nine, told my mother to watch out for additives, flavourings and colorants in foodstuffs. When I was 12 my father, a health professional, suggested that I start an exclusion diet after which he claimed to notice great changes in me. The changes though were short-lived, as my parents were about as good at seeing things through when it came to me as I was.

It wasn't until I came to London that I began to look into the matter seriously. I found that certain foods did indeed affect my behaviour such as oranges, cows' milk, chocolate, and sugar, often making me sick and lethargic within a few hours of eating. Sugar was a particular problem. Sally Bunday at the Hyperactive Children's Support Group (HACSG) helped me greatly at the time. The group, as I recall, didn't advocate any form of medication at the time and on and off I have stuck pretty rigidly to a certain exclusion diet. People are sometimes patronizing about it, saying: 'well, you've got great willpower to be able to do this!' Or, as my father once said, 'if it makes you feel better then stick to it'. Virtually no one took it seriously. But what I didn't understand at the time was that people in general didn't give a fuck. Why should they have?

Anyway, in 1995 I saw a TV documentary about ADHD. I recall trying to get the ADHD support group telephone number from the TV company the next day, and getting through to a rude and unco-operative young Irishman. I remember screaming down the phone at him: 'Give me your name now I'm going to have your job buddy!' Eventually I got through to the ADHD support group where I was given some book titles and advised to read everything I could on the subject. I subsequently called back sometime later and told the woman at the support group that reading these books had been a 'deja vu' experience. At which the lady said: 'I know what you mean.' And that's exactly what it was: the things I had read about in those books were exactly what I had experienced throughout my life. Reading individual accounts was like reading my own biography.

I subsequently saw a number of medical specialists – some of whom I felt I knew less about the condition than I did. This journey culminated in my treatment under the NHS at a famous English teaching hospital. Here, over six visits, I was examined, questioned and tested thoroughly both when I was on and off medication. The treatment led to a dramatic improvement in many areas of my life. At last I was being treated properly. But this is not to suggest that medication is the solution to everything. Far from it. One needs to also bear in mind the extent of emotional and psychological damage often suffered by people with ADHD. It takes much more than medication to overcome the years of rejection or admonition by parents, teachers, job managers and peers that

that can weaken the strongest of egos. The feelings of isolation and worthlessness imbued through recurring failure or non-completion of tasks. Medication just enables people to learn and understand what they couldn't understand or see before. I've seen the phrase 'like putting on a pair of glasses and being able to see clearly' and I could think of no more apt a statement to describe the purpose and value of medication in the treatment of ADHD.

Then comes the process of understanding that you're not stupid but in fact creative, intuitive, spontaneous and not weird. That your personality is not one to be ashamed of just because peers and elders called you 'weird' or 'mental' as a child and teenager. Most important is holding no resentment against those who gave you such a hard time. Rather, you have to try to understand where they're coming from. What I found most effective was a complete change of environment. Indeed coming to university was the best thing I ever did in my life. New people, a new understanding about yourself, a new start where nobody knows anything about you. This, however, is not an option for everyone so consideration of an emotional therapy programme is worth taking seriously. Though it may take three or four therapists before you find the right one.

This olive branch, however, needs some qualifying. It important to watch out for those in your family not prepared to accept the condition. Those closest to us can also be most damaging to us. Again you have to try to understand where they're coming from and avoid resenting anyone. This is difficult I know, but try. Indeed I would probably never have given any time to the idea of ADHD had things not continually prompted me to think 'hang on there's something up here'! Therefore, this is not a suggestion that you dump those who don't believe you. What is important is that you don't just waste emotional energy trying to force that inebriated horse whilst not being deterred by their lack of enthusiasm. On more than one occasion I have felt like a hypochondriac when around certain members of my family. I now realize that this was their problem; not mine.

My father used to say that I was the cause of all the trouble in the family. This I now know was not exclusive to me. Many families have a vacuum, where problems are said to arise and where blame starts: an easy target for family ailments. I would wager that in the majority of cases an ADHD sufferer – if in such a family – will be that vacuum. Again, don't get me wrong. Kids with ADHD, if not treated properly, can be a handful, but laying blame arbitrarily for structural and other family problems is in my opinion more damaging than any punishment. In a way, I got comfort from my parents' separation this year given that here I was 500 miles away. The upside is that I now understand myself more than ever before and feel very much at ease with myself.

I also can see quite clearly what I am turning into, and I don't like it. Now in theory, I could get help, and there's a strong argument to suggest that this would work out very well. But on a more realistic level I know that I don't have the energy left. Any energy that I did have was used up getting this far. My own limitations are also painfully obvious to me, and though this is obviously a major cop-out it is one by necessity rather than choice. I hope that parents and authorities will learn something from reading this and try to be more open-minded. Therefore, whilst what I am doing will seem to my closest friends and relatives to be done for purely selfish reasons I hope that this cause may get some more of the respect and recognition that it deserves.

To parents I would offer a word of caution. It is my opinion that the standard of medical knowledge on ADHD in this country is way too far behind that in America and Australia. There is, in my experience, hardly any focus on adults with ADHD in this country, in spite of the fact that many children carry the condition into adulthood. I also believe that private treatment for ADHD is over-priced. It is my opinion that parents should get to know absolutely everything about this condition and the options for treatment before going near any practitioner.

In response to the charge that ADHD is just another cop-out condition of the late twentieth century – a figment of the imagination – I would say it is fine to hold that view, so long as one realizes that it undermines many other (more widely accepted but sometimes less fully studied) medical conditions identified in the last 70 years or so. No doctor is well-qualified to understand and evaluate every possible condition therefore it is left to the specialists to learn about ADHD. If psychiatrists and neurologists are oblivious to this condition they shouldn't be practising.

There will, I am sure, be some parents who will say: 'I might have had ADHD too but I got through alright!' My answer to this is that maybe the parent who says this would have gone so much further, been so much happier or just felt much better about themselves, if they had had more recognition and support for this debilitating problem. It should also be pointed out that the world of the late twentieth century is not an easy place to live. Our parents grew up in times of greater prosperity and security, when jobs were expected to last for life. Now, unlike in our parents' time, staying in employment often depends on how sharp and trainable an individual is. The increasingly competitive job market extracts ever more from workers, in terms of stamina, skill and initiative. Society and the family are becoming ever more complicated. Meanwhile ADHD has been identified as a condition that acts as a serious handicap to some of the people who seek to participate in this competition. Information also abounds about the kinds of treatment and support that can help ADHD sufferers. These reasons alone make it essential that ADHD should become more widely recognized so that more people can gain access to the support they need.

References

Barkley R (1990) ADHD: A Handbook for Diagnosis and Treatment. New York: Guilford.

Blau G (1996) Adolescent suicide and depression. In G Blau, T Gullotta (eds) Adolescent Dysfunctional Behavior. London: Sage.

Part II
Supporting People with ADHD

Chapter 5
A Multi-Modal Approach to the Assessment and Management of ADHD

ROBERT E. DETWEILER, ANDREW P. HICKS AND MACK R. HICKS

Introduction

The authors demonstrate the nature and value of a multi-modal and multi-disciplinary approach to the assessment and management of ADHD drawing on their experience at the Centre Academy in London. It is suggested that the approach described here is good practice and that those approaches that do not incorporate multiple perspectives in the definition and management of ADHD are severely deficient.

ADHD as a diagnosis

As other contributors to this book suggest, the history of ADHD is both rich and varied. The modern history of its diagnosis began in the early 1900s when Dr George Still, a British physician, described attentional disorders in terms of a 'defect in moral control' thereby concluding that sufferers had insufficient moral fibre to stop themselves from being inattentive. By the middle of the twentieth century focus had shifted away from notions of moral deficiency to the view that the condition had biological antecedents that were outside the control of the individual. Preferred terms included brain dysfunction, hyperkinesis and hyperactivity. Another factor to emerge in the wake of these developments was the recognition that not all children who had difficulties focusing and paying attention were also hyperactive. Thus was born the modern conceptualization of the diagnosis currently favoured in the fourth edition of the American Psychiatric Association's Diagnostic and Statistical Manual of Mental Disorders (APA, 1994). This describes three types of attentional disorders:

- attention deficit/hyperactivity disorder, predominantly inattentive type;

- attention deficit/hyperactivity disorder, predominantly hyperactive-impulsive type; and
- attention deficit disorder, combined type.

The authors of DSM IV point out that there are no conclusive findings from laboratory or physical examination explorations that allow for a cast-iron physical test for the presence or absence of ADHD. Thus in spite of the widely researched and extensively theorized psychobiological understanding of the nature of ADHD, its assessment and diagnosis largely depend upon inferring the presence of the disorder on the basis of the observation of behaviour and the assessment of the individual's performance on different tasks. The assessment process, upon which the diagnosis depends, is therefore of critical importance. In our experience of working with children with ADHD at the Centre Academy, we have found that the most reliable assessment process must involve the very careful gathering of information from the parents, the child and the school, as well as a battery of neuropsychological tests and medical investigations. In short, assessment must be multi-modal. This in turn leads to the development of an equivalent multi-modal management programme, whereby interventions involving parents, the school, a psychologist and physician are often found to be necessary. We have found that the provision of a carefully monitored educational programme is always a key factor in the management of children with ADHD, whether they attend our own school or, after assessment, attend other schools.

It is clear that the environment can, in some cases, induce symptoms similar to those described in the ADHD diagnostic criteria. For example, a student with exceptional abilities who is placed in an unchallenging and unstimulating academic environment will, more than likely, become bored and inattentive. Conversely a child with learning difficulties will become disengaged with the work done in the class when he/she cannot keep up. Children with dyslexia will often find it difficult to pay attention in a reading class. Disturbances in children's home lives, such as divorce or family upheavals, can also cause otherwise capable students to focus their attention elsewhere to the detriment of their academic and social performance in school. For these reasons DSM IV requires that at least six symptoms of either inattention or hyperactivity-impulsivity or both must have existed for at least six months 'to a degree that is maladaptive and inconsistent with developmental level'.

Further, some of these symptoms must have occurred before the child was seven years old and be present in two or more settings. There must also be clear evidence of clinical impairment in social, academic and/or occupational functioning. Having established this pattern of symptoms, in terms of pervasiveness and chronicity, it must also be shown that the symptoms cannot be a function of some other disorder, such as autism. The systematic gathering of information from the parent, the child and the child's school by someone thoroughly familiar with the ADHD diagnosis is, therefore, essential in order to rule out problems that look like, but are not, ADHD.

The assessment process

At Centre Academy, in London, we have been evaluating children and adults for ADHD for over 25 years. The first stage in our procedures involves the gathering of information in three ways.

- *The parent interview.* First, the parents of the child suspected as having ADHD are interviewed in depth by our Director of Clinical Services, who is a psychologist. The Director knows the symptoms of the ADHD syndrome well and seeks to filter out those problems that are caused by temporary environmental stimuli and therefore have not been a pervasive part of the child's background.
- *The developmental checklists.* Second, our founder, Dr Mack R. Hicks, a clinical neuropsychologist, has designed two developmental check-lists – one for parents and one for teachers – which gather obser-vations about the child's behaviour in written format.
- *The child interview.* Third, the child's own perceptions and experi-ences, associated with the presenting problems, are ascertained through a clinical interview.

This combination of information gives a clear picture of the student's behaviour and the circumstances associated with it in a variety of settings. As indicative as this might be, however, it is not enough to be the sole determiner of ADHD.

The next step in our diagnostic process involves neuropsychological testing. The battery that we have designed:

- measures intellectual functioning;
- assesses the functioning of processing strengths and weaknesses (visual, auditory and visual motor);
- assesses achievement levels in fundamental school skills;
- measures both visual and hearing ability.

A computerized test measures vigilance and impulsivity. It also measures functions associated with the frontal lobes of the brain. These include finger oscillation, motor sequencing and confrontation tasks. It is the combination of the results of these tests that, when added to the infor-mation gathered in the interviews and through the checklists, may in some cases lead to a tentative diagnosis of ADHD.

The following example illustrates the way in which the information gathered during the assessment process can be combined to help determine the appropriateness of the ADHD diagnosis.

The student achieves low scores on the Digit Span subtest of the Wechsler (IQ test). This might indicate processing difficulties but the student shows strong auditory processing on the other tests and there are positive signs of ADHD on tests measuring vigilance and impulsivity. This suggests that the student's reported and demonstrated inability to recall details is due to wandering attention. The probability of ADHD is considerably increased when the interviews eliminate any obvious environmental causes for the presenting problems and suggest that the student has exhibited symptoms of inattention and/or hyperactivity for some time and in many different settings. Even though this battery of psychological tests did not indicate either hearing or vision difficulties (although it was capable of doing so), before the final diagnosis was made the student was referred for a medical examination to rule out either of these possibilities.

So far the assessment and diagnostic process has involved the skills of a knowledgeable interviewer, a clinical psychologist and a medical practitioner. Once the diagnosis of ADHD has been made, it is important to devote careful attention to informing the parents, the child and the child's school. These three elements form the core of the treatment team, as it is only when the school, parent and child are working together that an effective treatment programme can exist and the work of the physician and psychologist can be made effective.

The importance of the classroom for children with ADHD

The educational needs of the child with ADHD are considerable. Yet, because of dwindling resources, high student-to-teacher ratios and limited opportunities for flexibility in the mainstream classroom, many children with ADHD are not able to receive the full support that they require. The ideal classroom for the child with ADHD combines the seemingly contradictory attributes of consistency and flexibility. The classroom should be a consistent and predictable setting that provides much structure, limited distractions and flexibility in addressing each student's individual learning style. Other chapters in this book deal with classroom strategies for dealing with ADHD. In addition to the supportive work of Andrew Hicks, the work of teachers in classrooms at Centre Academy has developed through extensive practical engagement with the thousands of children with ADHD who have passed through our school. An example of our educational approach is provided through reference to David, aged eight-and-a-half, whose particular difficulties are presented here.

David: a case study

David has difficulty focusing and seldom remains on task for more than five minutes at a time. He is highly impulsive, has difficulty with selective and divided attention, and has particular difficulty with organization and visual motor skills. David dislikes school, is a class clown and is quick to test the rules and structure at school, although he is usually compliant. He wears down his mother at home, forgets to carry out domestic tasks that he has been given and has much difficulty getting ready for school in the morning.

The general classroom structure provided for David and his classmates includes the following:

- 10 or fewer children with a teacher and an aide;
- a room with four walls and no open space leading into other classrooms;
- no changing of teachers and no change in subject order from day to day;
- soundproofing and few distractions;
- daily individualized programmes and weekly schedules written and fixed to each desk;
- separate study carrels or 'offices' for each child;
- a time-out room nearby;
- computer, word processor, tape recorder, attention training devices in student 'office';
- a fan to block out extraneous noise;
- a monitoring system with aide marking papers and providing prompt feedback regarding the number of tasks accomplished and accuracy of work.

The curriculum

The curriculum is individualized for David, as well as the other students. This allows for self-competition rather than group competition, through the setting of attainment and achievement targets. The programme is designed to fit the different students' learning styles, by teaching through strong processing avenues (utilizing each child's preferred style of engagement with learning tasks) and remediating areas of weakness. Independence and self-reliance are taught through the self-paced programme. Students select the sequence of work with their teacher's approval and within the limits of their own individualized programme. This helps to teach organizational skills, personal responsibility and postponement of gratification. It also allows for purposeful movement to be built into the programme, as students must move about the classroom at frequent intervals to obtain materials or work on the computer or other audio-visual materials.

A major goal of the curriculum and classroom organization is to build students' self-esteem, helping them to bounce back from previous classroom failures. The curriculum is individualized to follow each student's central nervous system development rather than forcing him or her to conform to a fixed notion of their capabilities. This is accomplished, for example, on a daily basis, by evaluating the percentage of successfully completed number problems and the number of problems that need to be redone. When David, like other students, makes progress with a certain prescription of materials and methods, they are continued and increased in difficulty. When he is not making progress, different approaches are attempted.

Homework is also designed to be a successful experience and to decrease stress in the home. Difficult assignments are worked out in school, so homework is brief, enjoyable and focuses on areas of strength. Weaknesses are addressed in the classroom through remediation, much of which is designed to address attention skills, executive thinking and study strategies, such as the SQ3R method (Skim, Question, Read, Recite and Review). Compensatory mechanisms are also used, including typing and tape recording for oral reports.

Motivation and attention

Motivation and attention are addressed for all of the students through consistent reward systems and attention-training devices. Students earn points that count towards both short-term and long-term rewards (which we refer to as 'goals'). The more immediate rewards include activities at morning break time, lunchtime and the final period of the day. If classwork is not completed then students are required to complete it during the final period of the day. If David earns enough points for the week, then he has only recreational activities on Friday afternoon. An adequate number of points for the month results in a day off from school. Like many of his classmates, however, David prefers to come to school for fun and games rather than stay at home on the 'goal day'.

Individualized goals and special class goals are also developed. One example of a class goal was the provision of a special raw vegetable dip during activity for David's class. Some readers may not consider a raw vegetable dip an especially desirable reward. The important thing here was that the class agreed that it was highly desirable. This emphasizes the important point that what constitutes a reward can never be taken for granted and must always be determined through consultation with students.

Some students receive points for keeping their voices down. David receives a special assignment of reporting the time to the class every

30 minutes as he had previously caused disruption by constantly inter-rupting his peers to ask the time.

A number of different attention-training devices are used in the class-room. The Attention Training System (ATS) is a computerized response-cost system devised by Dr Michael Gordon, a clinical psychologist and member of the Centre Academy Advisory Board. The ATS enables the teacher to provide feedback to the student regarding on-task behaviour. Self-monitoring is also possible through a cassette tape with random beeps. The student records whether or not he or she is on task when each beep is heard and is rewarded for accurate reporting. Earphones are also used for taped messages, which take advantage of the child's special interests and encourage him or her to remain on task. A simple timer can also help increase sustained attention through breaking assignments into short sections and providing a short-term goal, such as completing the work within 10 minutes. Student and teacher work together to establish an appropriate amount of time for a particular schedule of work.

Meeting children's social needs

Socialization difficulties are also addressed systematically through the classroom structure and through work with parents. It is very difficult for parents or psychologists to offset the effects of 30 hours per week of negative social interaction in school. The most effective means of addressing social skills problems is in vivo, through structuring the child's environment to allow for success. This is critical for David, who, like so many other children with ADHD, has difficulty in relating to peers. The Centre Academy addresses David's needs as they exist, rather than starting with superficial stereotypes or parental projections regarding proper socialization. Sometimes, parents have nostalgic memories of the class dance or football game. They see these as impor-tant aspects of their own socialization and assume that their children need these experiences too. Unfortunately, as a result, this sometimes leads to their failing to recognize their child's true social needs.

A successful educational environment for students with ADHD enables them to develop basic trust and appropriate dependence. It also helps them overcome defensiveness and the tendency to project blame on to others. It furthermore helps reduce avoidance and impulsivity and the need to act out or be over-controlling. Students' social behaviour is gradu-ally shaped with these goals in mind. For example, David might work with one child on the computer, then another child in organized play, then another in free play before beginning to work with two or more children in each of these areas. The particular children interacting with David in these activities are carefully selected to provide him with the models or challenges that his programme of social development requires.

Good socialization also comes from the modelling of parents and authority figures. In the proper atmosphere David is able to have a very positive relationship with his teacher, who can help him to overcome past negative experiences and stereotyping of teachers. David also has the opportunity to deal with a female rule setter and authority figure – something he has had difficulty with in the past, but will gradually learn to accept as a result of the supportive environment provided by the school as a whole. David also writes or dictates to his teacher in his daily journal, recording experiences that are important to him.

David has a history of difficulties in relation to athletic skills – an area where academically unsuccessful students often achieve. David, however, has shown that he can be successful in physical education (PE) activities that do not require advanced athletic skills. For example, David was able to help raise money for his school through an event in which he walked around a track to obtain sponsor money. Regular activities can also help foster success and co-operation. For example, David may work with an older child in PE, with the older child kicking the ball in team kickball and with David running around the bases. The older student becomes a model and social tutor, thereby perhaps becoming a 'hero' for the first time, and the younger child learns valuable social skills from the older peer.

Essential to David's success is the co-operation of his parents and the integration of home and school strategies. At parents' night, David was able to show his classroom to his parents and then present a drama skit to the entire school, along with two other students. The clinical staff also work with the parents to address medication management, careful selection of sports and peer activities, home management and parent–child relations. Parents are discouraged from projecting their own experiences at a certain age on to their child. For David, and other children, it is important that his parents accept him as he is and work with his own needs and perceptions. David's socialization skills, self-esteem and academic function are expected to develop so that he can be a successful adult.

Working with parents

Assuming that the proper diagnosis has been made and that an appropriate educational programme has been implemented, it would be very easy to ignore the needs of the parents of the student with ADHD. The focus up to now has been on the 'subject' of this exercise – the child. The parents, however, have their needs too. It has already been noted that parental attitudes and beliefs can play an important role in helping the child with ADHD overcome his or her difficulties. This section considers some of the ways in which parents might be supported.

Once David starts to feel success because the educational programme has been geared to his needs, his parents too will feel relief. To have discovered information that sheds light on the possible underlying cause of previous anxiety and stress and to witness an effective programme of intervention may well help David's family put certain problems into proper perspective. Sometimes this is enough, but sometimes intervention is needed to help the family re-establish its equilibrium, which has been disturbed as a result of difficulties surrounding the child with ADHD. This is where counselling comes in.

Family dynamics can be severely strained by the presence of ADHD. David's parents, particularly his mother, have had to deal with problems relating to his difficulties in sustaining attention, his impulsivity, his failure to do normal household tasks, the disorganization/messiness of his room and sometimes oppositional behaviour in the face of pressure to conform. Until very recently David's parents have had to deal with these problems without either the knowledge of ADHD or peer or professional support.

In addition, they have shouldered the burden of popular disdain for parents who, it appears, cannot manage their own children and get them to behave as well as most children. They have lived with what is sometimes the intolerable stigma of being classed by others as failing parents, in spite of the fact that they have tried their best. Out of necessity, parent support groups have grown up to share the woes and successes of working with the child with ADHD. Schools have also added to parental stress. It is common for parents to dread the phone call from the school or the teacher and even worse the request to attend the school for a meeting to discuss their child's progress and behaviour. David's parents have been frequently told that their child is wilfully disobedient and disruptive, refuses to learn and will not pay attention when the class is being taught. From the school's point of view, in addition to the frustration generated by the child's lack of success, some anxiety is produced by the fact that school performance tables now rate schools publicly on attendance and exams. This anxiety is frequently shifted to the parents, who are told that children like David have a problem and that they are expected to solve it.

So far we have anxiety produced both at home and at school. Sometimes this creates conflict between the parents about how to handle the situation. One parent may be used to a very pragmatic way of solving problems – the 'try harder' approach; the other parent, by contrast, may compensate by becoming more sympathetic to the child's difficulties. This is a recipe for real internal discord, with each parent blaming the other for their child's problems.

With all of these dynamics working at once it would be unreasonable to expect the problems to be solved solely by finding and starting to repair the cause. This is where the trained ADHD counsellor can help the family understand the basis of the discord, to put it into perspective and to help family members back to a more balanced relationship. To do this, the counsellor needs to be fully aware of all of the ramifications of attentional problems on the family, the individual parents, the child and the child's environment. Integration is vital, so it is enormously important for the counsellor to be part of the multi-modal team working with the family with ADHD.

At Centre Academy our counsellors are attached to the school. This makes daily communication much easier. Information shared during counselling is never directly relayed to the school as it is confidential, but because the counsellors are fully aware of the school programme, the testing and background information on the child, and the daily successes and failures, they are part of the team that monitors and adjusts the programme frequently. We find that counselling is often most helpful when it has a directive component involving behavioural management at home.

Medical intervention

In addition to playing an important role in the process that led to the original diagnosis, the doctor can play a part in the success of the total programme and therefore is an important member of the multi-modal team. Even after all the intervention and strategies of the ADHD classroom are implemented, some students still find it difficult to focus and concentrate. For these students it is sometimes appropriate to consider the possibility of a trial on medication and the physician plays a key role here.

It is important to note that at Centre Academy a number of steps would have been followed before the point is reached at which medication is discussed with parents. These steps are:

- a reliable diagnosis of ADHD would have been made using the multi-modal approach;
- a structured, reinforcing and appropriate academic programme would have been put into operation;
- counselling for the student and/or the parents would have begun to help them understand the nature of ADHD and its manifestations;
- continual assessment of the effectiveness of the academic programme would have taken place and it would have been modified when needed;
- clinical observations of attention span and productivity would have been made within the programme;
- the propriety of medication as an option would have been discussed in the team of parents, teachers, counsellors and psychologists;
- if the parents and physician approve, a base rate of the quality and quantity of work without medication would be established;

- a two-to-three-week trial on medication would begin with everyone aware that it was a trial (during this trial any adjustments to the medication dosage and regimen would be made);
- at the end of the trial a comparison of attention span, ability to focus, and the quality and quantity of work would be made against the previously established base rate;
- the parents and physician would then decide whether to continue with the medication based on any improvements noted;
- once a year there should be a trial period off medication to determine whether continuation is appropriate.

Within the multi-modal team the physician plays a key role in the entire process of medical intervention, from discussing it with the parent, to the establishment of the regimen, to the review of the effectiveness, to the monitoring of its effect on the student's classwork. At Centre Academy our consultant paediatrician visits the campus twice per term to observe the students in the classroom and then reviews the individual students with the teachers. This way the paediatrician will have first-hand experience in seeing the child working in the academic environment before and after medication.

The importance of the assessment and intervention team

Gordon (1991) identifies five essential needs of the child with ADHD:

- The need for clearly specified rules, expectations and instructions.
- The need for frequent, immediate and consistent feedback on behaviour and redirection to task.
- The need for reasonable and meaningful consequences for both compliance and non-compliance.
- The need for programming and adult intervention designed to compensate for the child's distractibility, limited organizational skills and low frustration tolerance.
- The need for a well-integrated and functioning team of parents, teachers, administrators and clinicians who communicate often and work together to create a structured and supportive environment.

It is clear that the success of the first four items on this list is dependent on the functioning of the team. Just as the accuracy of the diagnostic process for ADHD is enhanced by involving a multidisciplinary team of professionals (the clinical interviewer, the psychologist, the physician, the parents and the school), the probability of success of any intervention programme for the child with ADHD will be enhanced by the continued involvement in monitoring and adjustment by the same professionals. In isolation, any one of them might get a distorted view of the whole child. Working as a team, however, means that they all have access to the same information and can share within the team their respective expertise to help the student to succeed.

References

American Psychiatric Association (APA) (1994) Diagnostic and Statistical Manual of Mental Disorders (4 edn). Washingon DC: APA.
Gordon M (1991) ADHD: A Consumer's Guide. New York: Guilford.

Appendix

Case study I: diagnostic testing – Peter R, the classic case of ADHD

Peter R, nine years and six months of age, was referred by his local education authority for diagnostic testing. During the initial session his parents indicated that Peter had been overactive since approximately the age of three and could not pay attention in school.

Peter's teachers felt he was not working to his full potential because of his short attention span and disruptive behaviour in the classroom. They suspected emotional problems and labelled him 'unmotivated'. Peter's parents indicated he had difficulty in art, physical activities and the lunchroom, as well as in the academic setting. He had difficulty reading in the classroom, but when they hired a tutor he was able to do rather well in the one-to-one situation. His grades were poor but he worked close to expectation level on school achievement tests.

Peter had poor organizational skills and difficulty following rules. He was impulsive both in and out of the classroom and his written work was messy, but if he slowed down and took his time, he could produce a presentable paper.

Peter had a tendency to touch and bump other children, but this did not seem to be premeditated. Peter seemed puzzled by his own behaviour and gave his parents the impression that he wanted to please them as well as his school. Peter seemed to want to please during testing, but he was easily distracted and was always in and out of his chair. He squirmed constantly, played with the tape recorder cord and frequently started a task before the examiner had completed the directions.

Neuropsychological testing gave evidence of classic signs of ADHD. On the WISC-IIIUK, there were significant variations in Peter's performance between subtests. This inconsistency between subtests or 'roller-coaster' effect is quite common in ADHD. The coding subtest score is usually low, but other subtests that purportedly measure attention, such as arithmetic and digit span, may or may not be low. It is more likely that they will be low on one testing occasion and high on another testing occasion.

This variability is also found in processing tests. Peter had a mental age of only five years and eleven months on Sound Blending on the Woodcock Johnson but reached 10 years and six months on Incomplete Words. He had a mental age below six years on the Digit Span subtest of the WISC-IIIUK and Memory for Words on the Woodcock Johnson.

At the same time, he placed at nine years and three months on Memory for Sentences. This inconsistency between subtests that measure similar avenues is often found in ADHD. Peter placed at only the 15th percentile on the Goldman Test of Auditory Discrimination without background noise and jumped to the 90th percentile when background noise was introduced. This result may seem to defy common sense but it is suspected that ADHD children will sometimes focus even harder for a short period of time when distraction is introduced. We have found that either the quiet or the noise subtest could be quite low with the other subtest high, and it is the separation between the two conditions that is significant.

At the same time, on our dictation test, with and without background noise, we usually find the background noise results to be lower. This was true with Peter who placed at a mental age of seven years and six months on dictation under quiet conditions and fell to five years and eight months with background noise.

Achievement testing also shows some degree of variability between similar achievement tests. Another interesting factor is that these achievement test scores average out close to Peter's expectancy based upon his chronological age and mental age. While some achievement scores are above his expected grade level and some are below, his average is close to his school placement. These tests are administered in a quiet one-on-one situation and even though his variability shows through, he is able to demonstrate what he knows, whereas this is not possible in the noisy classroom environment. Peter had difficulty with timed math computation, and this is often the case with ADHD. This difficulty may relate to Peter's visual motor weaknesses, as most children with ADHD suffer from dysgraphia and will have difficulty in any timed motor activity, whether writing or solving math computation problems.

Peter also had difficulty with verbal fluency when he was asked to give as many words as he could that start with a certain letter. He also had difficulty with confrontation tasks where he had to put up opposite fingers from those of the examiner. His impulsivity resulted in his putting up the same finger as the examiner on several trials. Peter produced only 14 words beginning with the letters F, A and S over three one-minute trials, and the average for his age is 22.6 words.

On finger oscillation (finger tapping using a telegraph key), Peter placed with 34 taps per ten-second trial with his dominant right hand

and fell to 21 taps with his left hand. There is ordinarily a 10% difference between the dominant hand and the non-dominant hand.

Performance on finger oscillation, along with performance on verbal fluency, motor sequencing and confrontation tasks, suggest frontal lobe difficulties. The frontal lobe is a major contributor to mediation of concentration and organizational skills. On the Gordon Continuous Performance Task, Peter had borderline scores on the Delay portion, which measures impulsivity and abnormal scores on the Commissions portion of the vigilance section. The Delay task requires Peter to push a blue button and then wait before pushing again. If he is able to delay his response, he receives a normal score.

On the Vigilance task, Peter was required to push the blue button every time a 9 came up after a 1. Errors on the commission portion mean that Peter saw the number 1 and impulsively responded to a number that was not a 9. Abnormal scores on the Commissions portion of the vigilance task give substantial weight to the diagnosis of ADHD because there are few false positives on this particular task.

In addition to formal testing, parent and teacher observations recorded on the Child Behaviour questionnaire and Developmental Checklist place Peter in the top 2% of children his age on inattentive and hyperactive scales. Observations are also significant in not placing Peter at high levels for depression, social withdrawal or aggression. As the above example indicates, there is no single definitive test for ADHD. Using a multifaceted battery, the experienced clinician has a much greater level of confidence in diagnosing ADHD.

Many researchers believe that testing adds nothing to the diagnosis of ADHD and that it should be based entirely on history and parent and teacher observations. The authors do not agree with this position. Formal testing provides a rich source of data that can compliment observation and history. This is especially true in the many cases where observation and history are clouded by differing opinions and inconsistency of data. After all, inconsistency is part and parcel of ADHD, and normative test data give structure to often confusing information. Formal testing also delineates other areas of weakness, such as dysgraphia, and rules out other disabilities, such as audiophonic dyslexia or visual dyslexia, which can coexist with ADHD.

Today's treatment of ADHD is a three-legged stool that includes education-remediation, parent training and medication. Formal testing is necessary to outline a proper course of remedial education.

Case study II: diagnostic testing – Scott C, a case of ADD and dyslexia

Scott C, 12 years and nine months of age, was referred for evaluation because of difficulties with academic work. Scott was not disruptive in the classroom. In fact, he was often quiet, and his teachers thought he was well-behaved, if not particularly bright. Scott's teachers were aware that he was having difficulty with reading, and he seemed to daydream much of the time. However, several other students demanded more of their time.

During the evaluation, it became evident that Scott actually had above average intellectual ability. However, his difficulties with concentration and auditory processing greatly interfered with his learning. While Scott did not display the hyperactivity or extreme impulsivity that many ADHD students display, he was experiencing frustration and disappointment because he was not progressing as well as other students of his intellectual capability.

While some inconsistencies and variability between subtests were present, Scott's overall pattern on evaluation suggested significant problems in areas related to attention, auditory discrimination, auditory memory and visual motor skills. On measures of auditory processing, Scott became quickly frustrated. He placed at the seven-year, zero-month level for Auditory Closure, the six-year, seven-month level for Sound Blending, and the 12th percentile for auditory discrimination with quiet background (5th percentile for auditory discrimination with noise background).

While Scott was reasonably good at mathematics, he did not perform well on the Arithmetic and Digit Span subtests of the WISC-IIIUK, seeming to struggle to manipulate math problems in his head and keep digits in proper sequence. On a task of requiring memory for words, Scott placed at a seven-year, three-month level. Not surprisingly, Scott had difficulty on a measure of reading decoding skills. He placed at a seven-year, six-month level when trying to pronounce words. However, he was able to perform somewhat better on a measure of passage comprehension, demonstrating some understanding and reasoning ability despite his poor basic reading skills. Scott placed below a mental age of eight on measures of oral and written spelling.

Scott demonstrated good intellectual ability on a number of measures, including the Block Design subtest of the WISC-IIIUK and a measure of receptive vocabulary skills. Scott's significant problems with reading were not the result of low intellectual ability, but were caused by his difficulty with auditory discrimination and perception, word-finding ability and other skills presumed to be mediated by the left hemisphere of the brain.

While Scott was able to show good understanding of receptive vocabulary, he had much difficulty on measures of expressive vocabulary or word finding. He had difficulty thinking of words beginning with particular letters, had some difficulty on a task of object naming, and struggled to come up with words to provide good definitions for vocabulary items.

In addition to these difficulties, which are associated with an auditory type of dyslexia, there was much evidence that Scott experienced difficulties with concentration and attention, even for visually presented material. On the Gordon Delay task, Scott was not at all impulsive and pressed the computer button fewer times than most individuals his age. On the Vigilance section, he did not press the button impulsively. However, he made a number of errors of omission as he did not always press the button when the target numbers were presented.

In addition to difficulties on the visual measure of attention and concentration, Scott performed well below age level on a task of crossing out target symbols on a page. This difficulty suggests that poor concentration, planning skills, and sustained visual-motor effort and speed may be present, despite Scott's generally good visual perceptual abilities as measured by Block Design, Object Assembly and Visual Closure measures.

An interview with Scott's parents further supported the notion that Scott struggled with concentration and attention across a number of settings, not just when reading or when required to pay attention to auditory-presented material. Parent and teacher checklists suggested a number of problems with following directions, inattentiveness, confusion, easy distractibility and poor concentration. Scott's combination of processing weaknesses is particularly devastating in the classroom. Difficulties with concentration and auditory processing make it nearly impossible to sustain attention and learn effectively when information is presented in a lecture format. Taking notes is particularly difficult for a student with this combination of ADD and auditory dyslexia. And because Scott did not create a behavioural disturbance in the classroom, some of his difficulties were not evident at an earlier age. Despite increasing frustration with his lack of progress, Scott was able to make use of his above-average intelligence to compensate for some of his processing difficulties. However, as the volume of work increased, Scott was not able to keep up.

In Scott's case, testing was essential in order to determine the nature of his learning problems. Because of the presence of audiophonic dyslexia, Scott is in need of further remedial intervention in addition to those measures necessary to treat ADD. Scott will not benefit from a pure phonics-based approach to reading, because his auditory channel is not strong enough to support such an approach. A more multi-modal remedial approach is recommended, including linguistic strategies and visual, tactile and kinaesthetic learning. As with other ADD children, it was essential that Scott have opportunities to learn in a classroom environment that limits distractions, provides much structure, breaks tasks into smaller units and provides individualized teaching that caters for his learning strengths. While significant behavioural problems were not present, parent training is still recommended in order to help Scott's parents understand the nature of his difficulties and ways to address them at home while being his advocate to the school.

Consideration of medication management of Scott's ADD is also recommended. Research on the use of stimulant medication suggests it may not be as effective for students with ADD without hyperactivity as for students who are hyperactive, but medication management can still be quite beneficial as a part of the overall treatment of the student with ADD.

Chapter 6
The Role of Medication in a Multi-Modal Approach to the Management of ADHD

GEOFF KEWLEY

Attention deficit hyperactivity disorder (ADHD) is internationally recognized as a problem of brain dysfunction with associated educational, behavioural and other difficulties. It is also believed to have a strong genetic component. Its core features are excessive inattentiveness and/or impulsiveness and hyperactivity. It is frequently associated with oppositional behaviour or conduct disorder, learning difficulties, low self-esteem, difficulties with social skills, and a wide range of other social and emotional problems (Barkley, 1998; Hinshaw, 1994).

Being caused by brain dysfunction, it is analogous with other conditions that are caused by physical dysfunction. For example, in asthma, the lungs are dysfunctional, the bronchi are tight and the air exchange is not proceeding normally. Lung function tests show an abnormality. In the same way, the brains of children with ADHD show abnormalities that may be correctable with appropriate medication. There are a number of ways of showing this, the most meaningful being through various scanning techniques, either single photon emission computerized tomography (SPECT) scans, which measure glucose uptake, or more practically by carrying out quantitative electroencephalogram (QEEG) studies.

Acknowledging that ADHD has a biopsychosocial (Tannock, 1998), as opposed to a simply biological or solely psychosocial basis enables the management of the condition to be much more effective; ADHD is eminently treatable, with a high success rate when a combination of various strategies is used. Untreated, ADHD frequently leads to academic and social failure and to psychiatric complications.

In understanding ADHD it is important to acknowledge that it rarely exists as a discrete condition and that it often coexists with various other problems, such as Asperger's syndrome, dyslexia, excessive oppositionality, anxiety and depression, obsessions, and co-ordination and speech and language difficulties (Hinshaw, 1994; Comings, 1990). No two children with ADHD present in the same way. Different children will experience

60

different complications and environments, and have different characteristics (such as IQ level). However, in acknowledging the broader concept
of ADHD there tend to be four main ways in which ADHD presents itself:

- *Hyperactivity alone.* These children are usually extremely active and
  meet the hyperactive criteria on traditional British and World Health
  Organization diagnostic instruments (WHO, 1990). Hyperactive
  children are usually pre-adolescent, but not necessarily so. There is
  an older, often adolescent, group where motor hyperactivity has not
  improved with time.
- *Diminished hyperactivity with persistent impulsiveness.* These
  children tend to have been hyperactive or overactive as pre-
  schoolers, and may have been trialled on dietary manipulation. With
  time, however, their motor hyperactivity has seemed to diminish and
  their problems relate more to verbal and emotional impulsiveness
  and poor concentration. Conventional 'hyperkinetic' assessment
  tends to overlook or minimize this very important group. With time,
  self-esteem and social skills often worsen with these children, and
  other difficulties frequently develop, such as conduct disorder,
  oppositionality and/or emotional problems.
- *Masking of core symptoms.* In some children the learning difficulties,
  oppositionality, conduct disorder, poor social skills, self-esteem and
  other difficulties can overshadow and mask the underlying core
  ADHD symptoms. Especially when the hyperactivity has diminished
  with time, these other difficulties become the most important and
  obvious day-to-day difficulties. It is vital, however, that the underlying
  ADHD be recognized and dealt with.
- *Predominantly inattentive ADHD.* These children have never been
  hyperactive or impulsive but are just unable to concentrate. They
  daydream, are 'spaced out', are not focused adequately to take part in
  learning, and may appear lethargic and apathetic. They only have
  difficulty with the predominantly inattentive ADHD criteria. They are
  differentiated from the diminished hyperactivity group where, in
  addition to the inattentiveness, there is impulsiveness and usually a
  previous history of overactivity. They may represent a different
  biological condition (Barkley, 1998).

The following description of John, aged 11, illustrates the less well-
understood predominantly inattentive subtype. John was described by
his teacher as:

> Bright, interesting and motivated on a one-to-one level, able to concen-
> trate well, retain information and to apply it at a later date. Conversely in
> class, or any small group, the reverse is true to a quite uncommon
> degree. He is unable to focus upon or follow through any task. All minor
> movements on the periphery of his field of vision, distractions and minor

comments from others break his concentration; he becomes listless, unmotivated and abstracted. He is not hyperactive or undisciplined, he simply 'absents himself'. However, subjects which hold his attention on a one-to-one level, in a group situation, fail to engage his interest.

Historical context

As we have seen, ADHD is a broad diagnostic category that encompasses much more than hyperactivity alone. It is important to note that the problems experienced by individuals with the ADHD diagnosis who are not hyperactive are often just as severe and debilitating as hyperactivity is for other children. One of the myths about predominantly inattentive ADHD without hyperactivity (sometimes referred to as ADD) is that it represents a milder condition and that it is probably not severe unless hyperactivity is present. Many parents of children with ADHD would disagree with this view and argue that the hyperactivity is the least of their problems and that the other problems cause them greatest difficulty. It is a common error for ADHD to be confused with hyperactivity.

Understanding about ADHD is also complicated by the widely held, but simplistic and inaccurate, view that poor parenting practices are always the primary cause of problem behaviour in children. This view is expressed almost daily in the media. The acknowledgement of a biological component in severe activity and attention problems is most widespread in North America. By contrast, an unpublished 1993 survey of UK child psychiatrists and community paediatricians found that a very low percentage of these professionals were aware of seeing significant numbers of children with ADHD (Kewley, Scott and Facer, 1994). It also found that the approach taken to behavioural and attentional problems tended to be almost purely psychosocial (focusing on family functioning) and dietary. Three-quarters of the paediatricians had never prescribed stimulant medication. This would suggest that, at the time of the study, ADHD was going largely unrecognized. A psychosocial diagnosis tends to mean psychosocial management, with little or no attention being paid to biological issues.

During the 1980s, ADHD was one of the most written-about childhood biological behavioural conditions (Barkley, 1998). There is, internationally, a very robust body of sound research literature that has now been present for many years, confirming that ADHD is a significant condition that may cause educational, behavioural and social problems. It has also been shown to be amenable to successful management (Barkley, 1998; Hinshaw, 1994; Goldstein and Goldstein, 1990).

There is a wide variation in practice between North America and the UK. Unfortunately, this variation disadvantages a great many children in the UK. It has been proposed that the incidence of ADHD is higher in North America, Australia and other such 'New World' countries because of emigration factors. It has been theorized that the more impulsive risk-takers were more likely to emigrate and may also have been involved in antisocial activity that may have led to their transportation (Hartmann, 1993). They may therefore have had a higher incidence of ADHD, conduct disorder and other conditions, and may then have subsequently interbred in their new abodes. Hinshaw (1994) accounts for such variations in less sensational but more scientifically plausible terms by pointing to the strong relationship between the estimates for the incidence of ADHD and national differences in assessment practices. Thus the fact that many UK paediatricians and child psychiatrists from the 1993 survey were barely aware of ADHD seems the likeliest cause for the lower incidence of the condition in the UK. It also suggests that there are likely to be a great many children with ADHD who are untreated and unrecognized (Kewley, 1998, 1999).

One of the reasons for this apparent British reluctance to embrace the concept of ADHD can be traced back to a possible misinterpretation of the classic study of behavioural and childhood problems on the Isle of Wight in 1964–5 led by Michael Rutter, a leading British Child Psychiatrist (Rutter et al., 1970). In this study it was acknowledged that the natural history of hyperactivity was that it frequently decreased over time but was replaced with other difficulties:

> Hyperactivity is age related and tends to be grown out of by mid-childhood [. . .] often to be replaced by under activity at about the time of adolescence. They will only rarely still be grossly hyperactive by ten years of age – most are likely to be handicapped in other ways . . . especially with aggression, destructive behaviour and antisocial activity.

Because hyperactivity lessens, it has been assumed that there are no other problems, or if there are, these also diminish. There is increasing recognition that children who have been placed in special schools for children with emotional and behavioural difficulty (EBD) may have untreated and often complicated ADHD. There is frequent similarity between the common and non-specific environmentally based diagnosis of emotional and behavioural disorder and the complicated symptoms of ADHD. Figures from the UK show that 2.1% of children have severe EBD problems and that there are 8000 children resident in EBD schools, costing approximately £300 million per year (BPA, 1993; POST, 1997). One small-scale study (Vivian, 1994) showed that 40% of a residential EBD population were still hyperkinetic and that 75% of the children had either conduct disorder or emotional disorders.

The following case study of Colin describes a typical pattern of childhood presentation of ADHD.

Case study

> Colin was aged 10 when he presented to the clinic. As a pre-schooler he had been very active and his mother had tried a number of dietary manipulations, which had taken the edge off his hyperactivity a little; however,

his problems had persisted. His hyperactivity lessened over the years, although he remained very fidgety and restless and tended to flit from one thing to another. He was very physically and verbally impulsive, and tended to do and say things that were quite inappropriate and at times dangerous. He was also emotionally impulsive with marked flare-ups in temper and outbursts, often in response to very minor triggers. At school his reports always said 'if only he would try to concentrate, Colin would do much better' and 'he must learn not to be so easily distracted'. As he struggled over the years his self-esteem lowered, he became more oppositional and had difficulty in keeping friends. His handwriting was 'atrocious' and the school gave him more and more support. Eventually he received a Statement of Special Educational Needs.

His father related to Colin's difficulties and felt he had struggled in the same way at school and that he still had difficulties with concentration and was often depressed. It sounded as though both Colin and his father may have had the same condition.

The assessment found that Colin had difficulty with all nine of the inattentive ADHD criteria both at home and at school and all of the impulsive criteria; he now only met two of the six hyperactive criteria, whereas he would have met all six when he was younger. He also met all of the oppositional defiant disorder criteria, had low self-esteem and social skills problems, and the educational psychology assessment showed moderate dyslexia.

As a result of working with the school to institute ADHD strategies and a positive approach, together with the use of Ritalin, there was a dramatic improvement. Relationships at home improved as did his schoolwork, he was asked out more, developed more friendships and he became much less oppositional. He still had many problems but all involved with Colin agreed that the use of medication enabled the other strategies to be more effective.

Assessment

A comprehensive assessment is essential for an accurate diagnosis of ADHD and to the exclusion of other conditions, as well as to ascertain exactly how much difficulty is being caused. The assessment must be carried out in a caring, professional and cost-effective way so that the child and family feel that the situation has been fully and carefully evaluated. It should not be overtly judgemental, nor seek to convey moral overtones. Such an approach is essential to establish an effective diagnosis and management strategy, and to develop the necessary rapport with the family.

The nature of the family interview, and the information obtained, depends very much on the interviewer's style and approach, but there is a well-documented history that must be ascertained as part of a thorough assessment. Some physicians prefer to do this purely on the basis of clinical judgement and their experience, but there are a number of standardized forms and computerized history interviews that can also be used. This interview is an essential part of the overall evaluation, and a great deal of information can be gained by listening to the child and his or her parents as they recount the areas of difficulties that have occurred over the years, the means by which they have coped, the amount of impairment that has occurred and whether or not the problems have worsened with time.

An astute interviewer is always on the alert for a history that does not ring true, a lack of consistency between the parents, and discrepancies between the comments of the school and the parents. No other person generally has a greater knowledge about a child than that child's parents. By approaching the interview in an open-minded, non-judgemental and empathetic way, a dialogue can be developed between the physician and the family. This is essential to long-term effective management. The interview also enables a view to be made of the relationship between the child and his or her parents.

Management

Following a thorough assessment and the diagnosis of ADHD, together with the profile of the associated co-existing conditions and the functional difficulties affecting the child, one is then in the position to plan effective management. The most effective approach is a multidisciplinary, multi-modal approach. All too often in the past the various strategies have been instituted separately. It is essential to use the most meaningful and effective strategies that are available. This may involve a medical approach in children with significant and persistent difficulties, but is not always the case. No one professional group 'owns' the management of these children and the ability of professionals to work together is crucial (Cooper and Ideus, 1996).

It is important to realize that ADHD is a progressive condition and the longer it has remained undiagnosed, the more the problems will have compounded, often becoming severe. There may have been years of recurrent embarrassment, loss of self-confidence, increasing learning delay, social skills difficulties and increased frustration. Inappropriate or wrong diagnosis and professional misunderstanding may have exacerbated the situation. Frequently such children have seen a wide range of other professionals whose perception of the difficulties may or may not have helped. If an inappropriate diagnosis of poor parenting had been made then the situation may have been exacerbated further. These problems are secondary to ADHD but are equally demanding of intervention.

Another area of difficulty that must be addressed at the management stage relates to the myths and misunderstanding that surround both the existence and nature of ADHD, and in particular the use of medication.

Misinformation has been fuelled by media 'hype' and by psychoanalyti-cally trained professionals who may not appreciate the biological component of ADHD and thus the role of medication. The side-effect profile of medication has tended to be grossly exaggerated. As a result, appropriate management is denied to many children. This situation mirrors that seen in the USA and Australia 10 to 15 years ago. Myth and misinformation sometimes become important barriers to effective management and must be addressed by open discussion and the sharing of information with parents and children.

Educational strategies are always important, whether or not medi-cation is used, and are discussed in detail in other chapters. Medication should be seen not as a threat but, where necessary, as an essential adjunct, providing a window of opportunity to allow the child to be more available for adequate teaching (Ideus and Cooper, 1995). Many classroom strategies helpful to children with ADHD can also be seen as good teaching practice that will benefit all children. However, children with ADHD need these strategies even more than those without the condition. Psychological, behavioural, psychiatric and other strategies are also often important when used appropriately in individual cases.

A team approach, with teachers' and parents' observation of students' concentration levels, their patterns of disruptive behaviour, their learning difficulties, social problems, distractibility and so forth, is essential to both the assessment and ongoing monitoring of progress.

It is important to recognize that children with ADHD can be very frustrating and unrewarding to teach. Teachers, therefore, need a great deal of support in coping with such children. Children with ADHD may fail even the best teaching strategies, in the same way that their problems may persist despite the most effective parenting. The stress that the child with ADHD may cause to both his or her parents and teachers may serve to aggravate the situation (Dendy, 1996).

Medication

The effective management of ADHD must be collaborative, involving a combination of education, medical and psychological strategies, where appropriate. Even when the child is being treated medically, day-to-day care is very much in the hands of the educator. Where medication is felt by the medical practitioner to be a possible strategy it must be discussed with the family and, if appropriate, with involved professionals, such as teachers. It should be pointed out, however, that a diagnosis of ADHD does necessarily automatically mean that medication must be used in its treatment.

In the past, the use of the hyperkinetic or hyperactive diagnosis tended to mean that children were not diagnosed unless they were very severely hyperactive. This meant that treatment often was not offered unless the child was in an extreme situation, as a last ditch attempt to overcome an increasingly deteriorating problem. In these circumstances medication was often the preferred treatment. Professionals dealing with ADHD tend to have a less rigid approach to the use of medication and will consider it more readily when other strategies have failed and the child is still struggling at home and/or at school; because of this, very significant medication usage differences have developed between countries such as the USA, Canada and Australia on the one hand and the UK on the other. These will be discussed further later.

The two medications that are available in the UK are methylphenidate (Ritalin) and dexamphetamine (Dexedrine). The third psycho-stimulant, pemoline (Cylert), is only available in the UK (on a named-patient basis). Both Ritalin and Dexedrine are internationally recognized as being indicated for use in ADHD when other strategies have failed. Guidelines for physicians for prescribing Ritalin indicate:

> Ritalin is indicated as part of a comprehensive treatment programme for attention-deficit hyperactivity disorder (ADHD) when remedial measures alone prove insufficient. Treatment must be under the supervision of a specialist in childhood behavioural disorders.

When used by experienced physicians there is a low incidence of short-term side effects. There is no evidence of long-term addiction to Ritalin when used for the treatment of ADHD, and no other significant side effects. Side effects, such as sleep problems, appetite loss and tics, occur in less than 5% of patients and are transient.

The effects of medication

Medication is one of the most effective forms of therapy for ADHD, when it is used correctly and in conjunction with other strategies. Most ADHD clinics report a success rate of 80–95%. This means that parents, child and schoolteachers generally report that there is a very significant ongoing improvement in symptoms and that the improvement outweighs any side effects. Parents, at follow-up, usually express the feeling that they would not wish medication to be withdrawn because of the very positive progress that is generally made. The school and the child also often express this view.

Prior to a decision being taken to prescribe medication, parents should have obtained information both from reading and from discussion with professionals, other parents and support groups. Parents must become informed so that they take the most appropriate advice from as many (reputable) sources as possible, be fully aware of the facts and data concerning ADHD, and not allow misinformation and personal bias to be passed off as fact.

In the UK, Ritalin is the most commonly used medication, although in other countries Dexedrine is used more widely. Both medications can correct abnormal brain function. Some children respond better to one medication than the other. They rarely result in troublesome side effects. When side effects occur they are dose-related and short-term, usually only lasting for about four hours. Parents and, where old enough, the child, should always be involved in the decision-making process.

When ADHD is present significantly and is unresponsive to other non-medical strategies, a decision needs to be made as to whether or not a medication trial is indicated. Failure to consider medication for a child with significant ADHD who continues to struggle and is unresponsive to other strategies is inappropriate. When severe enough, ADHD needs medical treatment, in conjunction with other appropriate strategies, in the same way that a diabetic or asthmatic needs treatment.

However, it is not always easy for parents to come to an informed decision about medication. The confusing myths and misinformation propounded by some professionals, and especially by the news media, have made it very difficult for parents and others to assess the real risks and benefits involved. Professionals treating ADHD must acknowledge the complexity of the condition and fully understand the issues involved. Parent support groups must avoid giving overly simplistic or inaccurate information on ADHD.

Medicating for ADHD is not like giving a course of antibiotics, with the expectation of a cure. ADHD may sometimes require ongoing medication for years, to replace the chemicals that appear to be deficient. Medication should be seen as providing a 'window of opportunity' to allow other strategies to be more effective. There is clearly little point in attempting complex teaching strategies, behavioural management or psychoanalysis if the child is unfocused and excessively impulsive.

Medication should be viewed as initially treating the core ADHD symptoms and usually having a flow-on effect to some of the other difficulties. It can have a very beneficial effect on the core ADHD symptoms and will generally improve concentration, impulsivity and hyperactivity. Short-term memory usually improves, as does the ability to learn and perform at school. Slowly one sees an improvement in self-esteem, socializing ability and in relationships, together with a decrease in mood swings. Off-task activity, impulsiveness and overactivity are also decreased. In particular, not only is the physical impulsiveness improved but frequently also the verbal and emotional impulsiveness. These symptoms are often very significant in overall day-to-day behavioural difficulty and are sometimes hard to disentangle from the mild-to-moderate oppositional defiant disorder symptoms that may also be improved once the key ADHD features are managed effectively. The effects of medication can be seen in about 20 minutes when the dosage is correct. The 'flow-on' improvements may take weeks or even months to appear.

For example, self-esteem and social skills difficulties tend to improve more slowly. There is frequently a fairly marked improvement in verbal expression and in clarity of speech. More complicated speech, and especially language difficulties, are slower to improve, but clinical experience suggests that many of the language disorders improve slowly with time, once the child is more focused and more socially aware. This allows the situation to stabilize and then enables the residual difficulties to be helped in a more cost-effective way.

In the classroom, improvement in concentration and in behavioural difficulties is usually seen fairly rapidly. If there are associated specific learning difficulties progress may be slower. It is frequently impossible to assess the severity of associated specific learning difficulties until the ADHD is treated.

Medication must not be seen as a magic cure and must always be used in conjunction with other strategies, but the change induced by medication is frequently striking. For the first few months one usually sees a very rapid improvement in the core symptoms, and often in some of the other features. A chronic, intransigent situation is often converted to one that can be improved and then managed more effectively. The initial rapid improvement that is often observed is usually slowly replaced by the realization after a few months that the problems will be ongoing, and possibly will be long-term, although much improved.

Clinical experience shows that in approximately 90% of children, there will be very significant improvement in response to medication. Ongoing difficulties persist for 40% of children with ADHD, even when under treatment, owing to the influence of co-existing conditions, such as conduct disorder and social, emotional and educational problems. It is not that all the problems cease for other the 60%, but it is the case that the medication and other treatment makes it possible to deal with these problems more effectively.

The following is a list of typical comments made by parents. It indicates the sense of satisfaction and surprise that they experience when their child with ADHD begins to make progress as a result of medication:

His progress is vertical!
He is now able to go on school trips.
Taking the Ritalin is like he is not on it, because off it he is so bad.
He can see himself as somebody now, not just the class clown.
He wants to learn now.
Whole demeanour is different.
Now happy to have him at their house.

I can't get over the transformation in his character.
I was choked when he got his first birthday party invitation. He's never had one before.

If medication does not help this does not mean that the diagnosis is wrong, although of course it should always be reviewed. Medication has been shown to be the most effective strategy for children with ADHD. However, for some children with milder symptoms, good educational and other management strategies alone suffice.

If there is failure to respond to one medication then the alternative stimulant should be tried. If the core ADHD symptoms are managed effectively but there is continued depression, obsessions, oppositionality or tics, then a second medication may be necessary to treat the co-existing features. When there is ongoing oppositionality, impulsiveness, tics, sleep problems or conduct disorder, the associated use of Clonidine can be very helpful. Antidepressants may help if there is depression or obsessions. Sometimes no one medication will control all the features of the syndrome and a second or even occasionally a third medication may be necessary. This should only be done by professionals who understand the complexity of ADHD. There is an increasing international literature regarding the safety and effectiveness of such combinations. This can be critical to the achievement of satisfactory management of children with multiple combinations of difficulties.

Occasionally professionals continue to attempt the management of children with moderate to severe ADHD without recourse to medication, even when they are continuing to struggle. Sometimes they can be contained within the school or family situation despite having ongoing ADHD symptoms. However, in the unstructured situation at home, they may have difficulties.

The decision to use medication is the parents', in conjunction with the paediatrician or psychiatrist. When a child has significant ADHD and is struggling, parents should be informed that their options are not just educational, psychological, behavioural and dietary but that the additional option of medication could also be considered. The common fear is that medication will be used indiscriminately and inappropriately. This is a danger to be guarded against but recent evidence (BPA, 1993) suggests that the UK has one of the lowest percentages of children on medication in the developed world (see Figure 6.1), suggesting that UK physicians are in general particularly cautious in their use of prescription medicines. Given the percentage incidence of UK schoolchildren having hyperactivity, this would appear to indicate undertreatment (Taylor and Hemsley, 1995).

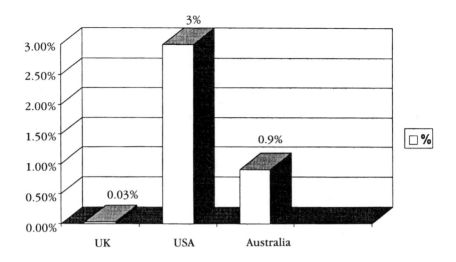

Figure 6.1: Medication usage.

The length of time a child will need to be on medication varies between individuals. It appears that prognosis is best when a child is treated before complications arise. However, as yet there are no firm data on this. Some children outgrow the need for medication during their school years and many more discontinue medication when they leave school. Although many of their ADHD symptoms may continue, provided they survive school with protected self-esteem and reasonable academic and behavioural achievements, they may be able to focus, or indeed over-focus, on things that they are really interested in and thus become successful in social and professional terms.

Some practitioners prefer Ritalin, others Dexedrine. Both may be very effective in some children; some children react better to Dexedrine, others to Ritalin. There is a large group of children who are responsive to both medications. Studies show – and clinical impression concurs – that more children will respond to Ritalin than Dexedrine. Both medications are widely used internationally as psychostimulants able to effectively help the core ADHD symptoms.

Side effects of medication

Side effects are best considered as either short-term lasting approximately four hours, or long-term. This distinction is important as short-term side effects are common and will only last for the duration of each dose. The most commonly discussed side effects include:

Short-term

Appetite suppression. This is probably the most frequent side effect that we see and although it often diminishes over the first few weeks of medication, it can persist. Rarely, however, is it severe enough to warrant cessation of medication. There is sometimes some weight loss over the first few months but it usually picks up later.

Abdominal pain/headaches. These occasionally occur in the first week or in the first few days but rarely persist.

Loss of sparkle or transient change in personality can occasionally occur. Some children become irritable, weepy, and quite angry and agitated. This occurs more commonly with Dexedrine.

Sleep difficulties. Too high a dosage of medication too late in the day can make it difficult to settle the child for sleep. Sometimes even a very small dosage at midday can do this and, in contrast, other children can take a large dose with the evening meal and still sleep well.

The rebound effect. Some children, especially those who are hyperactive, become even worse as the medication wears off. If significant rebound occurs it is important to ensure the doses are overlapping and this may mean a change of timing. In some children the medication only lasts 2.5 to three hours and more frequent doses may be necessary.

Tics. These involuntary movements or vocalizations occasionally occur with ADHD and, if severe, may be related to Tourette's syndrome. Although it is frequently said that Ritalin aggravates them, it sometimes actually improves them and they are not necessarily a contra-indication to the use of Ritalin.

Itchy skin, rashes, a feeling of depression, depression or mood change, or nausea can occasionally occur.

Some children actually talk more on medication and this can occasionally be a problem.

Feared long-term side effects

Possible growth retardation. Early studies suggested that height retardation could be a problem. More recent studies show that this is not the case (Hinshaw, 1994).

Possible addiction. This has not been substantiated in almost 50 years of stimulant usage (see Barkley, 1998; Hinshaw, 1994). Stimulants, in fact, help the child to focus more effectively. One never encounters a child who has a craving for his/her next dosage. Rather, as the dose wears off one often sees the previous difficult behaviour or poor concentration recur in the same way as an asthmatic will start wheezing once the treatment had worn off. The craving for the medication is simply not there, in fact often the children forget to take their next dose.

Avoiding side effects

Fine tuning. Dosage and timing adjustments are crucial to effective management. This can often make the difference between successful and unsuccessful management, avoiding rebound, using an effective dosage without side effects and avoiding any periods in the day when the child is unmedicated, all make a great deal of difference. It is important that the dosage and timing allow continuous cover during the day, so that there may be a need, for example, to use a second dosage at lunchtime if medication is wearing off in the late morning. Difficult periods before breakfast may necessitate a small dose on waking, and a larger dose as the child leaves the house for school.

In summary, where medication is appropriately used one would expect to see improvements in:

• concentration
• short-term memory
• distractibility
• oppositionality
• self-esteem
• social skills
• learning ability.

One would also expect to see a decrease in:

• aggression
• oppositionality
• hyperactivity
• off-task behaviour.

Rosenberg et al. (1990) sum up the argument for using medications:

These medications are solid, first line bread and butter type medications with a remarkably benign side effect profile and are not considered controversial [. . .] However ADHD is a condition with marked functional impairment, long-term morbidity and enormous consequences for the child and family.

Medication should be continued as long as it is helping significantly. Its use therefore needs regular review every six to 12 months.

Involving the school

It is vital that the school be fully involved in, and informed of, the outcome of the assessment process and treatment plans that are likely to affect the child in school. Any medication trial must involve the school. Where a school is against treating for ADHD, it needs to be determined whether this is on the basis of bias against the whole concept and against the use of medication without a full understanding of ADHD, or whether it is because the school authorities truly do not believe the child has significant difficulties. This can sometimes be very difficult to ascertain but usually with co-operation and good communication is it possible to do so.

Children with predominantly inattentive ADHD may be treated just during the school hours, usually with two doses per day only, provided that they cope with homework, that there are no significant behavioural problems and that self-esteem is reasonable. This, as always, is an individual decision.

Safety issues

It is always important that families, and especially teenagers, remember that the stimulants are controlled drugs. Medication must be kept at home in a safe place and the amount of medication being used carefully controlled by the parents. If this does not happen, teenagers may be tempted to sell their stimulant at school to their friends. This is sometimes done, because of their poor social skills, to make friendships. However, these difficulties are no different to those associated with many other medications, for example paracetamol. The simple point here is that there is always a need for care and caution in the giving and distribution of medications. The need for care and responsibility should not be seen as reasons for not using medication at all in ADHD.

Conclusion

Effective management of ADHD therefore involves a wide range of strategies, probably involving a number of professional groups. Medication should be considered for any child with significant ADHD and its use must be carefully considered, well explained to the parents, and carefully adjusted and monitored. To fail in any of these respects could not only lead to the treatment being unsuccessful but could also cause further problems for the already-distressed child and family. The failure to use medication appropriately in the past may also have helped create some of the inter-professional difficulties, myths and misunderstanding about ADHD. The use of medication in children with ADHD needs to be given its rightful place in the treatment of this biological condition. Its use should not be a threat to other professional groups but rather it should be seen as a necessary adjunct. The differences in approaches to diagnosing and managing between varying countries is very concerning. Although there is always a need for caution in diagnosis and in the use of medication, it would appear that there is currently significant under-usage of medication in the UK.

References

Barkley R (1998) Attention Deficit Hyperactivity Disorder. A Handbook for Diagnosis and Treatment 2nd Edition. New York: Guilford.

British Paediatric Association (1993) Health Services for School Age Children. London: BPA.

Comings E (1990) Tourette Syndrome and Human Behavior. Duarte, CA: Hope Press.

Cooper P, Ideus K (1996) Attention Deficit-Hyperactivity Disorder: A Practical Guide for Teachers. London: David Fulton.

Dendy C (1996) Teenagers with ADD. San Francisco CA: Woodbine Press.

Goldstein S, Goldstein M (1990) Managing Attention Disorders in Children. New York: Wiley.

Hartmann T (1993) ADD: A Different Perception. Novato CA: Underwood-Miller.

Hinshaw S (1994) Attention Deficits and Hyperactivity in Children. Thousand Oaks CA: Sage.

Ideus K, Cooper P (1995) Chemical cosh or therapeutic tool? Towards a balanced view of the use of stimulant medication with children diagnosed with attention deficit/hyperactivity disorder. Therapeutic Care and Education 4: 52–63.

Kewley G (1998) ADHD is underdiagnosed and undertreated in Britain. BMJ 316: 1594–5.

Kewley G (1999) Attention Deficit Hyperactivity Disorder: Recognition, Reality and Resolution Sussex: LAC Press.

Kewley G, Scott M, Facer R (1994) Study of ADD in the UK. Unpublished research report, Horsham, Learning Assessment Centre.

Parliamentary Office of Science and Technology report (POST) (1997, Feb.) Circular No 92.

Rosenberg Dr, Holttum J, Gershon S (1990) Textbook of Pharmacotherapy for Child and Adolescent Psychiatric Disorders. New York: Brunner/Mazel.

Rutter M, Tizard J, Whitmore K (1970) Health, Education and Behaviour. London: Longman.

Tannock R (1998) ADHD: advances in cognitive neurobiology and genetic research. Journal of Child Psychology and Psychiatry 39: 65–99.

Taylor E, Hemsley R (1995) Teaching hyperkinetic disorders in childhood. BMJ 310: 1617–18.

Vivian L (1994) The changing pupil population of schools with emotional and behavioural difficulties. Therapeutic Care and Education 3(3): 218–31.

World Health Organisation (1990) International Classification of Diseases. Geneva: WHO.

Chapter 7
ADHD – A Different Viewpoint I: Dietary Factors

JOAN KINDER

'In the treatment of the sick person, the physician must be free to use a new diagnostic and therapeutic measure if in his or her judgement it offers hope of saving life, re-establishing health, or alleviating suffering.'
Helsinki Declaration

Aim of this chapter

The aim of this, and the following chapter, is not to provide a self-help guide to the treatment of ADHD but rather to introduce the concept that there is almost always more than one way to approach any problem. This first chapter primarily addresses dietary and nutritional issues pertinent to the management of ADHD. The second chapter introduces a number, though not by any means all, of the complementary therapies that have yielded lasting benefit to large numbers of children with ADHD and their families. Although separate, the two chapters complement each other and are best read sequentially.

I hope that the information presented will whet the appetite of readers to explore approaches that have not yet gained acceptance by orthodox medicine. The information will hopefully also help dispel the myth that ADHD necessarily equates with treatment with methylphenidate (Ritalin). Naturally there will be cases in which methylphenidate, or other stimulant drugs, may be indicated, together, of course, with a package of multi-modal supportive and therapeutic input. From my perspective, however, the use of stimulant drugs should be reserved either for those children who have not responded sufficiently to other methods to enable them to enjoy a normal life, or for short-term treatment in cases that need immediate diffusion, whilst more definitive input with lasting benefit is being instituted.

At this point I would like to express my gratitude to all the complementary practitioners who kindly spared the time to share their expert knowledge with me regarding their own speciality.

Orthodox versus non-orthodox

'First do no harm' and 'assist nature' are two fundamental Hippocratic principles on which both ethical clinical medical practice and complementary practices are based (Davies, 1997).

Sadly, diagnostic and therapeutic measures that have not been conceived, gestated and delivered by orthodox Western medicine are still regarded with scepticism, cynicism and even downright hostility. It has been speculated that this negative attitude has been borne out of fear that established dogma, and the positions of figures eminent in their fields, might be threatened by the success of non-orthodox approaches. In addition, there is no doubt that any measure that facilitates self-healing is likely to reduce the need for pharmaceutical intervention, which would significantly alter profit margins in a currently thriving industry. There is, however, genuine concern in some quarters about the safety and efficacy of methods that are not subject to the rigorous scrutiny of authorized medical bodies.

In actuality, the relative risks of pharmaceutically orientated orthodox medicine compare unfavourably with those associated with complementary or non-orthodox practices (Davies, 1997). Take, for example, the significant death toll due to either accidental or intentional overdose of medications that are freely available to the general public 'over the counter'. Non-steroidal anti-inflammatory agents used in arthritis, for pain relief and reducing fever in children have been held responsible, either directly or indirectly, for numerous deaths annually in the UK (Davies, 1997). The widespread use of hormone treatments, both as the contraceptive pill and for HRT, in women has coincided remarkably closely with the increase in female cancers (Grant, 1994). The contraceptive pill has also been implicated in the genesis of ADHD in offspring (Grant, 1994). Unpleasant, and often dangerous, side effects of medications are commonplace. In contrast, how many people have died through eliminating junk food from their diets, from taking a vitamin and mineral supplement, a homeopathic remedy or from an aromatherapy massage?

High-tech medicine has achieved some spectacular results, but there is growing suspicion of its invasive procedures and powerful drugs. This, combined with an increasing interest in the holistic approach – in which the therapist considers how to treat the patient who has developed a particular disease, rather than targeting the disease that is affecting the patient – is making complementary therapies more attractive. Most therapists prefer the term 'complementary' to 'alternative', as it implies working with, rather than simply replacing, orthodox medical practices. In 1992 the Department of Health reported that up to 1700 general practitioners were using the services of a complementary practitioner compared to none a few years previously. This figure is certainly much higher now, and increasing numbers of doctors are undergoing additional training in one or other complementary field, such as acupuncture, homeopathy, Bowen therapy and others.

One branch of medicine that currently is considered non-orthodox is non-classical allergy, environmental and nutritional medicine. This includes food intolerance, which is highly pertinent to ADHD and will be the focus of this chapter.

Evidence-based diagnosis and treatment

A frequent criticism of non-orthodox practices is that they are not evidence-based. In 1986 the British Medical Association was quite damning in its criticism of complementary medicine, dismissing most of its claims as placebo effects. However, by 1993 the Association had reversed its position almost completely, calling for more research into the main therapies as a priority and suggesting an introductory course on the subject for medical students.

Perhaps the most important factor that separates orthodox Western medicine from almost all other healing systems throughout the world is the reluctance to acknowledge biological energy as the basis of our nature. Albert Einstein said: 'On such things as matter, we have all been wrong. What we have heretofore called matter is Energy. Energy whose vibration has been so lowered to be perceptible to the sense. As such there is no matter.' Phrases commonly used in everyday parlance such as 'being on the same wavelength' and 'sending out bad vibes' are indicators of the intuitive, albeit usually unconscious, general awareness of our intrinsic energetic nature.

Fundamental to the practice of most complementary therapies is the concept that the human being is a composite of mind, body and soul, all with their own discrete vibrational energies. A disturbance in the energy associated with any one of these inevitably will influence the function of the whole. Therapy aims to restore balance to flows of energy through the body, thereby facilitating a diseased part to heal itself with time. If issues are addressed at an early stage – not solely by suppressing symptoms using pharmaceutical agents – progress to a chronic state can be prevented. Most complementary therapists are also very conscious of the vital role of appropriate nutrition and will often advise on healthy eating and perhaps a change in lifestyle.

The very nature of complementary therapies, which base their approach on the unique individuality of the patient, adjusting treatment accordingly, does not readily lend itself to the classical double-blind placebo-controlled trials that are the gold standard for evidence-based medicine. However, if successful outcomes following treatment of millions of people daily worldwide is testament to their efficacy, this in itself is evidence.

Meanwhile, even within orthodox medicine it is not always possible to provide evidence that one treatment or procedure is safer or more effective than another. For example, how many people suffering with acute appendicitis would be prepared to sign informed consent for random allocation to either surgery or antibiotic treatment? Perhaps it has already been done! Consider also the drugs that have been 'proven' in extensive trials to be both efficacious and safe, yet subsequently have been shown to have disastrous side effects. And what evidence was there in the literature to support the first transplant surgeons in their belief that donated organs might be life-saving substitutes for diseased body parts? Research in controversial fields, which are not supported by the medical establishment, is hampered by lack of finance, equipment and manpower. Some pioneers have funded their own excellent research, following standard protocols, and at great personal expense, only to find their papers blocked from publication in scientific journals. Conversely, it has been known for mediocre studies within orthodoxy to find their way into journals of distinction.

Nevertheless, research in bioenergetics, and in the relationship of nutrition and diet to health, is ongoing, and eventually answers that will satisfy even the greatest of sceptics will be found. Meanwhile it is worth remembering that sailors were given lemons to prevent scurvy long before vitamin C was discovered!

Definition of ADHD

Synonyms of attention deficit hyperactivity disorder (ADHD) include hyperkinetic syndrome, minimal brain dysfunction and hyperactivity.

The classical behavioural characteristics that define ADHD are listed elsewhere in this book. The main features, in brief, are overactivity, inattentiveness, short attention span, impulsivity and aggressive behaviour. A significant number of children with ADHD are also clumsy and have excessive thirst.

Parents of a child with ADHD might define the syndrome as a devastating affliction which creates utter misery and chaos for all those involved, severely disrupting family life – often to the point of family breakdown – and causing psychological disturbance in siblings. In some families the risk of physical abuse, due to pure frustration, is very real. 'Do something, doctor, I can't cope with my child!' is the all too common plea of frantic parents of disturbed children brought for assessment.

Attention deficit hyperactivity disorder frequently co-exists with dyslexia, autism (in particular Asperger syndrome, usually associated with high intelligence), dyspraxia, learning difficulties, chromosomal abnormalities and sometimes with Tourette's syndrome.

Prevalence of ADHD

In the region of 10% of children in the UK display some kind of behavioural disorder. About 5% might be considered to have ADHD. In practical terms this means that it is likely that there will be at least one child in each class at school who will disrupt the smooth process of delivering the curriculum. The condition is commoner in boys than girls in the ratio of about 4:1. The majority are fair-haired with blue eyes.

The prevalence quoted relies upon diagnosis, and diagnosis depends to a degree upon the perceptions of those involved with the child.

Diagnosis and differential diagnosis of ADHD

None of the classical criteria for the diagnosis of ADHD are clear cut. Many children display behavioural features compatible with high scores on the various scales, which include the DSM, ICD 10, Conner's Scale and Encephalopathy Questionnaires. The score alone gives no useful information about the wide range of emotional and physical factors which may be contributing to the antisocial behaviour. Children presenting with ADHD should be screened for all of these by detailed history and examination coupled with appropriate investigations if necessary. In this manner an appropriate package of support and therapy can be instituted. In the majority of cases, particularly with schoolage children, this will involve liaison and co-operation between health professionals, education and often social services.

Factors contributing to the manifestation of ADHD are listed below:

Psychological

- frustration   sensory impairment (hearing, vision)
                speech and communication problems
                lack of consistent parenting
                boredom (for example in gifted children who are under-challenged)
- anxiety   parental discord or threats to the family, real or perceived
                changes in life (such as a new sibling, house move, change of school)
                illness
                hospitalization
                failed relationship with teacher
- fear   bullying (physical or verbal) at home or school
                abuse of any kind, verbal, emotional, physical or sexual
                irrational, perhaps implanted, fears (for example, from violent TV programmes)

Physical

- hearing difficulties (for example glue ear)
- visual impairment
- learning difficulties, including those associated with dyslexia
- chromosomal abnormalities (such as Fragile X, XYY syndromes)
- undiagnosed or inadequately treated asthma
- sleep apnoea or epilepsy (petit mal epilepsy may mimic concentration problems and attention deficit)
- chronic illness (for example cystic fibrosis, rheumatoid arthritis)
- heavy metal toxicity (for example lead, mercury)
- autism (especially Asperger syndrome)
- juvenile psychological, irritable bowel, migraine syndrome (PIMS)
- malfunction of the frontal lobes of the brain (frontal lobe deficit – learning, memory, behaviour) due to (a) birth defect (b) later physical damage (such as trauma or infection), (c) variable migraine-like changes
- food allergy/intolerance or nutritional deficiencies
- sensitivity to chemicals or other environmental factors.

In addition to the above, adverse psychosocial factors play a role in many cases. One study undertaken by Egger in Germany showed that 38% of children with ADHD came from families in which alcoholism was a problem, 10% had family members who had been in conflict with the law (data cited by Professor Joseph Egger at the inaugural meeting of the Allergy Research Foundation, Royal Society of Medicine, London, October 1996). There is a strong history of migraine and irritable bowel syndrome in these families.

Identification and treatment of physical problems such as glue ear, asthma, petit mal and sleep apnoea (Hansen and Vandenberg, 1997) often leads to resolution, or at least amelioration, of the behavioural problems. In this context, the importance of an expert assessment for intolerance to food, beverages, chemicals in food and the environment, and for nutritional deficiencies, cannot be overemphasized.

Granted, in some families food intolerance becomes a scapegoat for parents who are unable to face the less palatable possibility that domestic issues might be contributing to their child's bad behaviour. In others, parents of children who would benefit from dietary adjustment may themselves be 'grown up' unrecognized food-intolerant hyperactives, who are unable to cope with the discipline required for a change of diet and lifestyle. These people will often choose the easier option of palliative treatment with stimulant drugs for their offspring. Sometimes, however, even affected parents will modify their own diet along with that of their child, often with extremely rewarding results.

The outcome for untreated or inappropriately treated ADHD is not very good. Up to 60% will continue to have problems as adolescents and adults (Weiss et al., 1985; Gittleman et al., 1985; Satterfieldet al., 1982; Bakley et al., 1990). The sooner ADHD is diagnosed and therapy instituted the better the prognosis. Mothers of hyperactive children often describe increased foetal activity and how their child had 'tried to kick his way out of the womb'. In early infancy the baby may cry, scream, be constantly restless, require little sleep, suffer with colic, be difficult to feed and pacify, and will spurn affection. These babies are often very thirsty (mistaken for hunger) and may dribble excessively. As time progresses they start head banging and rocking the cot and may have breath-holding attacks, fits and tantrums. Sometimes these symptoms are associated with signs such as catarrh, cradle cap, waxy ears, bowel disturbance, vomiting and skin problems, and even non-infective high fevers. Often symptoms are ascribed to 'a virus' and treated with antibiotics 'to be on the safe side'. Antibiotics do not kill viruses, but they can wreak havoc with gut flora. This sort of history is a powerful indicator that appropriate dietary and environmental intervention instituted at this early stage may completely eliminate the symptoms and prevent years of distressing problems.

Contributing causes: supporting evidence

Food intolerance

Hyperactivity is commonly associated with conditions such as migraine, irritable bowel, arthritis, urticaria (hives), eczema, rhinitis, asthma, Crohn's disease, food aversions and addictions, clumsiness, unreasonable thirst, bed-wetting and sleep disturbance – which are also often present in family members of hyperactive children. All of these may respond to dietary intervention (Brostoff and Gamlin, 1989/1992). In adults, PIMS seems to occur more frequently in people with a history of hyperactivity in childhood. This condition often responds to a simple change in diet. Professor Joseph Egger, an enthusiastic researcher in the field of nutritional medicine, claims that up to 70% or more of children with ADHD can be helped by diet. Through his work with double-blind, placebo-controlled trials, subsequently verified by others, Professor Egger has brought a sound scientific basis to the nutritional approach to ADHD (Swanson and Kinsbourne, 1980; Egger et al., 1985; Carter et al., 1993; Boris and Mandel, 1994), which is now gaining credibility and support, including from doctors eminent in the British National Health Service and some members of parliament.

There are still some, however, who remain unconvinced about the effects of food and food additives on the brain. This is despite the wealth of accrued supporting evidence from numerous studies and publications (Millstone, 1997; Feingold, 1981, 1982; Slauss, 1981; Rowe and Rowe, 1994; Weiss, 1983; Walker-Smith, 1986), including hundreds of references listed in an extensive bibliography entitled 'Food Sensitivity and the Brain'. I quote a statement representing the stance of the body of sceptics regarding this issue: 'The persistence of belief in a dietary basis for behavioural disturbance in the face of all scientifically valid studies failing to confirm any link sounds a cautionary note for those who believe that medicine based on rationality should be the basis of our practice' (David, 1992). In real-life terms, perhaps the most compelling evidence for the efficacy of dietary modulation, in a significant percentage of children with ADHD, is the testimony of tens of thousands of parents of hyperactive children in the UK alone, whose lives have been transformed by eliminating offending foods from, and correcting nutritional imbalances in, their child's diet (see the Hyperactive Children's Support Group Database). In the words of Albert Einstein: 'Pure logical thinking cannot yield us any knowledge of the empirical world; all knowledge of reality starts from experience and ends in it.'

Several hypotheses incriminating specific dietary factors have been developed over the years, including the Feingold hypothesis, which advocates that foods with a high salicylate and chemical additive content are responsible for symptoms (Feingold, 1981, 1982). Some children with ADHD improve using only this diet, which is promoted by the Hyperactive Children's Support Group (HACSG) but most require more rigorous exclusions. Other theories, such as the German phosphate hypothesis, have been discredited. Some studies that appeared to disprove the link between diet and behaviour were flawed in that chocolate drinks were used to disguise placebo and the chocolate itself was causing the reaction!

The commonest trigger foods for hyperactive behaviour seem to be:

- colouring (especially azo-dyes)
- flavouring
- preservatives
- cow's milk
- chocolate
- cheese
- wheat
- tomato
- sugar
- orange
- MSG (monosodium glutamate, E621, flavour enhancer).
  (HACSG database)

Other fairly frequent triggers include fish, egg, citrus fruit, banana, berry fruits, chemicals in the environment (such as perfume), cigarette smoke and, in some cases, tap water.

Affected children are often described as having a Jekyll-and-Hyde personality. Some parents express concern that their child might be schizophrenic, so bizarre and unpredictable is their behaviour (there is evidence that some cases of schizophrenia might respond to dietary modulation: Klee et al., 1979; Singh and Say, 1976; Davies and Stewart, 1987). In some people the reaction to a triggering substance can be dramatic, and an intelligent, rational and articulate person can be transformed into an incoherent whirling dervish. I quote an abridged version of an account written by a successful lawyer during a bad food allergic phase, taken from Dr Alan Franklin's chapter in the book *The Secret Life of Vulnerable Children* (Varma, 1992):

> Hypoactivity produces more less the opersit feeling to brain fag. Everything becomes sharper, the feeling of pain, cold heat as if the nerves are tort. But like brain fage thereis an absance of fear. It starts oftern slowly, but not nesesarlly so, and yhe feeling is like running round and roun an anormouse spring sometimes seeing to sliral upwards, or feeling as is one is an aturntable with someone starting to turn it egain faster & faster. Alough one pftern feelstired the brain starts to speed up at the same time demandingaction and however tired you fail to obay at your peral, the longe you mage to stop the action the more intence it will be. The driving forse within the brain feels very like a strong wind, you may desperatly wasnt to stop but can't.. Whille you feel out of control the brain pushes to move faster and faster.
>
> You can build a mountain, but if anyone asks you why you would like to hit them . . . I tend to knok thins over and if the slightes difficulty arises I stop & do somethig else.. As an adult I felt that I must be able to try and think my way through it but have only tried once, never again, I thought I was going mead. An Adult should have more control that a child for them it must be hell, an adult can keep away from people a child can't. Whille I realise that some restrant must be tried, the hell this must cause is indiscrible.
>
> Any form of ristrant will only add fule to t he fire..If the child must be contained may I sujest a padded cell. One of the main problems isthe desire for excitment,speed. When thebody says stop, the brain scea s GO..One thing is very clear to a HP pesron they are never at fault it's alwas the other person. They oftern look as is thy are high, as with drugs. I never go to a lector in t is state as I will not learn anything, and will only antagisze the speacker by stiring having to speak to get rid of the pentup felling Whille the activity sounds great to many people it is the feeling of being driven with the lack of control that creats the feeling of desparation..so that when you finaly crah the brian fag, somby-like state, is oftern a reliefe., particularly I'm sure to the parent.

If, during assessment of a child with ADHD, food intolerance seems possible, the most successful method of accurately diagnosing trigger foods to date has been the 'oligo-antigenic' or few food diet, with challenge (Egger et al., 1985; Carter et al., 1993).

Children should not be put on restrictive diets without medical and dietetic supervision, nor without addressing other factors that may be contributing to their disturbed behaviour. In addition, it is important that children on a few food diet are not made to feel that they are being punished for something they cannot help. Positive reinforcement with treats (not forbidden foods!) are part of the programme. On the diet sometimes the child's behaviour worsens initially due to withdrawal of an offending food to which the child has become addicted, such as sugar, milk or wheat. During digestion wheat and milk may give rise to opioid-like peptides named exorphins, which are pharmacologically active and can affect the brain (Klee et al., 1979; Shattock and Savery, 1997). As these peptides are recirculated via the kidney, to truly reduce levels it is best to avoid wheat for at least three months when on an elimination diet. Undertaking a diagnostic elimination and challenge diet is no light matter and families often need considerable support. It may even be necessary to admit the child to hospital for the elimination phase.

Once the provoking foods have been identified, compliance with an appropriate diet is important. This can be difficult, especially for older children who function independently and go out in groups with their friends. For those who find it excessively difficult to adhere to long-term dietary regimes, which isolate them from their peers at a vulnerable time of their lives, desensitization is possible using a variety of methods, one of which is enzyme-potentiated desensitization (EPD), which is described briefly later. EPD has been shown to be effective in food intolerant children with ADHD (Egger et al., 1992). Other methods such as homeopathy and the Miller neutralization technique may also be helpful (Miller, 1997).

Most children with ADHD who are food intolerant additionally have an imbalance, and often deficiency, in nutritional factors such as vitamins, minerals, trace elements and essential fatty acids. Nutritional supplements are usually required.

Blood tests, skin tests and other standard methods for diagnosing allergy do not seem to be very successful with food intolerance. An IgG Elisa assay has been developed but is not yet widely used. If atopic allergy (eczema, asthma, hay fever) co-exists, IgE antibodies to foods or other allergens are sometimes found. Alternative diagnostic methods such as applied kinesiology, vega testing and radionic hair analysis have helped some people. One newer and promising non-invasive diagnostic technique is computerized electrodermal screening. This method measures changes in electrical energy flow through the body in response to an applied challenge with specific frequencies generated by the computer. The computer has been programmed to deliver pulses that correspond to the substance requiring testing.

Chemical intolerance; vitamin and mineral status

A study of over 1200 hyperactive children, undertaken by Dr Neil Ward of Surrey University, in conjunction with the Hyperactive Children's Support Group, showed that more than 60% reacted adversely to synthetic colourings, flavourings, preservatives, chemical detergents and perfume – as well as to cow's milk and other food products (Ward, 1997).

Blood, hair, urine and sweat were analysed for mineral and heavy metal status. Compared with controls, the ADHD group had significantly lower levels of iron and zinc, and exceedingly high levels of aluminium, cadmium and lead. Cigarette smoke is known to increase the cadmium and lower the zinc status of the body. A large number of the ADHD group were passive smokers. Passive smokers in the non-ADHD group had much higher initial levels of zinc. It is possible that baseline low levels of zinc render ADHD children more vulnerable to the effects of smoke.

In another study the azo-dyes tartrazine and sunset yellow were shown to dramatically increase urinary zinc loss in many hyperactive children (Ward et al., 1990). They also inhibit the digestive enzymes trypsin (protein) and α amylase (carbohydrate). Incomplete digestion per se reduces absorption of nutrients. It also generates small protein molecules named peptides which, if they gain access to the system, may either be recognized as 'foreign', triggering an immunological response, or may directly affect the brain. Even small doses of tartrazine may provoke dramatic adverse behavioural reactions in zinc-deficient ADHD children within 30 minutes of exposure. Amaranth caused increased urinary loss of magnesium in this group of children.

Vitamins, minerals and trace elements are vital co-factors for the function of enzyme systems in the body. Common deficiencies occurring in ADHD, in addition to zinc and magnesium, include vitamins B_1, B_6, C, and essential fatty acids (EFAs). Many environmental pollutants, including food additives and chemicals used in agriculture and in the home, block receptor sites on enzymes for vitamin B_6, so that even if dietary intake is adequate, enzyme function is impaired. Deficiencies in B_1, B_3, B_6, B_{12}, iron, zinc, magnesium and calcium can all affect behaviour (Davies and Stewart, 1987).

Case study

RT is a 12-year-old hyperactive boy of high intellect but underachieving at school. Although his parents are divorced, the arrangement is amicable and he has regular positive contact with his father whilst living with his mother. Both his father and paternal grandmother smoke. His mother regularly wears perfume. RT has a history of uncontrollable, sometimes violent, rages. His general health is said to be good but he suffers with

headaches, nasal congestion, waxy ears and clumsiness. He also has difficulty getting up in the morning. He is known to react adversely to
chemical additives, which he largely avoids, but still has problems characteristic of ADHD. Examination showed a well-grown boy with bitten
fingernails that were covered with white flecks (usually a sign of zinc
deficiency). He also had large tonsils. RT's father had a history of hyperactivity. The treatment plan included avoidance of smoke, perfume and
other chemicals as much as possible. He was given information about the
commonest food triggers of hyperactive behaviour and headaches,
advised to avoid junk food and was prescribed a zinc supplement and a
good-quality vitamin and mineral supplement. Lavender oil bath soaks at
night were also suggested.

On review three months later the response was described as
'brilliant'. RT had had no headaches, his nose was clear, he was getting
up in the morning without trouble, and said he was feeling happy and
less stressed. His mother reported a complete change saying that he was
now generating an aura of peace and calm! School and homework had
improved and he was already achieving two grades higher than before
treatment. RT had found that, in addition to chemical additives in food,
chocolate, orange and squashes with preservatives affected him. The
quality of his diet had improved. He loved the lavender bath soaks. His
mother was convinced that the zinc had played a major role in the
improvement. He was praised for his achievement and advised to
continue the zinc supplement until all the white flecks had disappeared
from his nails and then to wean off, but to remain on the vitamin and
mineral supplement for several months longer.

Essential fatty acid deficiency

Omega-6 and omega-3 fatty acids are considered essential because we
cannot synthesize them in our bodies and are dependent on dietary
sources. They are ubiquitous in food, especially grains and vegetables
(omega-6) and seafoods (omega-3). Until relatively recently infant
formulae contained very little in the way of EFAs and generations of
bottle-fed babies were almost certainly deficient in these nutrients.
Essential fatty acids are major structural components of cell membranes
and influence membrane fluidity and transport of ions across them. The
omega-6 EFAs are distributed evenly in the tissues whereas the omega-3
EFAs are concentrated in a few tissues, notably in the brain.

Once ingested, EFAs are converted, via a number of complex
enzymatically controlled steps, to biologically active hormone-like end
products called prostaglandins. Prostaglandin E_1 (PGE$_1$), derived from
the omega-6 EFAs, is an extremely active substance that influences the
function of virtually all tissues in the body, including the immune system
(Davies and Stewart, 1987; Graham, 1984; Horrobin, 1980). It has anti-
inflammatory and possibly neurotransmitter effects. Deficiency may

contribute to the manifestation of allergy, antisocial behaviour and thirst. One of the enzymes involved in the omega-6 pathway, the delta-6 desaturase enzyme, seems to be congenitally deficient in some people with ADHD, especially if they also suffer with atopic allergy (eczema, asthma, hay fever) (Graham, 1984). It also seems to be deficient in cystic fibrosis. Delta-6 desaturase depends upon adequate supplies of zinc, magnesium and vitamin B_6 for its function. Its activity is inhibited by a number of factors, including suboptimal levels of the above nutrients, excess sugar in the bloodstream, some viral infections, saturated fat, cigarette smoke, stress, ageing, ionising radiation and others. A further enzymatically controlled step in the pathway is inhibited by azo-dyes, salicylates, deficiency of vitamins B_3, C, D and calcium, and also by opioids of wheat and milk (Graham, 1984). The omega-6 EFAs also give rise to PGE_2 series, which are pro-inflammatory.

Omega-3 EFAs are metabolized via a different pathway, yielding yet another series of prostaglandins, the PGE_3 series. A balance between all three is essential for health.

Many studies have demonstrated the important role of EFAs in ADHD (Bundy and Colquhoun, 1981; Stevens et al., 1995; Mitchell et al., 1987). Deficiencies can lead to disturbed function in any tissue or organ in the body (Davies and Stewart, 1987; Graham, 1984). Symptoms include dry skin, lumpy skin on the upper arms and thighs, cradle cap in babies, excess thirst, fluid retention and behavioural problems, especially ADHD, amongst others. Dyslexic children are likely to have low levels of omega-3 EFAs (as well as zinc) (Grant, 1994). Up to 50% of ADHD children are also dyslexic (data cited by Professor Joseph Eggar in his presentation at the inaugural meeting of the Allergy Research Foundation, Royal Society of Medicine, London, October 1996).

Shortage of omega-6 EFAs (hence PGE_1) can be addressed by supplementing the diet with oils rich in one of the intermediates in the pathway, gamma-linolenic acid (GLA). This also bypasses the possible block caused by deficiency and/or inhibition of delta-6 desaturase. Good sources of GLA are evening primrose oil, borage oil (star flower) or blackcurrant seed oil. Omega-3 chain deficiencies are supplemented with flax seed oil, food-quality linseed oil or fish oils containing eicosapentaenoic acid (EPA) and docosahexaenoic acid (DHA). Aspirin and non-steroidal anti-inflammatory drugs such as ibuprofen, used to reduce fever or relieve pain, block some of these pathways, as do steroids. They are best avoided in children with ADHD who are food sensitive, unless absolutely necessary.

Glyconutrient deficiency

In Darwinian theory we learn that survival depends upon our ability to adapt to all challenges we encounter. By definition our environment is hostile, which means that we must develop extremely efficient mechanisms for maintaining homeostasis. The triad of genetic predisposition (inherited constitution), environmental challenge (toxins, infections, etc.) and nutritional state all interact and contribute to the outcome. Satisfactory adaptation leads to health. Partial adaptation leads to disease, and failure to adapt leads to death. Since we have, to date, survived as a species, it follows that we must be genetically programmed for health. In a healthy body the millions of processes constantly and silently correcting any imbalances in, and repairing damage to, our diverse systems must be working together in sophisticated harmony. The maintenance of the stability of this internal milieu is known as homeostasis. For the components of these systems to function effectively, accurate internal communication is vital. The key to success in the battle for survival is communication.

Many biological 'messengers', such as hormones, neurotransmitters and a multitude of molecules involved in the immune system, have been identified and their roles elucidated. However, one neglected area in the field of medicine is glycobiology, which deals with the role of carbohydrates in biological events, in particular with relation to communication between cells. In its most basic form this communication occurs at cellular level – individual cells must 'talk' to each other. If the language of cells is garbled, so that the message is unclear, health problems occur.

According to John Hodgson:

> Almost without exception, whenever two or more living cells interact in a specific way, cell surface carbohydrates will be involved. From the first meeting of sperm and egg, through embryogenesis, development and growth, carbohydrate molecules confer exquisite specificity upon cell–cell interactions. (Hodgson, 1990)

Any molecule in which a sugar (carbohydrate, saccharide, glyco-) is bound to the functional part of another molecule is called a glycoconjugate – for example, a sugar with a lipid forms a glycolipid and a sugar with a protein forms a glycoprotein. Both of these types of molecule are fundamental structural elements in cell membranes. Glycoproteins seem to play a key role in cellular communication, including that between neurons in the brain.

Originally, proteins were thought to be the primary communication molecules, but their structural simplicity limits the number of configurations that are possible in combining with other molecules. The structurally more complex carbohydrate molecule is much more versatile. For example, up to tens of thousands of different oligosaccharide configurations are possible with four sugars, whereas only 24 oligopeptide configurations are possible with four peptides (Stryer, 1995).

Glycoproteins are assembled in the endoplasmic reticulum (factory house) of cells under instruction from messengers sent by the DNA in cell nuclei. Many genetic diseases are associated with altered glycoproteins. These include the collagen diseases such as rheumatoid arthritis (Axford, 1997). ADHD, as noted earlier, has a strong familial link with rheumatoid arthritis. Research in the field indicates that eight monosaccharides (sugars), commonly found in human glycoproteins, are vital for the synthesis of the highly specific structures at receptor sites in cell membranes, which are essential for accurate communication. These sugars are: galactose, glucose, mannose, N-acetylgalactosamine, N-acetylglucosamine, fucose, xylose and N-acetylneuraminic acid (Stryer, 1995; Murray, 1996).

The raw materials required to build glycoconjugates are provided by plants. Ultimately only plants are able to capture the sun's energy to create carbohydrates. The biological signal for the plant to synthesize these molecules is maturation of the fruit, vegetable and seed. Fruits and vegetables that are picked unripe will not have reached this stage. If, in addition, they are grown in soil deplete in micronutrients, are then subjected to processing and lengthy storage, followed by overcooking, there is very little in the way of nutritional value left. The average modern child prefers milk products, crisps and biscuits to a plate of fresh steamed vegetables and fish with fruit for dessert. Working people find it easier to cope with the demands of job and home if they buy processed food, denuded of nutrients and laden with chemical additives, which is further adulterated by microwave cooking. It is hardly surprising that there has been a significant increase in allergies, behavioural disorders, chronic diseases and ill health, when we consider the burden we are asking our bodies to carry, with inadequate supplies of vital nutrients with which to do it.

Early studies have been undertaken in the USA looking at the role of glyconutrient supplementation using phytonutriceuticals in children with ADHD (Dykman and Mckinley, 1997; Dykman and Dykman, 1999). The products used in the studies were obtained by flash freeze drying a range of fresh raw fruits and vegetables, grown naturally and picked at their prime. The technique used protected the essential components of the whole food, and the supplements contained no chemical additives. The studies were not placebo-controlled, but they indicated significant health benefits and reduction in the frequency and severity of symptoms of ADHD.

Before leaving the topic of glyconutrition, the reader should note that the unique power of human breast milk to protect and promote good health in human babies is because the saccharides (sugars) required to synthesize molecules and cells involved in immune defence are only naturally provided in human milk, not in cow's, goat's or sheep's milk, or formulae made from them. These necessary saccharides are galactose, fructose, glucose, N- acetylglucosamine and N-acetylneuraminic acid (Dr H Reg McDaniel, personal communication). It is important that the nursing mother has a diet able to provide these elements.

The nutritional status of both parents prior to conception, and of the mother during pregnancy, can profoundly affect the outcome for the child. Optimal nutrition and a healthy lifestyle in these early days will promote accurate communication between dividing and developing cells, making it less likely that the child will be born with defects, either of gross structure, of neurological connections or, more subtly, at a cellular level. It may also reduce the risk of a genetically defective gene being 'switched on' in utero.

Brain changes in ADHD

Frontal lobe deficit is associated with difficulties with learning, memory and behaviour. Single photon emission computed tomography (SPECT) brain scans performed in Denmark on people with ADHD and reversible frontal lobe deficit (food-related) have demonstrated reduced perfusion of the frontal lobes of the brain, which improves with diet (Henrikson et al., 1989). In some there was also reduced perfusion in the basal ganglia where complex movement is co-ordinated (a significant number of hyper-active children are also clumsy). Abnormalities in the basal ganglia in ADHD have also been demonstrated by magnetic resonance imaging (MRI) scans in a recent American study (Mataro et al., 1997).

Positron emission tomography (PET) scans performed in the USA on a similar population showed reduced glucose utilization in the frontal lobes (Zametkin et al., 1990). The changes were reversible and brought on by trigger foods. Both this and the Danish studies provide evidence that frontal lobe deficit has a physical cause, though the mechanism by which changes are effected has not yet been elucidated.

EEG abnormalities

Many hyperactive children have difficulty getting to sleep and then wake frequently. In one randomized sleep-monitoring study, the EEG (brain wave) and oculography (eye movement) responses in a study group of known food sensitive hyperactive children, both on and off diet, were recorded (Kiefer et al., 1991). Rapid eye movement (REM) sleep, which seems to be important for concentration and memory, increased signifi-cantly when avoiding provoking foods. By adjusting the diet it was possible to normalize sleep patterns and improve mental function. Disturbance of sleep for any reason, including sleep apnoea and snoring siblings, will have similar effects (Hansen and Vandenberg, 1997; Fishbein, 1970). One method of torture during the Second World War was to repeatedly wake the prisoner during REM sleep, which caused severe mental disturbance (cf junior doctors in the UK 10 years ago!).

Computerized analysis of EEG in food intolerant children has shown increased electrical activity over the frontal lobes during challenge with provoking foods (Uhlig et al., 1997). The electrical activity decreased on an appropriate diet. This is interesting since we know that patients with migraine can suffer seizure activity during a migraine attack, and the link between migraine and hyperactivity has already been established (Egger et al., 1989).

With the combination of reduced blood flow, reduced glucose utilization and increased electrical activity in the frontal lobes, it is hardly surprising that there are significant differences on psychological testing of ADHD children when they are on an appropriate diet.

Some practitioners in the USA are using melatonin to help sleep disturbances in ADHD (personal communication).

Case study

John was referred at the age of four-and-a-half for possible epilepsy. He had been suffering trance-like episodes for almost two years. The onset coincided with a fall downstairs, though he had not seemed traumatized at the time and no medical advice had been sought. The 'episodes' had been increasing in frequency and severity and were accompanied by quite bizarre behaviour. One night he bounced up and down on his bed, squealing and giggling for several hours, but was unresponsive to his parents. Recently the episodes had started to occur at mealtimes. His eyes would glaze over and roll up, he would put his thumb in his mouth, would then leave the table and dance around with little jerky steps, backwards and forwards, and might burst out laughing. When his parents remonstrated, he might cease momentarily but would then continue with a vengeance. During attacks no colour change or vomiting was ever noted. He denied head or tummy pain. His bowels were regular. He did have asthma, controlled by inhaled steroids, and mild eczema. He also bedwet intermittently. John was described as hyperactive much of the time. He had mood swings and tantrums, poor concentration and his sleep was restless. He was clumsy and unco-ordinated. At school he was said to be socially immature and to have poor concentration.

The pregnancy had been uneventful, though he had been active in utero. Delivery had been slow and difficult and John had narrowly escaped Caesarian section for foetal distress. He required a whiff of oxygen but then fed well from breast and bottle.

As a baby he suffered with tantrums and would head bang. His development was mostly normal though his speech was slow and he had ambivalent handedness. His diet lacked vegetables, which he refused to eat.

John's father had asthma. Both parents suffered with intermittent migraine with visual loss. His sister had very severe infantile eczema that had responded excellently to dietary intervention.

Examination was unremarkable apart from a pale, sallow complexion, a very large head (like his father), ambivalent handedness, poor co-ordination and massive white flecks on his fingernails indicating probable zinc deficiency.

His parents were concerned about either a brain tumour or schizophrenia.

An EEG showed generalized bursts of abnormal activity.

A CT scan showed a tiny infarct in the left parieto-occipital region.

Anticonvulsants had been recommended by another paediatrician but the pointers indicated a dietary cause for his problems and his parents preferred to avoid medication unless absolutely necessary. He underwent electrodermal intolerance testing and was put on a diet avoiding cow's milk products, chocolate, cheese, banana, orange, apple, tomato and all chemical additives. He also showed sensitivity to the natural phenoloic malvin. The family were already geared to diets because of John's sister's food intolerance. Nutritional supplements were given including extra zinc.

Within two weeks the 'episodes' had almost stopped. He was eating a healthier diet, though still rather low in vegetables, and was sleeping soundly. On one occasion he reacted adversely to pickles, given as a treat.

John is now a healthy, happy boy who has lost his previous symptoms and has made excellent progress at school. His parents cancelled his follow-up EEG appointment as he is now so well.

Gut factors

Many children with ADHD also suffer with abdominal symptoms, including pain, bloating or irregular bowel habits. In one study, 17 children in this category, who were known to be wheat sensitive, were examined for coeliac disease by suction biopsies of the bowel (data cited by Professor John Eggar in his presentation at the inaugural meeting of the Allergy Research Foundation, Royal Society of Medicine, London, October 1996). None had coeliac disease. Some showed secondary lactase deficiency acquired due to long-term irritation of the bowel by foods to which it was sensitive.

In addition, the biopsy samples showed a significant increase in receptor density for a substance called vasoactive intestinal peptide (VIP) in the duodenum during avoidance of provoking foods. In the brain, VIP is able to constrict blood vessels, which might explain the reduced perfusion in the frontal lobes in some hyperactive children on food challenge. It might also explain the transient visual loss or seizures associated with migraine. The possibility of using blood VIP levels as a diagnostic tool for food-induced ADHD, migraine or epilepsy is being explored.

A significant number of children with ADHD suffer with symptoms compatible with gut parasites or abnormal gut flora, which often follows treatment with oral antibiotics. Many of these children have had several courses of antibiotics for ENT problems or mucus on the chest, often starting before their first birthday. Antibiotics tend to kill off beneficial or friendly micro-organisms (bacteria) in the intestinal tract, allowing the overgrowth of fungal or yeasty elements such as candida. The condition is popularly dubbed 'the candida syndrome', though this may be a misnomer. In the 'syndrome' the integrity of the gut wall seems to be impaired due to irritation and inflammation caused by allergenic substances produced by the abnormal flora. The resulting increased bowel permeability permits the transfer of peptides from incompletely digested protein and harmful substances, such as the phenolic compound p-cresol and aldehydes generated by this altered flora, into the bloodstream. This has led to the term 'the leaky gut syndrome'. Many children with ADHD do respond, sometimes quite dramatically, to a diet avoiding foods that promote the growth of fungal and yeasty elements, such as sugary and yeasty food, perhaps also supported with antifungal medication or herbals (Brostoff and Gamlin, 1989/1992; Truss, 1978; Crook, 1984; Anthony et al., 1997). One practitioner in the USA, who has treated thousands of children with ADHD, has found gut parasites of one kind or another in most of the children she has seen (Joyce Baker, personal communication). In many of the children the behavioural manifestations of ADHD abated when the parasites were eliminated. This could have been due to an increased uptake of nutrients, which previously were being consumed by the 'visitors', and/or a reduction in the amount of p-cresol and aldehydes being produced by the abnormal gut flora. Frequently there is a history of thrush in the mother. The children characteristically have a pallid complexion, violaceous shadows around their eyes, bloating of the abdomen and catarrh.

Genetic factors

Although no specific gene for ADHD has yet been identified for certain, ADHD does seem to be a genetic disorder, as evidenced by twin studies, which show up to 100% concordance for ADHD in monozygotic (identical) twins and only 50% concordance for dizygotic (non-identical) twins (data cited by Professor John Eggar in his presentation at the inaugural meeting of the Allergy Research Foundation, Royal Society of Medicine, London, October 1996). In addition, there is a very strong familial incidence of ADHD together with migraine, irritable bowel, rheumatoid arthritis and addictions such as alcoholism, cigarette smoking and drug abuse amongst others.

Methylphenidate influences the reuptake of the neurotransmitter dopamine in the brain (Ding et al., 1995) and transiently improves brain perfusion during treatment (Lou et al., 1989). Research generated from this finding has demonstrated a possible abnormality in the dopamine transporter gene. One might postulate that abnormal glycoprotein synthesis, perhaps due to a combination of faulty genetic coding together with nutritional deficiency, might be involved.

Some children with ADHD seem to congenitally lack certain enzymes. Delta-6 desaturase has already been mentioned in the context of EFA metabolism. Another of these enzymes is phenol-sulpho-transferase- P (PST-P), which is found in the gut and brain. The primary role for this enzyme is to detoxify phenolic compounds by adding a sulphate group to them. Its function is sulphate dependent, as are other detoxification processes in the liver and brain. The enzyme's action is inhibited by red wine, and certain food colourings, as well as amines present in cheese, chocolate and banana, amongst others (Brostoff and Gamlin, 1989/1992; Waring and Mgong, 1993; also Robert Sinaiko's address at the Annual Conference of the Feingold Association in Fort Worth, Texas, June 1994, and the letter by Vivette Glover in *The Lancet* of 5 April 1986).

A primary source of sulphate is the amino acid cysteine, which is released during the complete digestion of protein. Under normal circumstances about 25% of dietary cysteine is absorbed. Protein digestion may be impaired in some allergic children with ADHD due to reduced stomach acid, which is necessary for the action of the protein-digesting enzyme pepsin. In addition, azo-dyes, such as tartrazine, used as food and medication colourants (including in antibiotics), have been shown to inhibit another protein-digesting enzyme, trypsin. Low cysteine levels due to dietary deficiency or poor digestion, coupled perhaps with abnormal function of enzymes controlling the conversion of cysteine to sulphate, reduce the amount of sulphate produced. In addition, excessive utilization of sulphate in detoxification processes, for example of paracetamol in the liver, further reduces the pool.

Sulphate deficiency in itself both impairs the function of PST-P and limits the liver's detoxification capability. It also seems to affect the quality of mucus produced in the gut (and airways), which instead of being negatively charged – due to the sulphate ions – fluid and smooth, becomes positively charged, thick and lumpy. This mars its protective function. The gut wall becomes 'leaky' and, as mentioned above, peptide molecules generated by incomplete digestion of proteins more readily pass into the circulation and thence may gain access to the brain. Normally, the negative charge and smooth fluidity of healthy, sulphate-rich gut mucus repels harmful bacteria, most of which also carry a negative charge. Bacteria and other microbes are more readily attracted to sulphate-depleted, positively charged mucus, to which they may adhere, become established and produce increased amounts of toxic compounds, such as p-cresol. Since both PST-P activity and the protection of cells lining the gut are impaired by sulphate deficiency, toxic phenolic compounds may accumulate and enter the circulation. These compounds are soluble in both fat and water, and thus are also able to cross the protective blood–brain barrier and wreak their effects on the brain (Waring and Mgong, 1993).

The structure of some neurotransmitters (molecules that carry chemical messages across gaps between nerve cells) is based on the phenol molecule. Because of a similarity in shape, extraneous phenolic compounds can latch on to receptors, which should be specific for these neurotransmitters, and interfere with normal neurotransmission. They may either mimic the natural neurotransmitters – send false messages, block the receptors – or use up the PST-P in the brain that would normally inactivate the transmitters once their job was done. The net effect is neuro-excitation manifesting rather like static (Waring and Mgong, 1993; also Robert Sinaiko's address at the Annual Conference of the Feingold Association in Fort Worth, Texas, June 1994, and the letter by Vivette Glover in *The Lancet* of 5 April 1986).

Phenolic compounds are ubiquitous in our diet. Some of the foods in the Feingold diet that do not have a high salicylate content do have a high phenol content. Many phenolic compounds are harmless. Some are toxic. One such toxic compound, p-cresol, as mentioned above, is produced by organisms in the gut. Others, such as the petroleum-based food additives butylated hydroxyanisole (BHA) and butylated hydroxytoluene (BHT), used as antioxidants, frequently cause problems for food-intolerant children with ADHD. Detoxification of both phenolic compounds and aldehydes (which, as mentioned earlier, also may be produced by abnormal gut flora) is sulphate-dependent.

Perfume, cleaning materials and cigarette smoke contain significant quantities of phenolics. Sensitivity to environmental phenols could explain why the behaviour of some children with ADHD deteriorates in specific locations. I have known children who have reacted to the cleaning agents or felt tip pens used at school, and others who were only hyperactive at home, but were found to be sensitive to cigarette smoke, mum's perfume or dad's aftershave!

An excess of phenolic compounds in the gut, from dietary sources or produced by gut flora, combined with congenitally defective detoxification mechanisms, perhaps a lack of sulphate and a 'leaky' gut, are ideal conditions for the toxins to enter the circulation or lymphatic system and access the brain, where their presence is manifested as behavioural disturbance. Homeopathic potencies of phenolic compounds, including neurotransmitters, have helped some children, as has homeopathic sulphur. Others seem able to absorb both magnesium and sulphate ions through their skin during soaks in Epsom salt (magnesium sulphate) baths. Magnesium sulphate given by mouth, however, may precipitate diarrhoea and very little is absorbed.

Paracetamol detoxification in the liver uses up sulphate, therefore its use is best avoided in children displaying hyperactivity (or autistic features) unless absolutely necessary, as it could worsen the situation. This is particularly relevant for screaming hyperactive babies who are given Calpol to quieten them down. This practice could actually be exacerbating the situation and accelerating a decline.

Neurotransmission

The brain is made up of nerve cells (neurons) with long extensions called axons. At the ends of the axons are terminal processes that house vesicles containing chemicals called neurotransmitters. Neurons form complicated communication networks in the brain, yet nerve cells do not actually touch each other. Between them there is a minute gap called a synapse. Thoughts are formed when a tiny electrical current passes down the axon to the terminal process of the presynaptic neuron, triggering the release of neurotransmitters from the vesicles. These cross the synapse and attach to specific receptor molecules on the post-synaptic neuron, setting up an electrical signal that is perceived as a message. When the transmitter has done its job it is inactivated by enzymes in the synaptic gap so the message generated is clear, without background 'noise'. The production, release and decommissioning of neurotransmitters after use is all carefully regulated. If the process is disturbed, changes in mood, behaviour and thought processes occur. Adequate supplies of essential nutrients are vital for the enzymes that control all these processes.

A number of neurotransmitters are involved in behaviour including noradrenalin, serotonin, dopamine and acetylcholine. Gamma amino butyric acid (GABA) is an inhibitory transmitter, preventing excess release of excitatory transmitters.

Opioid peptides from milk and wheat that have gained access to the brain from the gut may initially increase brain signals but later decrease them. Many food-sensitive children experience a 'buzz' after a milk or wheat 'fix', followed by tiredness and lassitude. According to some researchers, over a period of time opioid peptides can damage neurons and 'prune' brain connections. As the brain connections regenerate poorly after early infancy, prompt recognition of ADHD, autism and dyslexia and institution of appropriate management is mandatory to prevent long-term effects on the brain. Opioid peptides also inhibit colon motility. Many children with constipation, especially those who are addicted to milk, improve when cow's milk products are removed from their diet (Shattock and Savery, 1997).

Some foods rich in amines, such as banana, cheese, chocolate, as well a host of phenolic compounds, may impede decommissioning of neuro-transmitters after use either by direct inhibition of enzymes or by competing for PST-P sulphation in the brain. Migraine triggered by these foods is a probable indicator of PST-P deficiency. Frequently one or both parents of a hyperactive child suffer with migraine. Organophosphates (OPs) and other toxic compounds used widely in agriculture, and also for the treatment of head lice in children, are fat soluble. Grains, unless organic, are impregnated with these noxious chemicals, which are not destroyed by cooking. OPs accumulate in fatty tissue, including in the fatty sheaths surrounding nerves in the brain. They block enzyme systems and can interfere with neurotransmission (Anthony et al., 1997). Omega-3 series EFAs are important in maintaining the integrity of the neuronal sheaths.

It would be unwise in the extreme to treat head lice in children with ADHD with pesticides. In fact, their use in anyone carries a significant risk.

Possible mechanisms affecting neurotransmission

Allergic

The immune system mounts a response to peptide amines that have reached the brain from the gut as a result of incomplete digestion and 'leaky gut'. The prolonged allergic inflammatory response damages the presynaptic terminal with reduction in availability of neurotransmitters. There is a compensatory increase in postsynaptic receptors to catch the reduced amount of transmitter. The postsynaptic neuron is now more 'excitable' and finds it difficult to differentiate between true and false transmission, with resultant background 'noise'.

Orienting response

In order to accomplish a task the brain needs to be able to focus on that task, screening itself from all non-priority information. In so doing it is working in its focused, organized state. At other times it needs to be alert and ready to respond to a variety of possibilities, receiving information from different sources which it is able to collate. This is the receptive, disorganized state. Normally the brain is able to switch back and forth between these states, a phenomenon called the orienting response. ADHD children do not seem to have this capability. They are able to focus on their own ideas but find it difficult to switch to the receptive state which is required for learning. The stimulant drug methylphenidate locks the brain into the organized state, and although children are able to focus on their tasks better, they are usually not as receptive to assimilating different concepts.

Gut

The gut flora are disturbed – perhaps due to altered charge (positive instead of negative), this being due to reduced sulphation of the mucus or to excessive use of antibiotics – with overgrowth of abnormal bacteria and/or fungal elements and perhaps parasites. Production of phenols and aldehydes by fungi/bacteria leads to overload of the PST-P detoxification mechanism. Phenols accumulate in the brain and, because of increased receptors, are able to latch on, creating 'background noise'.

False signals

These may result from the reduction in availability of PST-P sulphation in gut and brain, together with excess phenolic, opioid or other peptide amine compounds. 'Communication' may also be impaired by deficiencies in essential 'sugars' necessary for the formation of glycoproteins at receptor sites.

Use of Ritalin

This stimulates release of transmitters from presynaptic neurons. This ultimately leads to their depletion, followed by compensatory increase in receptors and later background noise. New receptors develop fairly rapidly but remain for a very long time, even after the need for them has been removed.

Vaccination

The role of vaccination in the manifestation of ADHD is not proven. Research is currently being conducted that might provide evidence linking the onset of symptoms in genetically predisposed individuals to some challenging event in their lives, such as vaccination. There does seem to be circumstantial evidence for the link with autism in some cases, and since autism and ADHD are closely related, it would seem reasonable to keep an open mind on the subject. It would be sensible to ensure that any child manifesting signs of ADHD should be physically well at the time of vaccination, as even a heavy cold is a challenge to the immune system, and the additional stress of vaccination may make a vulnerable child more sensitive to other stressors, such as dietary factors and environmental chemicals.

Prognosis

Some children do seem to 'grow out of' ADHD, but these are few. About 60% will go on to have severe problems as adolescents and adults (Weiss et al., 1985; Gittleman et al., 1985; Satterfield et al., 1982). In addition to the features of ADHD, a significant number also demonstrate features of conduct disorder, which includes violence, stealing and verbal abuse (Loeber et al., 1991). For these children, generally, the prognosis is not very good if they remain untreated or are treated inappropriately.

Research undertaken independently by Mannuzza in New York (Mannuzza et al., 1989), Mark Wolfgang in the USA (Wolfgang et al., 1972) and David Farrington, criminologist, in the UK (Farrington, 1993) has shown that the vast majority of crime (in particular violent crime, such as armed robbery, rape, assault and battery) is committed by about

6% of the population, known as chronic offenders. Many of these offenders have problems with addictions, including alcohol, cigarettes, coffee, Coca-Cola and street drugs as well as prescribable medications. Although it is recognized that most human behaviour is the product of social factors, it is noteworthy that the common marker in two-thirds of these chronic offenders is hyperactivity at the tender age of six! If the underlying issues contributing to hyperactive behaviour were addressed early, or even preconceptionally, this would impact on the majority of all crime and would have enormous beneficial implications for society, including education, health and policing. Of course, not all children meeting the diagnostic criteria for ADHD at the age of six will progress to delinquency and criminality, but the risk is significant. Many will be unhappy people as adults, partly because they failed to achieve at school and without qualifications are unable to secure employment that is rewarding intellectually and financially, partly because they may still be carrying the burden of poor self-esteem and an inability to tolerate stress. Many, in fact, have above average IQs.

During 1991 and 1992 Peter Bennett, a police inspector at the time, conducted a pilot study called The Shipley Project, in which he used diet, nutritional supplements and low-dose enzyme-potentiated desensitization (EPD – see below for an explanation of this technique) on a group of delinquent adolescents, who had already been in serious trouble with the law on a number of occasions. Eight out of ten co-operated. This group showed remarkable changes in behaviour, and the cost to the community in terms of vandalism and police time fell considerably. Most of the youngsters chose to continue with the diet after the study had ended (Bennet, 1992).

A number of other studies, undertaken by Professor Stephen Schoenthaler on inmates of various penal institutions in the USA, have shown statistically significant reductions in antisocial behaviour and acts of violence within the institutions when the prison diets were changed and supplemented with vitamins and minerals. Many thousands of dollars were saved in repairs to property and costs of legal proceedings as a result (Schoenthaler, 1985; Schoenthaler et al., 1997).

Treatment options

Dietary intervention and nutritional support

Some 60–70% of children with ADHD will respond to dietary intervention. Sometimes all that is required is avoidance of key trigger factors for ADHD. At other times a diagnostic elimination with a challenge diet may be needed. There is no universally correct diet for children with ADHD. Each child will need his or her diet to be modified individually according to information obtained in a detailed history. This is time-consuming but essential. Restrictive diets should only be undertaken under the supervision of a doctor or dietician/nutritionist with experience in the field of nutritional medicine. Merely providing hand-outs does not work. In addition, it can be dangerous to stay on an unsupervised long-term diet as nutritional deficiencies may develop. During the diet, chewing gum, coloured toothpaste and tap water may be unsuspected triggers for bad behaviour.

Many, if not all, children presenting with ADHD consume inadequate amounts of key vitamins and minerals. Almost always zinc, magnesium, some of the B vitamins and essential fatty acids are lacking, which will undoubtedly contribute to the manifestation of the disorder. Most will require nutritional supplementation. It is safe for most children to be given a good-quality, low-dose vitamin and mineral supplement (additive free), which will help protect them from infectious diseases and reduce the need for antibiotic therapy. Minor ailments can often be dealt with using complementary therapies – for example, camomilla, biochemic tissue salts or a roman chamomile compress for teething. Mucus and nasal congestion with colds often respond to inhalations of lavender, myrtle and eucalyptus oils.

If a prescribed diet does not seem to be working, suspect sabotage – for example, food swapping at school, grandmother's visits, cheating when at a friend's or when spending the weekend with a parent who is estranged from the main family following divorce. For cases in which compliance with dietary changes for any length of time seems impossible, desensitization is probably indicated. If the diet is adhered to and definitely does not work, other factors should be considered, such as those outlined earlier in the text: thyroid disorder, lead poisoning, the effects of maternal smoking during pregnancy, metabolic disorders, genetic disorders, foetal alcohol syndrome, etc. There will be some cases in whom no cause can be identified. These may respond to other therapies. For some, stimulant drugs may be needed in the short term. If coeliac disease is diagnosed, avoidance of gluten will probably be life-long.

The role of phosphatidyl serine as a supplement for some children with ADHD has awakened interest in some quarters, though most of the research has been conducted on the elderly (Klinkhammer et al., 1990; Zannoti, 1987). This phospholipid (along with others) appears to be important for the structure and function of cell membranes in the brain, and deficiency results in reduction of cognitive function. In addition to improvements in perception, memory and recall, ability to concentrate and focus upon tasks have been shown to improve. More general functional improvements reported with treatment include mood and attention, behaviour, social interest and participation, reduced withdrawal, improvement of sleep patterns and better motor reactions. Supplements specifically for children with ADHD are sold 'over-the-counter' in the USA.

Enzyme-potentiated desensitization (EPD)

This method for desensitizing patients against allergies was first discovered in the late 1960s/early 1970s by Dr Len McEwen, when he found that a single dose of grass pollen, together with the enzyme beta-glucuronidase, could be as effective as a long course of conventional desensitizing injections (McEwen and Starr, 1972; McEwen, 1973, 1975; Fell and Brostoff, 1990). Since the dose of allergens used in EPD is much smaller than those used in the conventional method, this treatment is also safer. In fact, extremely low doses of allergens are used. These are mixed with beta-glucuronidase and administered either by injection into the skin or by applying a plastic 'cup' containing the desensitizing mixture to a small area of scarified skin, usually on the forearm. The 'cup' is left in place for at least 24 hours. The latter method is usually more acceptable to children than injections.

Large quantities of beta-glucuronidase are present in certain white cells in our bloodstream called macrophages and polymorphs. These are involved in the immune defence of our bodies. During an inflammatory or allergic reaction significant amounts of the enzyme are released into the tissues from these cells. The activity of beta-glucuronidase is triggered by the presence of certain simple sugars, which are also released locally from more complex molecules as a result of the inflammatory process. In nature, the quantities of free beta-glucuronidase and the simple sugars that trigger its activity, which are normally present at sites of inflammation, will significantly increase the immune response to the antigen responsible. EPD utilizes this principle, but the doses used for treatment are much smaller than those occurring naturally. In Dr McEwen's words: 'the "whispered" natural message of EPD to the immune system generates a new family of cells. After three weeks, when they are all mature, these will travel around the body actively switching off allergies' (McEwen and Starr, 1972; McEwen, 1973).

As EPD is using one of nature's own pathways, it is easily influenced by the body's hormones, nutrition and the environment, and certain preparatory and precautionary measures have to be employed during the days either side of a therapeutic session. The greatest risk is in the 24 hours following treatment. During this vulnerable period excessive exposure to allergens from other sources can actually reverse the effect of EPD for the allergen concerned. In order to avoid failure certain instructions need to be adhered to regarding (1) avoidance of allergens, (2) diet, (3) water intake, (4) vitamin and mineral therapy, (5) preparation of the gut (many children with ADHD have gut parasites, commonly fungal elements such as candida). In addition, EPD should not be performed if the patient is unwell with an infection. Certain drugs and medications can also interfere with the response. A comprehensive booklet explaining EPD has been produced for patients by Dr McEwen.

The effectiveness of EPD in the treatment of allergies associated with ADHD has been demonstrated in controlled trials (Egger et al., 1992). For children with ADHD who have been shown to have significant food sensitivities, but who cannot or will not adhere to a diet for any length of time, desensitization is of great value.

Drug therapy

Psychostimulant drugs unfortunately do not alter the ultimate prognosis in ADHD (Hechtman et al., 1984). They do increase perfusion of the frontal lobes of the brain but only transiently and are of help only for the duration of action of the drug, which is approximately four hours. Those children who are using the drug sodium methylphenidate (Ritalin) usually need doses in the morning before going to school and again at lunchtime to enable them (or their teachers) to cope through the school day. If they also have an evening dose their sleep is disturbed and they require yet another drug to counteract the effect of the methylphenidate. Harmful side effects may occur, which include insomnia, irritability and excitability, nervousness, night terrors, euphoria, tremor, dizziness, headache, convulsions, dependence and tolerance, sometimes psychosis, anorexia, gastrointestinal symptoms, possible growth retardation in children, dry mouth, sweating, tachy-cardia (and angina pain), palpitations, increased blood pressure, visual disturbances, cardiomyopathy with chronic use, choreoathetoid movements, tics and Tourette's syndrome in predisposed individuals, rash, urticaria, fever, arthralgia, alopecia, exfoliative dermatitis, erythema multiforme, thrombocytopenic purpura, thrombocytopenia and leucopenia.

It is not unreasonable to use Ritalin in desperate situations, such as when diet and other input do not work, which may be the case in a small proportion of children, perhaps with adverse family circumstances, when it is not possible to follow recommendations. In these cases the use of the drug offers the opportunity for the child to attend school and gives him or her the potential to learn, as well as alleviating some of the strain at home. However, as mentioned above, the use of the drug in childhood does not affect the final outcome for adults, who manifest the same disturbed behaviour as those who have received no treatment at all (Mannuzza et al., 1989; Hechtman et al., 1984).

Between 60 and 70% of these adults have problems of self-identity, criminal behaviour, alcoholism, short attention span and so on. The patients who adhere to the diet continue to do well, relapsing if they come off it. At this point, a word of caution: pyschostimulant drugs are definitively contra-indicated for use in autism, and a significant number of children manifesting characteristics of ADHD are autistic, often at the higher end of the spectrum – with high intelligence, such as those with

Asperger syndrome. It is imperative that all children presenting with behavioural characteristics compatible with ADHD are thoroughly assessed (preferably by a paediatrician or other professional familiar with the use of dietary intervention), so that other contributing factors are dealt with and so that all other therapeutic interventions are instituted before resorting to drug therapy.

Prevention

Distraught parents often comment that their hyperactive child is quite different from the other children in the family. They want to know why this is so, whether there is something they have done wrong and whether it is likely to happen again.

Naturally, genetic factors play a decisive role in the outcome of any pregnancy but there are measures that parents can take that will reduce the risk of having a child affected by ADHD. Unfortunately, public awareness of contributing factors is almost non-existent, and we have all become so accustomed to abusing our bodies and minds in the chemically laden society in which we live that this pattern becomes an accepted way of life. Many people are addicted to their lifestyles and find the prospect of radical change daunting.

Preconception care of both parents is the best starter for those who are motivated. It is particularly recommended for couples who have family members with ADHD, migraine, irritable bowel, rheumatoid arthritis or allergies, amongst others. The Foresight charity runs a programme for assessing would-be parents and they have also produced two extremely useful books to aid the preparation for pregnancy (Barnes and Bradley, 1994; Bradley and Bennett, 1995).

There is no doubt that parental habits before conception can alter outcomes for the offspring. Alcohol is a well-recognized teratogen (damages DNA and causes foetal abnormalities). Smoking reduces body levels of zinc and increases toxic elements such as cadmium. Zinc is necessary for the efficient functioning of hundreds of enzymes and is vital for the formation of DNA in the developing foetus. It is essential for normal immune function and for the normal production of neurotransmitters. Significant zinc deficiency in parents can cause congenital defects and is a powerful factor in the manifestation of disorders such as ADHD and dyslexia in offspring (Grant, 1994; Davies and Stewart, 1987). Zinc requirements increase during pregnancy.

It would be sensible for parents to avoid smoking, alcohol, stimulant drugs – including coffee and cola drinks – and chemicals in their food and environment as much as possible for several months prior to conception, as well as thereafter. Analysis and correction of any imbalances in their nutritional status should be addressed and any recognized or hidden infections sought and dealt with. Dental work should be carried out well before conceiving. Stress hormones released in pregnancy can affect the baby, so relaxation methods such as yoga, pleasant walks, restful music and perhaps Bach flower remedies are often helpful. If there is a family history of food intolerance, the offending food is best eliminated from the mother's diet both during pregnancy and breast-feeding. Appropriate nutritional supplementation will improve both the parents well being and the outcome of the pregnancy.

After delivery, breast-feeding promotes colonization of the baby's gut with friendly bacteria, increases the intake of EFAs, which aid brain development, provides more zinc than formula feeds, provides protective immune antibodies and also the vital 'sugars' necessary for the baby to develop its own healthy immune responses. Even a single bottle of formula in the early days in an 'at risk' baby could trigger later milk intolerance. Unless absolutely necessary, treatment with antibiotics, paracetamol and ibuprofen should be avoided. The weaning diet should contain wholesome food, rather than processed food. I usually advise against introducing wheat and regular cow's milk products until after the first birthday in 'at risk' babies. Avoidance of exposure to cigarette smoke, aerosols in the home, perfumes and aftershave all help reduce the risk in this vulnerable population.

Closing comment

Improvement in the care of children with ADHD by removing provoking factors for disease and disturbed behaviour, restoring normality to the gut and correcting nutritional imbalances would confer long-term benefits for health and well being on affected children and their families. It would also have considerable financial implications for the NHS, education, social services and the Exchequer in general, taking into consideration the potential millions of pounds saved in reduced criminal behaviour in later life by adults who were hyperactive as children. In the words of Jonathan Brostoff, Professor of Allergy and Environmental Health at the University College London Medical School, England:

> We owe it to ourselves, to our children and, if we are in the professions, to our patients and clients, to act on the knowledge we have, especially if the interventions with potentially profound benefits are so simple, such as elimination diets and nutritional support.

References

Anthony H, Birtwhistle S, Eaton K, Maberly J (1997) Environmental Medicine in Clinical Practice. Southampton: BSAENM Publications.

Axford J (1997) Glycobiology and medicine: an introduction. Journal of the Royal Society of Medicine 90: 260–4.

Bakley RA, Fischer M, Edelbrook CS (1990) The adolescent outcome of hyperactive children diagnosed by research criteria: 8-year prospective follow-up study. J Am Acad Child Adolesc Psychiatry 29: 546–57.

Barnes B, Bradley SG (1994) Planning for a Healthy Baby. London: Vermilion.

Bennet P (1992) Medicinal Crime Prevention. Yorkshire Medicine 4: 19–21.

Boris M, Mandel FS (1994) Food and additives are common causes of the attention deficit/hyperactive disorder in children. Annals of Allergy 72 (May): 462–8

Bradley SG, Bennett N (1995) Preparation for Pregnancy: An Essential Guide. Glenderule, Argyll: Argyll Publishing.

Brostoff J, Gamlin L (1989/1992). Food Allergy and Intolerance. London: Bloomsbury.

Bundy S, Colquhoun ID (1981) Is a lack of essential fatty acids a possible cause of hyperactivity? Medical Hypothesis 7: 673–9.

Carter CM, Urbanowicz M, Hemsley R, Mantilla L, Strobel S, Graham PJ, Taylor E (1993) Effects of few food diet in attention deficit disorder. Arch Dis Child 69: 564–8.

Crook WG (1984) The Yeast Connection. Jackson: Professional Books.

David TJ (1992) Food and Food Additive Intolerance in Childhood. Oxford: Blackwell Scientific.

Davies S (1997) Scientific and ethical foundations of nutritional and environmental medicine. Part III: Pharmacodoxy - the teaching of pharmacotherapeutics as a first line treatment in clinical medical practice; a consideration of Hippocratic and Darwinian evolutionary principles. Journal of Nutritional and Environmental Medicine 7: 219–32.

Davies S, Stewart A (1987) Nutritional Medicine. London: Pan Books.

Ding YS, Fowler JS, Volkow ND, Logan J, Gatley SJ, Sugano Y (1995) Carbon d-threo-methylphenidate binding to dopamine transporter in baboon brain. Journal of Nuclear Medicine 36: 2298–305.

Dykman KD, Mckinley RN (1997) Effect of glyconutritionals on the severity of attention-deficit hyperactivity disorder. Proceedings of the Fischer Institute for Medical Research 1(1): 24–5

Dykman KD, Dykman RA (1999) Effect of nutritional supplements on attention-deficit hyperactivity disorder. Integrative Physiological and Behavioural Science 33(1): in press.

Egger J., Carter CM, Graham PJ, Gumley D, Soothill JF (1985) A controlled trial of oligoantigenic diet treatment in the hyperkinetic syndrome. Lancet 1 (9 March): 540–5.

Egger J, Carter C.M., Soothill J, Wilson J (1989) Oligoantigenic diet treatment of children with epilepsy and migraine. Journal of Pediatrics 114: 51–8.

Egger J, Stolla A, McEwen LM (1992) Controlled trial of hyposensitisation in children with food-induced hyperkinetic syndrome. Lancet 339:1150–3.

Farrington DP (1993) Childhood origins of teenage antisocial behaviour and adult social dysfunction. Journal of the Royal Society of Medicine 86: 3–17.

Feingold BF (1981) Dietary management of behaviour and learning disabilities. In SA Miller (ed.) Nutrition and Behaviour. Miami FL: Franklin Press, pp. 235–46.

Feingold BF (1982) The role of diet in behaviour. Ecol Dis 1: 153–65.

Fell P, Brostoff J (1990) A single dose desensitisation for summer hay fever. Results of a double-blind study – 1988. European Journal of Clinical Pharmacology 38: 77–9.

Fishbein W (1970) Interference with conversion of memory from short-term to long-term storage by partial sleep deprivation. Behav Biol 5: 171–5

Franklin AJ (1992) The secret life of hyperactive children In V Varma (ed.) The Secret Life of Vulnerable Children. London: Routledge.

Gittelman R, Mannuzza S, Shenker R, Bonagura N (1985) Hyperactive boys almost grown up. Psychiatric status. Arch Gen Psychiatry 42: 937–47.

Graham J (1984) Evening Primrose Oil. Wellingborough: Thorsons.

Grant E (1994) Sexual Chemistry. London: Cedar Publishers.

Hansen DE, Vandenberg B (1997) Neurophysiological features and differential diagnosis of sleep apnoea syndrome in children. J Clin Child Psychol 26(3): 304–1.

Hechtman L, Weiss G, Perlman TJ (1984) Young adult outcome of hyperactive children who received long-term stimulant treatment. Am Acad Child Psychiatry 123: 261–9.

Hodgson J (1990) Capitalizing on carbohydrates. Bio/technology (8 February), pp. 108–11.

Horrobin DF (1980) The possible role of PGE1 deficiency in the immunological abnormalities seen in schizophrenia. In G Hemmings (ed.) Biochemistry of Schizophrenial Addiction. Lancaster: MTP Press.

Kiefer Ch, Voderholzer U, Degner H (1991) Schlafveranderungung bei Kindern mit nahrungsmittelinduziertem hyperkinetischen Syndrom. In B Kohler, R Keimer (eds) Aktuelle Neuropadiatrie. Berlin: Springer-Verlag, pp. 361–5.

Klee WA, Zioudrou C, Streaty RA (1979) Hyperactive Children's Support Group Database. 'Exorphins: peptides with opioid activity isolated from wheat gluten, and their possible role in the etiology of schizophrenia'. In NS Usdin (ed.) Endorphins in Mental Health Research. New York: Oxford University Press, pp. 209–18.

Klinkhammer P, Szelies B, Heiss WD (1990) Effect of phosphatidylserine on cerebral glucose metabolism in Alzheimer's disease. Cognitive Degeneration 1: 197–201.

Loeber R, Lahey BB, Thomas C (1991) Diagnostic conundrums of oppositional defiant disorder and conduct disorder. J Abnorm Psychol 100: 379–90.

Lou HC, Henrikson L, Bruhn P, Borner H, Nielsen JB (1989) Striatal dysfunction in attention deficit and hyperkinetic disorder. Arch Neurol 46: 48–52.

Mannuzza S, Klein RG, Konig PH, Giampino TL (1989) Hyperactive boys almost grown up. Arch. Gen Psychiatry 46: 1073–9.

Mataro M, Garcia-Sanchez C, Junqué C, Estévez-González A, Pujol J (1997) Magnetic resonance imaging of the caudate nucleus in adolescents with attention deficit hyperactivity disorder and its relationship with neurophysiological and behavioural measures. Arch-Neurol 54(8): 963–8.

McEwen LM (1973) Enzyme potentiated hyposensitisationl II. Effects of glucose, glucosamine, N-acetylamino-sugars and gelatin on the ability of β-glucuronidase to block the anamnestic response to antigen in mice. Ann. Allergy 31: 79–83.

McEwen LM (1975) Enzyme potentiated hyposensitisation V. Five case reports of patients with acute food allergy. Ann. Allergy 35: 98–103.

McEwen LM, Starr MS (1972) Enzyme potentiated hyposensitisation I. The effect of pre-treatment with β-glucuronidase, hyaluronidase and antigen on anaphylactic sensitivity of guinea pigs, rats and mice. Int Arch Allergy 42: 152–8.

Miller JB (1997) A double-blind study of food extract injection therapy. Ann Allergy 38: 185–91.

Millstone E (1997) Adverse reactions to food additives: the extent and severity of the problem. J of Nutr and Environ Med 7: 323–32.

Mitchell E, Aman M, Turbott S, Manku M (1987) Clinical characteristics and serum essential fatty acid levels in hyperactive children. Clinical Paediatrics 26: 406–11.

Murray RK (1996) Harper's Biochemistry (24 edn) Stamford CT: Appleton & Lange.

Rowe KS, Rowe KJ (1994) Synthetic food colouring and behaviour. A dose response effect in a double-blind, placebo-controlled, repeated measures study. The Journal of Paediatrics, 125: 691–8.

Satterfield J, Hoppe CM, Schell AM (1982) A prospective study of delinquency in 100 adolescent boys with attention deficit disorder and 88 normal adolescent boys. American Journal of Psychiatry 139: 1795–8.

Schoenthaler S (1985) Nutrient levels and antisocial behaviour in juvenile institutions: a quasi-experimental interrupted time-series, an extended time series, and an inter-state double-blind placebo-controlled challenge study. A paper presented at the American Society of Criminology meeting, 16 November 1985, San Diego.

Schoenthaler S, Amos S, Doraz W, Kelly M, Muedeking G, Wakefield J (1997) The effect of randomized vitamin-mineral supplementation on violent and non-violent antisocial behaviour among incarcerated juveniles. J Nutr and Environ Med 7: 343–52.

Shattock P, Savery D (1997) Autism as a Metabolic Disorder. Sunderland: University of Sunderland, Autism Research Unit.

Singh MM, Say SR (1976) Wheat gluten as a pathogenetic factor in schizophrenia. Science 191: 401–2.

Slauss A (1981) Diet, Crime and Delinquency. Berkley CA: Parker House.

Stevens LJ, Zentall SS, Deck J, Abate ML, Watkins BA, Lipp SR, Burgess JR (1995) Essential fatty acid metabolism in boys with attention-deficit hyperactivity disorder. Am J Clin Nutr 62: 761–8.

Stryer L (1995) Biochemistry. New York: WH Freeman, p. 477.

Swanson JM, Kinsbourne M (1980) Food dyes impair performance of hyperactive children on a laboratory learning test. Science 207: 1485–7.

Truss CO (1978) Tissue injury induced by candida albicans: mental and neurological manifestations. J Orthomol Psychiat 7(1): 17–37.

Uhlig T, Merkenschlager A, Brandmaier R, Egger J (1997) Topographic mapping of brain electrical activity in children with food-induced attention deficit hyperkinetic disorder. European Journal of Paediatrics 156(7): 557–61.

Varma V (ed.) (1992) The Secret Life of Vulnerable Children. London: Routledge.

Walker-Smith JA (1986) Milk intolerance in children. Clinical Allergy 16:183–90.

Ward NI, Soulsbury KA, Zettler VH, Colquhoun ID, Bunday S, Barnes BJ (1990) The influence of the chemical additive tartrazine on the zinc status of hyperactive children – a double-blind placebo-controlled study. Nutritional Medicine 1: 51–8.

Ward NI (1997) Assessment of chemical factors in relation to child hyperactivity. J of Nutr and Environ Med 7: 333–42.

Waring RH, Mgong JM (1993) Sulphate Metabolism in Allergy Induced Autism. Relevance to the Disease Aetiology. Biological Perspectives in Autism, Deptartment of Biochemistry, University of Birmingham, England.

Weiss B (1983) Food Additives and Environmental Chemicals as Sources of Childhood Behaviour Disorders. American Academy of Psychiatry.

Weiss G, Hechtman S, Milroy T, Perlman T (1985) Psychiatric status of hyperactives as adults: a controlled prospective 15-year follow up of 63 hyperactive children. J American Acad Child Adolescent Psychiatry 24: 211–20.

Wolfgang M, Figlio R, Sellin T (1972) Delinquency in a Birth Cohort. Chicago:

University of Chicago Press.
Zametkin AJ, Nordahl TE, Gross M (1990) Cerebral glucose metabolism in adults with hyperactivity of childhood onset. New England Journal of Medicine 323: 1362–6.
Zannoti A (1987) Pharmacological properties of phosphatidylserine: effects on memory function. In WB Essman (ed.) Nutrients and Brain Function. New York: Karger, pp. 95–102.

Further reading

Barnes B and Colquhoun ID (1984) The Hyperactive Child. Wellingborough: Thorsons.
Dobbing J (ed.) (1987) Food Intolerance. London: Baillière Tindall.
Feingold BF (1975) Why is your child hyperactive? New York: Random House.
Flack S (1987) Hyperactive Children – A Parent's Guide. London: Bishopsgate Press.
Franklin AJ (1988) The Recognition and Management of Food Allergy in Children. Carnforth: Parthenon.
Hanssen M with Marsden J (1987) E for Additives. Wellingborough: Thorsons.
Mackarness R (1994) Not all in the Mind. London: Thorsons.
Minchin M (1986) Food for Thought. A Parent's Guide to Food Intolerance. Oxford: Oxford University Press.
Rapp DJ (1979) Allergies and the Hyperactive Child. New York: Sovereign Books.
University of Edinburgh Deptartment of Medicine (1992) Food Sensitivity and the Brain. Edinburgh: The University of Edinburgh.

Useful addresses

1. Action Against Allergy, PO Box 278, Twickenham, Middlesex TW1 4QQ; Tel. 0181 892 2711. (A registered charity campaigning for greater medical recognition of allergy and food intolerance. It stocks a wide range of books on allergy and intolerance, including many not published in the UK. Send stamped addressed envelope for information.)
2. Allergy Research Foundation, The Middlesex Hospital, Mortimer Street, London W1N 8AA; Tel. 0171 380 9351. (Research only).
3. Biolab Medical Unit, 9 Weymouth Street, London W1N 3FF; Tel. 0171 636 5959. (Offers comprehensive nutritional testing and treatment in which nutrition plays a part. Patients must be referred by a doctor.)
4. Biotech Health, 26 High Street, Petersfield, Hants GU32 3JL; Tel. 01730 233 414. (Clinic for electrodermal testing. Will also provide lists of local practitioners.)
5. British Society for Allergy, Environmental and Nutritional Medicine (BSAENM), PO Box 7, Knighton, LD7 1WT; Tel. 01547 550 380. (An organization for doctors and other professionals interested in food intolerance, chemical sensitivity and related matters.)
6. Enzyme Potentiated Desensitisation. McEwen Laboratories, 12 Horseshoe Park, Pangbourne, Berkshire RG8 7JW; Tel. 0118 984 1288.
7. Foresight, The Association for the Promotion of Preconceptual Care, 28 The Paddock, Godalming, Surrey GU7 1XD.

8. Hyperactive Children's Support Group (HACSG), 71 Whyke Lane, Chichester, East Sussex, PO19 2LD; Tel. 01903 725 182.
9. Kindercare, 4 Old Mansion Close, Ratton Manor, Eastbourne, East Sussex BN20 9DP; Tel. 01323 505839. Meridian Stress Analysis – testing for food intolerance and nutritional advice.
10. The National Society for Research into Allergy, PO Box 45, Hinckley, Leics, LE10 1JY; Tel. 01455 851546.
11. Society for the Promotion of Nutritional Therapy, PO Box 47, Heathfield, East Sussex, TN21 8ZX; Tel. 01825 872921. (Stamped addressed envelope for list of practitioners.)

Chapter 8
ADHD – A Different Viewpoint II: Holistic and Other Approaches

JOAN KINDER

Introduction

Chapter 7 presented nutritional factors as significant and treatable elements contributing to the manifestation of the syndrome. The prime objective of this chapter is to heighten awareness of the immense benefits for health offered by a variety of complementary therapies, which also have a role to play in the management of ADHD. Due to space limitations only a selection of the many potentially useful therapies will be described. Once again, I would like to thank the various complementary practitioners who have contributed to this chapter by sharing with me information about their specialities.

Complementary therapies aim to address issues at an early stage, not by suppressing symptoms using pharmaceutical agents but by facilitating a person to 'self-heal' – to attain harmony of mind, body and soul. This accords totally with the two fundamental Hippocratic principles cited in the first chapter: 'first do no harm' and 'assist nature'. Most serious conditions – excluding accidents – do not arise suddenly; they develop gradually over time, often many years, and only become apparent at an advanced stage. The art is to identify an imbalance at an early stage and employ measures to restore equilibrium thus preventing the development of disease.

The holistic model, which is the hallmark of complementary practice, recognizes the unique individuality of each person and that, although a person may present with a set of symptoms that are characteristic of a particular 'syndrome', for example ADHD, the contributing factors may be diverse and therapeutic approaches may need to be adjusted according to the person's specific needs at any particular time. We are all dynamic beings, constantly changing and evolving. An appropriate therapeutic approach prescribed at one stage of our development may not be as effective at another time. For most cases of ADHD, a multi-modal approach, including psychological support and often speech therapy, will be required for the child and the affected family. Complementary therapies 'complement', rather than interfere with, more conventional therapies, and as such should be welcomed rather than reviled.

Whatever symptoms a patient may present with, in good medical and non-medical healing practice a diagnosis will be formulated only after taking into account all aspects of the patient – including lifestyle, diet, events at and attitudes to school or work, medical history, emotional state and past experiences, together of course with observation and examination.

Treatment options

Acupuncture

Acupuncture is one of several aspects of traditional Chinese medicine, which also includes moxibustion, herbalism and exercise, and can be traced back as far as the Stone Age. It began with the discovery that stimulation of certain areas of the skin affected the functioning of the body's internal organs. Acupuncture is effective in a wide variety of physical and emotional conditions through its power to stimulate the body's own innate healing resources. There are an estimated three million practitioners worldwide. Many doctors in the UK are using the technique as part of their healing repertoire. In some health authorities acupuncture is available on the National Health Service.

In traditional Chinese medicine the aim of therapy is to unblock or restore balance to flows of energy, known as Ch'i, in the body. These flows follow specific channels, called meridians. As yet the anatomy of meridians has not been defined, but they are distinct from blood, nerve or lymph channels. There are 14 meridians in all, of which 12 are associated with the body organs. If the flow of energy in a meridian is impeded, the energy associated with the organs and tissues along the line of that meridian will be disturbed and the organs will malfunction. Once normal flow is restored, the affected part of the body will be able to heal itself with time, according to its genetic blueprint, provided that the condition has not progressed to such a level of chronicity that irreparable damage has occurred. There are two main energies, Yin, which is often denoted as female, and Yang, which is male. These must be in balance for health. The pulse is a particularly important indicator of the health of an organ and will always be palpated by an acupuncturist.

The emphasis in traditional Chinese medicine is on prevention rather than cure. In former days, patients in China would visit their practitioner for prophylactic therapy. If the patient subsequently became ill the practitioner would not be paid – a definite financial inducement to keep one's patients well! Hyperactivity is rare in China.

In Chinese medicine, hyperactivity is a symptom of heat in the body. Heat can be caused by foods such as cow's milk, oranges, sugar, artificial flavours and colourings, amongst others. Heat may also linger in the body after a febrile illness or immunization. It can be generated due to tension in the family, a shock during or after birth and even by the mother's diet during pregnancy. Heat causes the restless agitation, the violence and poor sleeping that so often are part of the hyperkinetic syndrome. In Chinese medicine a poor diet or an allergic reaction to food generates heat, which affects the heart. Since the heart is believed to house the mind and spirit, heat in the heart gives rise to irritability and insomnia. Prolonged heat or poor food can also adversely affect the function of the spleen, leading to the production of mucus (phlegm). Mucus production is associated with so-called 'damp' foods, which include cow's milk, cheese, butter, sugar, banana and mushrooms. The combined effect of both heat and phlegm results in severe disturbance of the mind with mania. Treatment aims to clear the heat and calm the child. Dietary modification prevents recurrence of the heat.

The acupuncture points used will depend upon whether the assessment shows that the child has a weak or strong constitution, if there is an excess or lack of energy and whether he or she is hot or cold. Often hyperactive children have pale faces with red cheeks and tongues. Acupuncture is usually effective in treating ADHD. If there is no mucus, about five to ten sessions will be required. If there is mucus, more may be necessary. The speed of improvement varies according to the patient, not the complaint. Sometimes improvement is noted after the first visit.

Treatment consists of inserting fine, stainless steel, sterile, disposable needles into specific acupuncture points along the meridians. In certain cases warmth may be applied to the various acupuncture points, perhaps burning specific herbs or other substances. This is known as moxibustion, and the two methods are often used in combination.

The question everyone asks is 'does it hurt?' The answer is that the needles used are very fine, unlike those used for injections. Sometimes a little prick may be felt when the needle is inserted, and sometimes there is a slight tingling or dull ache as the needle reaches the acupuncture point, 4–5 mm below the surface of the skin. The sensation only lasts a second or two, and is rarely described as painful. In traditional acupuncture between four and eight points are used at each session.

Aromatherapy

'The way to health is to have an aromatic bath and scented massage every day.'

Hippocrates

Hippocrates, the revered father of medicine, had great insight into the therapeutic value of many of the natural approaches to healing used in ancient Greece. The Greeks, in turn, had acquired much of their knowledge from the ancient Egyptians. Although the Hippocratic oath is the cornerstone on which the principles of modern medicine are founded, his methods have long since been superseded by modern practices. Perhaps there would be less chronic disease now if some of the ancient methods were taught in medical schools and if aromatherapy were available on the NHS.

Aromatherapy is an ancient art, dating back to at least 3000 years BC, when it was used by the ancient Egyptians. Since then, aromatic oils have been used to prevent and cure all manner of ailments, from painful conditions, allergies and contagious diseases to emotional and psychological problems.

Aromatherapy, as its name implies, exerts its effects to a large extent via the sense of smell, or olfaction. The olfactory nerves lie in the upper part of the nose and are connected directly to the brain. Because of this, the sense of smell is the most immediate of our senses. Aromatic oils are volatile – they vaporize very readily when exposed to air. Minute particles dissolve in the moist secretions inside our nasal passages and in this form can be detected as aromatic particles. From the main bodies of the olfactory cells, fine filaments or 'cilia' project. At the tips of these cilia are receptors that have many different shapes. The molecules of aromatic particles also have different shapes. When an aromatic molecule meets a smell receptor that matches, a reaction is triggered that sets up a signal that is transmitted to the limbic area of the brain, where it is perceived as smell. The interpretation of the signals as smells depends upon previous experience and associations, for example, the smell of a rose or of cooking onions.

The nose can register as many as 10 000 types of smell sensation, yet the number of different receptors is considerably less than this. It is possible that combined signals from different receptors create complex smell sensations. Another hypothesis is that the vibrational energy of aromatic molecules may play a role in the brain's ability to distinguish between the myriad of smells that exists.

One very important part of the brain that is associated with responses to smell, through links with the limbic system, is the hypothalamus, situated at the base of the brain. This structure is involved in regulating many vital body activities including endocrine function – the secretion of hormones affecting growth, sex, metabolism and other functions – and the autonomic nervous system, which controls unconscious activities such as heart rate, breathing, temperature regulation, digestion and gut motility. We have all experienced a physiological response, for example, to the smell of freshly baked bread, by feeling hungry and noting increased salivation. On the other hand, smells such as bad eggs or vomit may induce us to vomit. Certain perfumes or odours may arouse sexual feelings. Some responses are learned responses, but nevertheless have a physiological basis. Some children (and adults), whose bodies are overloaded with toxic substances and who may have high concentrations of chemicals, such as hydrocarbons, in the fatty tissues of their brains, may become quite ill or behave abnormally in response to inhaled particles such as those in cigarette smoke, exhaust fumes, outgassing from new carpets and furniture and aerosol sprays used in the home, to mention but a few. The repeated stress response to these negative aromatic encounters will ultimately lead to exhaustion of the body's response mechanisms – in particular the adrenal gland's production of stress hormones – and result in stress-related illness. A positive encounter with a pleasant aroma may help redress the effects of the negative experiences.

The right side of the brain is believed to be primarily associated with intuitive thought and behaviour, whereas the left relates more to logical and intellectual processes. If the two hemispheres are in harmony we experience feelings of calm and well being. Pleasant aromatic experiences seem to promote synchrony of the hemispheres.

Professional aromatherapists currently use about 300 aromatic oils, but the average household could probably fulfil most of its needs with about ten. Each oil has its own range of properties including antiviral, antibacterial and antifungal, anti-inflammatory, antitoxic, antispasmodic, antidepressant, diuretic, analgesic, sedative, uplifting, hormone-balancing and calmative effects. The properties depend upon the combination and proportions of the naturally occurring chemical components within the oils. Chemists have isolated active substances from oils, which have been shown by practical usage to exert healing effects, and medications have been developed using concentrations of these ingredients. However, each oil may contain up to 200 or more different ingredients, and the interaction between them is synergistic – it confers added 'power' to the property of the oil, perhaps also preventing or reducing unwanted or harmful side effects, which come as part of the package with artificially produced medications. Having said this, oils used in aromatherapy also need to be used appropriately to prevent unwanted effects.

Although some aroma oils in their very purest form can be used internally, it could be dangerous to ingest them without expert advice, and therefore extreme caution is advised. In France 'aromatherapists' who prescribe aroma oils for internal use are medically qualified doctors. In the UK almost all aromatherapists are not medically qualified, and very few would recommend oral treatment. One of the great beauties of aromatherapy, however, is that pure oils are very efficiently absorbed through the skin and mucous membranes of the respiratory tract, and are easily eliminated from the body in urine and faeces, perspiration and exhalation. The safest and most effective way to use the oils is by external application or inhalation.

Essential oils are extracted from certain varieties of plants, trees, shrubs, herbs, grasses and flowers. Different oils are concentrated in different parts of the plant – leaves, blossoms, stalks, roots, bark, fruits, berries, twigs and so forth. The extraction process can be extremely laborious and some oils are very expensive because they require enormous amounts of raw material to produce small volumes of oil – for example 60 000 rose blossoms to produce one ounce of rose oil, and 8 000 000 hand-picked blossoms of jasmine to produce one kilogram of oil.

Each oil contains a range of chemical components including terpenes, alcohol, esters, aldehydes, ketones and phenols. The combination, quantity and purity of the components in the oils contributes to the fragrance and the therapeutic efficacy, therefore it is always worthwhile seeking advice about which brand of oil to buy in order to ensure that the desired effect is achieved. Only *pure* oils should be used. Contaminants alter the properties.

So how are the oils used? The commonest and perhaps most effective method is by therapeutic massage, which has the duel benefit of physically relaxing the muscles and also inducing relaxation by using oils whose fragrances have pleasant associations. It is important that oils selected for their therapeutic value are also aromatically pleasing for the recipient of treatment. There are qualified aromatherapists in most towns who usually charge fairly modest rates for a session and are willing to give advice on home use of the oils.

The amount of oil used will depend upon the age of the person being treated. For small babies the oils should always be diluted with an organic carrier oil, such as grapeseed, evening primrose or calendula oil. As a general guide the doses should be as given below.

Baths

- Babies (0–12 months) – 1 drop (diluted with a carrier oil).
- Small children (up to 5 years) – 2 drops.
- Juniors (5 – 7 years) – 3 drops.
- Juniors (8 –12 years) – 4 drops.
- Adolescents (13 years +) – 5 drops.
- Adults – 6 drops.

Just sprinkle the oil into warm water in the bath, using no bubble bath, mix well and soak for 10–15 minutes. Avoid contact with the eyes, and it is better not to drink the water!

Massage

- Babies (0–2 months) – 1 drop in 15 ml carrier oil.
- Babies (3–12 months) – 1 drop in 10 ml carrier oil.
- Small children (up to 5 years) – 2 drops per 10 ml carrier oil.
- Juniors (6–12 years) – 2–3 drops per 10 ml carrier oil.
- Adolescents (13 years +) – 3–4 drops in 10 ml carrier oil.
- Adults – 5 drops in 10 ml carrier oil.

There are other ways of delivering the oils, such as by compresses, inhalations, hand and foot baths, diffusers or even a drop or two of oil on the sheet at bedtime.

For the ADHD child, massage has the benefit of positive physical contact between the parent and the child, whose relationship may be less than agreeable for much of the time. It is surprising how many hyperactive children enjoy an aromatherapy massage and do calm down. A simple massage of the hands and feet addresses all the reflex zone points of the body and therefore helps balance the body's energy flow.

The two most suitable oils for babies and small children are **Roman chamomile** and **lavender**. They have significant calming effects as well as a host of other properties. Both are very safe, even for a woman who may be pregnant, though excess lavender should be avoided in early pregnancy. Roman chamomile has been dubbed 'the children's oil'. For crying babies who will not sleep and have colic, a gentle massage of the tummy, back and feet using a suitable dilution of Roman camomile may be all that is needed. It will also help calm the mother. Other useful oils for babies are **mandarin**, **tangerine** and **geranium**.

For the older child who may have angry, aggressive tendencies and sleeps poorly, **lavender** is often very effective. **Ylang ylang** is also useful for these children, particularly if the symptoms are linked with poor self-esteem.

Older hyperactive children may be helped by **marjoram**, though I tend to avoid this in the very young and it should not be used if the mother is pregnant. **Clary sage** is another useful oil, especially if the behaviour is stress-related and associated perhaps with obsessive, compulsive tendencies with hostility as well as overactivity. Again, this oil should be avoided in pregnancy (apart from at delivery – but that is another story).

Juniper is a cleanser of both the physical and 'subtle' body and helps remove negative energy. It can be used together with the Bach remedy **crab apple**.

Vetivert is a wonderfully earthy, grounding oil. It is a panacea for stress and tension and helps balance the central nervous system. It has been called the 'the oil of tranquillity'. Some children, however, do not find the aroma pleasing, so an initial 'smell' test would be wise.

There are a host of other oils that have calming properties and may be useful in ADHD but, as with any other of the complementary approaches to healing, the choice should be made taking into account all the facets of the child's personality, experiences and behaviour, as well as his or her response to the aroma.

When using the oils a drop or two of one or more of the Bach flower remedies, appropriate for the child, can often enhance the effectiveness of the treatment. For example, **Roman chamomile** blends well with the Bach remedy **impatiens** for anger and irritability. **Jasmine** (a very expensive but highly effective oil) blends with **larch** to inspire confidence. **Marjoram** blends with **vervain** to calm and relieve tension, and **rose** (another very expensive but powerful oil) blends with **holly** where there is jealousy. It would be sensible to seek the advice of an accredited practitioner or to attend a short introductory course on the use of aromatic oils before embarking on home use of this extremely pleasant and valuable therapy. Where expensive oils are required, a practitioner will be able to make up a massage blend that will reduce the cost.

Bach flower therapy

This is an extremely gentle but effective therapy, safe even for babies and pregnant women. The remedies are non-addictive and even in overdose are harmless. Dr Edward Bach, a visionary physician, who had worked as a consultant bacteriologist and also practised homeopathy in the 1930s, discovered them. Dr Bach had become disillusioned with the limitations of modern medicine as practised at that time. He believed that there must be a more effective answer in nature to the needs of mankind, particularly those associated with spiritual and emotional disquiet. The 38 Bach remedies are the fruits of his labour of love. As with homeopathy in general, and other complementary therapies, the remedies exert their effects by balancing energy in the body. They are beneficial not only to humans but also have powerful effects on animals and, indeed, plants.

Apart from rock water, whose source is obvious, all of the remedies are prepared from wild flowers. They have been selected for their ability to treat the personality and distressing emotions of the sufferer rather than physical symptoms of disease. However, because of the inter-relationship between the mind, body and soul, disturbance of one will inevitably influence the others. The judicious selection of appropriate Bach remedies may be invaluable in aiding recovery from physical and mental disturbances by the balancing effect they exert on the 'higher self'. Bach remedies are useful adjuncts to other therapies, such as aromatherapy and Bowen therapy. The remedies are obtainable from most health shops and from many pharmacies. There are also a number of very useful books on their usage.

All children suffer at times from a range of disturbing emotions, including fear, terror, depression, jealousy, insecurity and anger. As a rule children do not hide their feelings, but it is not always easy to identify the root cause or causes of deviant behaviour, which may be the manifestation of underlying emotional or spiritual distress. The selection of appropriate Bach remedies requires knowledge of the child's current circumstances and behavioural patterns as well as insight into the basic personality of the child. Previous experiences, including prenatal events, will have contributed to the development of his or her personality, and Bach flower remedies may be helpful in addressing these issues.

As with all healing practices, the essence of treatment is the intent. In other words, the attitude and motives of the therapist, whether a professional or a family member, will contribute to the outcome. Sceptics will talk about placebo effects, which undoubtedly exist, but consider the following: some readers will remember school experiments demonstrating the presence and shape of the magnetic field around a magnet using iron filings. They will also remember the change or distortion of the field, evidenced by a change in the pattern of iron filings, when another magnetic field was brought into its vicinity. Also in school experiments it was possible to demonstrate the reciprocal relationship between magnetic fields and flows of electrons in a conductor of electrical current. Our electrical power at home is delivered within a particular frequency band, and items of electrical equipment are designed to function effectively only within a limited frequency range. If the parameters fluctuate, the equipment malfunctions. Within the electromagnetic spectrum, energy of different wavelengths has different properties, from infrared to ultraviolet, through the colours, X-rays, radio- and microwaves, etc. We know that some of these rays affect us adversely because the frequency is incompatible with our own and disrupts our normal functioning. This property is exploited in the treatment of cancerous cells using radiotherapy, but can have disastrous effects on healthy cells.

Our brains are powerhouses of energy. Our nerves conduct electrical energy. We generate heat, which is energy. There is a magnetic field around our bodies, present as a result of the electrical activity and energy associated with our body. This field is mystically known as the aura, but there is no mystique about it – it is a fact of life and basic to bio-energetic medicine. All healing approaches throughout the world, apart from Western orthodox medicine, recognize and utilize the fundamental concept that we are essentially energetic beings. When one person approaches another, the magnetic fields surrounding them and the frequency of vibration of their energies interact. Fields can change depending on the state of physical, mental and spiritual health and well being of the individual. How many times have you heard people comment on 'bad vibes' emanating from someone, or experienced a prickly skin sensation, a distinct feeling of being ill at ease in the presence of another person, sometimes even before seeing that person or hearing him or her speak? In respect to giving treatment, therapists often talk about 'tuning in' to their patients in order to optimize the results. In the same way, choosing or administering Bach remedies should be a positive exercise, undertaken with loving intent, thereby delivering not only the remedies but also the positive energy to accompany them.

Useful remedies for children showing symptoms of ADHD include:

- **Cherry plum**, which is a must when the child feels he or she is losing control – 'going over the top' – especially if the child feels he or she wants to hurt someone, scream and throw things about.
- **Chestnut bud** is useful for those who fail to learn by experience and repeatedly make the same mistakes despite being reminded. These children find it difficult to pay attention and they may be slow learners, often forgetting routine things, such as bringing their physical education kit home.
- **Chicory** helps babies who are very demanding, always seeking attention and hating to be alone. This remedy is also useful for older children who tend to manipulate those around them, using emotional blackmail as one of their tools. They may even feign illness to get their own way. Chicory is appropriate for children who often have tantrums when thwarted.
- **Heather** is used for children who are exceptionally egocentric, the whole world revolving around them. They can be loving in a good phase.
- **Holly** may help a child who is jealous, envious, revengeful or suspicious, but can be loving.
- **Impatiens** is often given to babies who scream for attention and demand immediate gratification. Early treatment may abort the development of this aspect of the child's character within the spectrum of ADHD. It may also be valuable for the older child whose needs must be met immediately.
- **Vervain** is perhaps the most frequently used remedy for ADHD. It can help those highly strung children who are tense, frustrated and hyperactive, often requiring less sleep than average. The children often are very bright, lively and enthusiastic about what they are doing but do not know where to draw the line. Vervain used together with a lavender oil massage is a good combination.
- **Willow** may be useful for a child who is resentful and perhaps bitter, feeling that he or she has not been given a fair deal and people do not understand him or her.

Of course it is necessary to consider the whole child. Other personality 'type' remedies may need to be added to a blend. Some children are anxious or depressed and need appropriate remedies. Others are afraid to try new things for fear of failure and may be disruptive to avoid the situation, in which case larch is helpful.

One remedy that is invaluable for a household in which one (or more) members have ADHD tendencies is 'rescue'. This is a composite of five other remedies and is useful for any crisis situation, for anyone. It helps pre-examination nerves, pre-driving test anxieties, fear of giving birth, dread of one's hyperactive child coming home from school, and it helps the child who may well have fears and phobias contributing to his or her disturbed behaviour. Four drops of this remedy are usually used, diluted in drinks or, in a crisis situation, even dabbed on the temple.

Bach remedies do not 'change' a person. The 'type' remedies help the person to achieve equilibrium and allow the positive aspects of his or her character to emerge. The situational remedies help people cope with the circumstances in which they find themselves, often facilitating a change of attitude, which in itself may help change the adverse situation.

Administration in ADHD is usually by mouth. A couple of drops of each remedy required are taken from the stock bottle and diluted in spring water (or filtered water, or even juice if the child will not drink anything else). This can then be sipped over a period of time, although most children seem to drink it in one gulp. At least three doses per day will be needed. They are more effective if taken at a separate time from food. Sometimes two drops can be applied directly under the tongue, but this is less palatable for most children due to the pure brandy that is used as a preservative. If a practitioner makes up the remedy blend it will be in a 30 ml brown glass dropper bottle, which should be stored away from heat and light and extreme cold, as well as sources of radiation and microwave ovens. Some aroma oils are best avoided when using the diluted Bach blend, which exerts its effects homeopathically. These include peppermint and eucalyptus.

Some families have tried one or two Bach remedies and found that they have not been as helpful as they hoped. There are a number of possible reasons: (a) the choice of remedy was not appropriate for the child, (b) the remedy was stored incorrectly or had been kept for too long (usually it is recommended that a diluted blend is used within three months), (c) the remedy was always taken with food, (d) it was given with negative intent as a punishment or corrective 'potion' to change the child to someone the giver might like better, (e) the circumstances contributing to the problem were overwhelmingly powerful and would also need to be addressed in order to optimize the effect. The majority of families, however, do find the remedies to be very helpful. They are also a useful adjunct to other therapy, and do not interfere with standard medical or complementary practice.

Other flower essences are also available, including the Bailey essences, which are usually composites of wild flower extracts.

Case study

JH is a six-year-old boy who was referred for ADHD. He was described as having a Jekyll-and-Hyde personality, with marked mood swings, attention-seeking behaviour, poor concentration, constantly fidgeting and fingering objects, and requiring special needs input at school. He had set fire to his bedroom and had cut his hair with scissors. He suffered from constipation, catarrh, itchy bottom and allergic conjunctivitis. He was described as a 'nervous' child, not naturally affectionate and preferring the company of older children rather than his peers.

His mother was a passive smoker in pregnancy. JH was born 10 days late by rapid delivery but inhaled meconium and was taken to the special care baby unit, where he had two stomach washouts. He did not sleep all the way through the night until he was three and even now he gets up for a drink. He developed eczema at the age of one. His mother is a patient person. His father works away from home part of the week. He has two half sisters.

Examination was unremarkable apart from pale skin, a blocked nose and mouth breathing. He also had a birthmark at the base of his spine. He wandered round constantly fingering things during the consultation. He created the impression of having low self-esteem and of being a bit depressed. His mother suspected food intolerance. Extensive testing for food and environmental sensitivities was unrewarding. However, he appeared to need a number of Bach remedies including cerato, chestnut bud, chicory, heather, holly, hornbeam, impatiens, mustard, oak pine, rescue, scleranthus, vine, walnut and water violet. This seemed quite a combination but we decided to try it.

A few weeks later his mother reported that JH had been a lot better. He had been a good boy all round, a lot happier, brighter and healthier. His teachers were pleased with his improved concentration and sitting still in class. His work had improved so much that he had moved to the 'bright' group from the special needs group.

Bowen therapy

The Bowen technique is a dynamic system of muscle and connective tissue therapy which was developed in Australia by Mr Tom Bowen after the Second World War. Although Mr Bowen worked without manuals or charts, the details of his technique were observed and recorded by Oswald and Elaine Rentsch, who studied with him for two-and-a-half years. Mr Bowen verified their documentation as being an accurate representation. Since his death, Oswald and Elaine Rentsch have been teaching the technique in Australia, New Zealand, North America, the UK and Europe. The number of accredited practitioners is growing rapidly as the technique has been proving highly effective in helping a wide range of ailments. In particular it produces lasting relief from pain and discomfort, but can also have dramatic effects on behaviour. Bowen therapy is a gentle technique that uses precise moves on specific soft tissue points of the body to stimulate energy flow, empowering the body's own resources to balance and heal itself. Each individual move may produce a positive effect, but the full benefit of the technique is gained through a complementary series of moves. Between moves there are frequent pauses to allow the body time to benefit from each. Only a limited number of sequences are needed during each session.

An individual move consists of identifying the structure that is to be addressed (such as a muscle, tendon or nerve sheath) with the thumb or fingers. The skin slack over this tissue is gently tractioned in the opposite direction to the intended move. Then the muscle is challenged with gentle pressure in the direction of the intended move. Finally the skin is allowed to move across the structure to the limit of available skin slack.

The technique is safe to use on anyone from pregnant women, through newborn babies to the aged. The only contra-indications are the 'coccyx' procedure in pregnancy and 'breast' moves for tenderness if silicon implants are present.

Because the Bowen technique allows the body to heal itself with minimal intervention it does not interfere with the effectiveness of other disciplines. However, other forms of manipulative therapy performed up to four days before or five days after a Bowen therapy session may interfere with the effectiveness of the Bowen treatment.

No one really knows how the technique works, but it is believed that the moves made set up vibrational patterns that correspond to particular areas of the body. The body then attempts to alter its vibration to match these ideal vibrational patterns and, in so doing, brings itself to harmony. An analogy would be a musician playing a stringed instrument. Changing the point at which a string is pressed creates a vibrational pattern that corresponds to a specific frequency, manifested as sound. If the string is not 'in tune' with the other strings, even if the point held is correct, the sound will be discordant, the frequencies not in harmony. Once the string has been adjusted, or tuned in, and the instrument is played sensitively the required sound is created.

Because of its overall balancing effect on the body, the technique has a calming effect in some children with ADHD. Once the first couple of moves have been achieved the child will often lie still and allow the therapy to continue. I have seen very agitated children transformed after a session. Their parents can hardly believe that it is their child! It is probably necessary for most children with ADHD to have several sessions, also using other non-intrusive inputs such as dietary changes in order to achieve lasting benefit.

It is important to note that the Bowen technique is not a massage. It is not acupressure or chiropractic. It is not directional energy work, physiotherapy or neuromuscular re-education. Bowen technique is not fascia release, lymphatic drainage or an emotional release discipline. Having said this, one of the striking results of the work is that people report a lightening of their spirits and often subtle refocusing of troublesome emotional patterns. It is an holistic approach that addresses physical, emotional, cognitive and spiritual aspects of the individual concerned. Just one Bowen move on the body actually addresses the whole person. Growing numbers of professionals in the health service as well as in complementary medicine are studying the technique and using it in their practices.

Although relatively new to the arena of light touch therapies, the Bowen technique has already established itself and is well worth considering for the ADHD child.

Colour therapy

Colour, like sound and radio waves, is an energy, but vibrating at a much higher frequency. Light splits up into all the colours of the rainbow when it reaches the visible area of the electromagnetic spectrum between ultraviolet and infrared. In keeping with other energies within the spectrum, each of the light colours has its own specific vibrational frequency, its positive and negative attributes and also its own complementary colour. Both colour and its complementary colour are used in colour therapy. Examples are blue and orange, red and turquoise, yellow and violet, green and magenta.

According to Theo Gimbel, an expert in colour therapy, colour influences the focusing of the eye. Blue focuses in front of the retina, red behind and green on the retina. Blue is the kindest colour for the human eye. Green light in excess, for example in video display units, can be damaging to the eye, as it can be to other tissues that are rapidly dividing and are therefore vulnerable. For example, pregnant women should be cautious in using VDUs with green screens. Green light can, however, be useful as a complementary adjunct in the treatment of cancer.

Cells on the retina receive light and transmit nerve impulses to the brain, which are perceived as 'vision'. The cells are called rods and cones according to their shape. The rods are responsible primarily for night vision but are not sensitive to colour or fine detail. The cones are used in bright light and for distinguishing colour. The eye can distinguish about 7 500 000 hues. When light of a particular colour impinges on these cells they naturally produce the complementary colour. During this change the cells contract and expand. The muscles of the iris will also be activated and the pupil size will alter. This is a healthy experience and helps retain the vitality of the organ. However, in certain conditions, including food intolerance and toxic overload, the process becomes pathological. Some children have difficulty changing focus when their gaze shifts from their writing page to the blackboard, and the pupil size vacillates, a condition known as hippus. If they are having visual difficulties this will cause frustration and affect their attention span. Some opticians and orthoptists are interested in the role of colour in conditions such as dyslexia, which we have noted earlier to be very closely connected with ADHD, and autism. With the use of specially selected filters, either in spectacle lenses or placed directly on reading material, quite dramatic results have been achieved. One boy I saw for behavioural problems that were considered to be ADHD, had poor self-esteem, was being bullied and was having special needs input at school, and had a personal and family history typical of the genetically linked hyperactivity/conduct disorder families. I sent him for assessment for visual dyslexia and learned later that a specific combination of ancient light filters transformed his reading ability so dramatically that both his mother and the orthoptist wept for joy! His behaviour improved concomitantly.

Theo Gimbel has developed an 'eye strengthening chart' using the eye's ability to produce complementary colours, thus helping to improve function.

It is not only through our eyes that colour is absorbed into our being. The whole of one's bodies is sensitive to light, just as it is to any electromagnetic radiation, and the electromagnetic field that surrounds each one of us is constantly filled with changing vibrating colours. There are stock phrases such as 'red with anger', 'green with envy', 'got the blues', 'in the pink', but do we question the origin of these expressions? We use some people, described as clairvoyants, who are able to 'see' the colours contained in the electromagnetic fields surrounding us – the aura. Housed within the aura are energy centres, or chakras. There are seven main chakras, each associated with an internal organ, primarily the endocrine glands, and displaying a colour of the rainbow. The colours of the aura change according the vibrational energy produced by a person at any one time. They reflect the state of health and well being of the individual. As with any other interacting electromagnetic forces, the application of colour will influence the fields. How many of us feel good in summer when we are bathed in light, and how many suffer the condition known as SADS (seasonal affective disorder syndrome) when deprived of blue skies and sunshine?

In general, colour therapy uses only the positive aspects of colours, which means that only the brighter colours are used. For example, bright red is the symbol of life and vitality, it energizes and stimulates, being a good colour for paralysis. However, it is also a contracting colour and is best avoided in asthma, which improves with blue, an expansive colour. Because of its powerful stimulating and energizing properties red is best not used where there is anxiety or emotional disturbance. As such, it may not be considered to be a suitable colour for children with ADHD, but they do tend to love red. In fact, children's perception of, and emotional response to, colours is quite different from that of adults. For example, yellow for an adult indicates a sunny extrovert nature, though for a child it may be associated with insecurity and fear. Generally young children like the primary colours, bright red, blue and yellow, and also green. The subtle appreciation of colour develops later.

Green is the colour of balance and harmony, bringing the negative and positive aspects of the person's being into balance. It also has a 'cleansing' effect.

Blue symbolizes peace and tranquillity. It creates a sensation of space and expansion. It is a colour that slows things down, and is useful to treat fear, tension and insomnia, which may occur in ADHD. If used with its complementary colour, orange, it brings about a state of peaceful joy. Sometimes children with ADHD reject blue because it has a numbing effect on them. They often prefer the vibrant red.

Indigo, although representing the night, which can be a fearful time for some children, is a combination of deep blue and a small amount of red. It broadens the mind and frees it from fears and inhibitions and can have a powerful effect on mental complaints. It is also associated with the eyes, ears and throat and is often recommended for children with ADHD. Indigo with orange or coral is said to be 'magic'.

Violet pertains to spirituality and insight. It is useful for people who lack dignity and self-respect, for those who do not really love themselves, and therefore are unable to relate well to others. This colour may be helpful in some children with ADHD. It is a healing colour for people with psychological disorders such as schizophrenia.

Bubblegum pink is a colour used in prisons, as it calms down new inmates. This is probably a good choice for children with ADHD as well, as it has tones of red but is not as invigorating. The link between ADHD in childhood and criminal activity in adult life has been proven.

The colours required for treatment will vary according to the general personality of the child and his or her state of being at the time of assessment. In the home it is useful to have white walls that can then be decorated with different coloured pictures, or illuminated with different coloured lights as situations change.

There is a great deal more to colour therapy than is presented here and the advice of a colour therapist is recommended when considering this type of approach.

Herbal medicine (phytotherapy)

Plants have always been part of our lives, providing food, shelter, beauty and healing for any manner of ailments. It is believed by some that wild herbs growing in abundance in a particular locality may be the ones needed for healing the people living there. For example, dandelions are an excellent liver tonic. If they grow in profusion in someone's garden, perhaps the person living there is suffering from liver maladies manifesting as explosive temperament, chronic fatigue, depression, indecision and anger. Nature seeks balance.

Herbalists, like other complementary therapists, treat people rather than diseases. However, although each case is treated individually, some herbs figure prominently for certain conditions. In ADHD, **ginkgo biloba** helps increase cerebral perfusion, as do **betonica**, **scutellaria** and **vinca minor**. Ginkgo is reputed to restore memory to those who tend to forget things all the time, and to increase concentration and focus.

Cat's claw enhances immune function. It is anti-inflammatory, aids digestion and decreases gut permeability to partially digested peptides, which can trigger allergic responses in the brain.

Vallerian root has been used traditionally for calming and relaxing nervous tension. It may also be combined with other herbs, such as **hop grains** and **lemon balm**, to make a highly effective remedy for older children who have trouble sleeping. **Chamomile** has a calming effect and can be used in babies and small children.

Echinacea has powerful immune system stimulating properties and protects against illnesses that might otherwise require antibiotic therapy, which could disturb gut function and lead to food intolerance and accumulation of toxic products from overgrowth of harmful microorganisms in the gut. This process and the significance for ADHD have been described in Chapter 7.

Aloe vera is a wonderfully healing plant. Its leaves contain a complex starch composed of mannose sugars joined in chains, called polymannose or mannans. Mannans enhance immune function. They also improve the effectiveness of vaccines, with the production of higher antibody levels. This, in its turn, could prevent the persistence of the virus present in the vaccine, thought by some to play a role in the etiology of ADHD/autism. Aloe vera is extremely useful for aiding healing of a dysfunctional gut, especially if inflammation is present. This increases intestinal absorption of nutrients, which together with a reduction in toxic compounds reaching the brain, improves symptoms of ADHD.

Caution is advised in self-medicating with herbs; combining them requires a certain degree of knowledge. Herbs are the basis on which modern pharmacology is founded and do contain active principles that could be detrimental to health if taken inappropriately. The advice of a qualified herbalist is recommended if following this route.

Homeopathy

Homeopathy is another natural healing process in which remedies assist the patient to regain health by stimulating the body's natural healing forces.

Although the principles of homeopathy have been recognized since the time of Hippocrates and the ancient Greeks, modern practice owes its origin to the work of an eighteenth-century physician, Hahnemann. Hahnemann believed that existing medical practices did more harm than good. He began to search for an alternative that would be safe and effective.

After years of close observation and careful experiment, Hahnemann established the three basic principles of homeopathy:

- A medicine that in large doses produces symptoms of a disease will in small doses cure that disease.
- By extreme dilution, the medicine's curative properties are enhanced and all the poisonous or undesirable side effects are lost.
- Homeopathic medicines are prescribed individually by the study of the whole person, according to his or her basic temperament and response.

In homeopathy there is no single remedy to treat a specific disease state.

Recovery during homeopathic treatment is aided by paying attention to general health measures such as appropriate diet, rest and fresh air. Responses and length of treatment vary according to the chronicity of the problem. Babies and small children usually respond extremely well due to their high intrinsic vitality and lack of accumulated 'blocks' – the 'garbage' of life. Homeopathy is also effective for animals.

In many instances homeopathic treatment may avert the need for more drastic intervention, such as surgery (for example insertion of grommets for glue ear), or the use of drug therapy, such as Ritalin in ADHD, which is palliative rather than curative and may produce harmful side effects.

Homeopathic practitioners generally prefer to work with the medical profession, and many are themselves medically qualified doctors. Homeopathy is recognized by the General Medical Council and there are several homeopathic hospitals in Great Britain funded by the NHS, including those in Tunbridge Wells, London and Glasgow.

As mentioned above, homeopathic remedies are selected after taking into consideration the temperament of the patient, the symptoms, both physical and emotional, and inherited factors. These latter are termed 'miasms'. The help of a qualified homeopath is recommended if homeopathic treatment is to be optimized. Not only the correct remedy but also the correct dilution for a particular problem must be identified. The greater the dilution the greater the potency. Often very high-potency remedies are required for mental problems.

Sometimes what appears to be a perfect fit for the person is not as effective as would be hoped, in which case there could be a miasmic block that will need clearing first. Sometimes, once this has been dealt with, all the other problems seem to resolve spontaneously. Below are a few remedies that are frequently useful for children and adults with ADHD.

Sulphur is useful for children who are very 'busy', always fidgeting and fingering things, although not usually violent or aggressive. They are untidy people, the sort of children who within minutes will have all the contents of a toy box strewn over the floor. They tend to get red hands and feet and sweat, and may have dry, itchy skin, which they scratch causing soreness. These children may suffer with boils and develop redness and sores round orifices such as mouth, nose and anus. Often they sleep poorly, awaking at the slightest sound, and cannot get to sleep again because their brains are too active with floods of ideas. They tend not to feel the cold and walk around in T-shirts even in cold weather.

Tuberculinum is a miasmatic remedy – it deals with a problem that has come with the genetic package. The remedy, or nosode, as it is called, is derived from tuberculous cells, but is not infective. People who suffer with an inner restlessness, always rushing around and unable to concentrate, may benefit from tuberculinum. These are people who also tend to be destructive, who smash chairs against the wall, throw plates or punch holes in the door. They often have poor self-esteem.

Medorrhinum is another miasmatic remedy used in ADHD. This one is made from gonorrhoea cells.

Other remedies that may be used for aggressiveness include belladonna, stramonium and hyoscyamus. These are all linked with hyoscine and atropine and are used for violent, dramatic behaviour in restless individuals.

Lycopodium is a remedy that often helps with attention deficit, usually in children who are anxious, insecure and lacking confidence – especially when anticipating a new challenge. They may cover up these feelings of insecurity by difficult behaviour. They frequently suffer with digestive problems, including acid reflux, bloating of the abdomen with wind and a full feeling after very little food. They also frequently have difficulty passing water and there may be a red deposit in the urine, which clears after treatment. They are often intolerant of cow's milk products. Although these children are anxious they generally manage to cover it up and give the appearance of coping. Lycopodium may also be helpful in dyslexia.

Argentum nitrum is also for anxiety and lack of confidence, but these people are so affected that they are not able to do things. They become anxious gibbering wrecks at the thought of undertaking some perceived challenge. Like the people who need sulphur, these prefer cold weather, walking around in shirt-sleeves in the snow. They enjoy the mixed flavour of salt and sweet.

Phosphorus may help with some of the children who show poor concentration at school and may disrupt the class. They are generally likeable people and may be popular class clowns.

Pulsatilla is a remedy for children who can be irritable, cry easily and have mood swings. They often suffer with catarrh. When small they can be clingy, demanding and attention seeking, yet they are also very loving.

Silica may be used for children who may behave badly but who have poor self-confidence. It is a remedy for the 'lack of grit' person. Children needing silica are often anxious. They give up easily in difficult situations but can be very obstinate and irritable and are capable of getting into rages.

Aconite is useful where there is fear and ignatia is often helpful for panic.

Homeopathy can be combined with a number of other disciplines, but may be neutralized by certain aroma oils, such as peppermint, like that found in toothpaste (toothpastes for homeopathic users can be purchased at most health stores), eucalyptus, often in decongestant preparations, and clary sage.

Osteopathy

Osteopathy requires several years of training. Some osteopaths undertake additional training in paediatric osteopathy, which includes cranial osteopathy. This is not to be confused with cranio-sacral therapy that may be performed by non-osteopathically trained therapists.

The cranium is the housing for the brain and comprises the skull bones and the meninges, a triple-layered membrane. The outer layer of the meninges, the dura mater, as its name implies, is tough and protects the inner surface of the skull bones. Beneath this is the arachnoid mater and closely attached to the brain is the pia mater. There is a space between the arachnoid mater and the pia mater filled with cerebrospinal fluid, which contains nutrients for the brain and spinal cord. The meninges form a continuous membrane surrounding the brain, looping down between the right and left hemispheres and forming a division between the upper and lower parts of the brain. They extend all the way down the spinal column wrapped around the spinal cord and are attached at their lower end to the sacrum. Osteopaths believe that the meninges are constantly under tension and the dura is known as the 'reciprocal tension membrane'. Although the meninges are always under some tension, this may be greater than it should be, which will create pressure in the head, rather like a permanent mini tension headache. This being the case, concentration is impaired and it is much more likely that when people become angry or upset they will lose control and often display temper tantrums. This can occur at any age. People with increased dural tension are often described as having a

Jekyll-and-Hyde personality. Of course there are other triggers for this type of behaviour, not least diet and environment factors. When an experienced osteopath puts his or her hands on someone's head he is able to detect tension in the skull and also in the tissues of the scalp. Increased tension of the meninges is said to feel akin to an over-pumped tyre. Just as a violinist is able to detect fine variations of pitch when tuning in his instrument, those practised in using their hands as instruments develop the same degree of sensitivity.

All children showing characteristics of ADHD display this tension of the dura. Frequently there is also increased tautness of the diaphragm, the muscle lying between the chest and abdomen, whose movement is vital for respiration. Tautness of the diaphragm is often linked with emotional tension. If an experienced osteopath detects both dural tension and diaphragmatic tautness, even if a child seems well behaved and controlled during the consultation, the diagnosis is confirmed.

A number of factors can contribute to an increase in tension of the meninges, not least of which is diet. Others include:

- Prenatal shock, such as emotional trauma (death in the family, husband leaves wife) or physical trauma (amniocentesis, significant illness), which causes increased release of stress hormones and altered biochemistry, which can affect the foetus.
- Drugs – recreational, cigarettes, medications – including those used at birth, such as drugs used for induction of labour, epidural analgesia (especially if a top-up is given), pethidine.
- Shock to the baby, for example a physical shock such as lack of oxygen at birth, perhaps due to the cord being around the neck.
- Postnatal shock, for example domestic violence, physical or verbal. Atmosphere of stress.
- Later on, in some children, chickenpox can cause tightening of the membranes that might by this time have begun to relax.

Treatment involves very slow release of membrane tension by 'taking' the membranes to where they want to be.

There are basically two ways of releasing a restriction: either by applying a force across it to 'break the lock' or by enabling it to move in the direction it wants to go. In muscle spasm one can either stretch the muscle against the cramping force or compress it further. The same principle applies to the meninges and to the diaphragm. In babies, however, one always takes the membrane in the direction it wants to go. Release of tension in the meninges may have the added benefit of facilitating freer flow of cerebrospinal fluid carrying nutrients to the brain and removing waste products.

Two cautions apply in children with ADHD:

- These children are often disturbed by change so it is necessary to release the membrane very slowly, little by little. If the release is too fast it may evoke a strong emotional response, creating increased hyperactivity and further tightening of the membrane. It is, therefore, imperative to work at the speed dictated by the child. The number of treatments required will vary, perhaps three sessions for some children, ten in others. Often a periodic top-up treatment is advantageous, even when improvement has occurred.
- In the initial stages of treatment children often will not stay still long enough to be touched – the only place perhaps being the feet whilst they are otherwise being distracted. Using the feet it is possible to start to relax the diaphragm and by the second or third visit the child will allow contact.

Response is variable, some benefit enormously, some recurrently redevelop tensions, perhaps due to dietary factors or domestic or school circumstances. The simultaneous input of other therapies may be needed, such as psychological support, Bach flower remedies, speech therapy or remedial help at school.

In an ideal world prevention is better than cure. If it is not possible prenatally to avoid predisposing factors then a paediatrically trained osteopath available at delivery might be able to prevent some infants from developing problems such as vomiting, colic, crying and poor sleeping, with later manifestation of hyperactivity, by releasing tensions in the meninges and diaphragm at birth.

Reflex inhibition – brushing

The relationship between hyperactivity, autism, Gilles de la Tourette syndrome, dyslexia and dyspraxia has already been noted. It is, therefore, not surprising that therapies that are helpful for one condition are often found to be helpful for others within the 'family'. One such therapy has been developed by Stephen Clarke at the Centre for Developmental and Learning Difficulties in Berkshire, a modification of earlier work pioneered 20 years ago by two Britons, Peter Blythe and David McGlown. Clarke uses a technique based on the theory that learning difficulties, such as dyslexia, and related problems such as hyperactivity and dyspraxia, and even autism, are caused in some children by the presence of immature neurological reflexes. He believes that children with the above problems have reflexes that have not completed their normal developmental sequence, starting in foetal life. Each reflex has its own particular function to perform before it is either inhibited or transformed by the brain. If the sequence is interrupted, normal development fails to take place and the child or adult is impaired in some way. The type of impairment depends upon the reflexes affected and this will depend upon the genetic makeup of the foetus, the nutritional status, the insult to which it has been exposed and in particular, the timing of the insult during the course of development.

A baby is born with a set of primitive reflexes that are designed to help it survive its first few months of life. These are intimately connected with the development of the central nervous system. One by one, during the first 18 months of life, these reflexes disappear or mature into adult reflexes. One of these reflexes, the moro reflex, is manifested in the baby as a startle with arms and legs flung out to the sides, fingers and toes splayed, and a look of surprise followed often by crying. This should disappear within the first three-to-four months. It normally develops into the adult type startle reflex which causes us momentarily to freeze involuntarily when surprised or shocked, followed by recovery and voluntary response to the situation. If the maturation of the moro reflex fails to occur, a child will react to the world with the infantile response, causing the production of an excess of adrenalin and hypersensitivity to stimuli such as bright lights, sudden noise and movement, sometimes with tears and/or tantrums – a distinct disadvantage in the school environment.

Paediatricians and paediatric healthcare teams are well aware of the importance of the sequential changes in these reflexes, and developmental surveillance programmes are in place throughout the UK in order to detect, at the earliest opportunity, deviations from the norm. Teams of physiotherapists, speech therapists and occupational therapists based in paediatric developmental units become involved with these children and their families and, ideally, a programme of therapy designed to help each individual is implemented. In reality, lack of manpower resources often makes it difficult to offer an optimal service, and many families are turning to complementary practitioners for help – a sad reflection on the state of the NHS in its fiftieth year.

Clarke has found that by using a small, soft, dry paintbrush to gently stroke certain lines on the body, face, hands and feet, it is possible to either inhibit or stimulate a reflex. This brushing is repeated each morning and evening for a prescribed number of strokes (maximum 40) for a period of 4–6 weeks. Before embarking on a programme a complete assessment of the child (or adult – it is never too late!) is undertaken to evaluate the potential for response to this approach. If accepted on to the programme the first step is to identify the point at which the reflexes failed to develop normally, starting at the earliest foetal reflexes and working forward. The method uses the brain's natural function to trigger the next reflex in the developmental sequence, thus speeding the remedial process. Other workers in the neurodevelopment field have instituted programmes involving intensive input of 8–10 hours a day for children with significant neurological problems, which in many cases has been highly effective, but in comparison with the brushing technique also highly labour intensive. It is also very important to recognize that it is essential that the correct information is fed back to the brain, otherwise abnormal reflexes, postural tone or incorrect movement patterns may be fed back to the brain, ensuring that the abnormality remains unremediated. An individual programme is designed for each patient.

Mr Clarke has found that a great number of dyslexic children he has treated are also hyperactive and both conditions improve using this therapeutic approach.

A pilot study to evaluate a programme of reflex inhibition and stimulation on children who have dyslexia (specific learning difficulties) was reported in 1996 by Pam Henley.

Reflexology

Reflexology is an holistic therapy used to discover where a problem is occurring in the body. It is not a diagnostic technique per se. For example, it may be possible to identify that there is a problem with the kidneys or the adrenal glands, but it is not possible to say exactly what the nature of the problem is. Reflexology is also able to stimulate the natural healing processes of the body. As with many of the therapies relying on self- healing, the subject often feels worse before getting better as the body throws off toxins and readjusts its function. This process is popularly known as the 'healing crisis'. After an authentic reflexology treatment it is common for people initially to experience nightmares, nausea or diarrhoea. The occurrence of a reaction is a good reason to continue treatment as the body obviously has considerable waste to clear and a great deal of healing to achieve.

So how does reflexology work? No-one really knows, despite the fact that the technique, or variations of it, has been used for many thousands of years. In keeping with most of the ancient healing practices, reflexology relies on the premise that parts of the body are linked by flows of energy. In acupuncture and acupressure these are called meridians. In reflexology there are ten energy zones in the body from head to toe called the longitudinal zones. There are five longitudinal zones on each foot; one linking the great toe to the brain and the thumb. There are also transverse zones across the body and feet, for example the shoulder zone runs across the base of the toes, the waist zone runs transversely across the mid foot and the pelvic zone across the heel. There is also a relationship between hands and feet called crossed reflexes.

Reflexology unblocks energy flows within the meridians and is a very effective therapy. For example, emotional problems often reside in the solar plexus. The reflexology point for this is mid-foot. Treatment of the foot can often trigger a powerful release of emotional energy. Stimulation of the tips of the big toes reflexly affects the brain. People with brain problems such as epilepsy should avoid overstimulating the tip of the big toe in particular, as this could possibly trigger a seizure. It is also important that shoes are not too small.

Morrell reflexology is slightly different from traditional reflexology. Instead of the firm pressure usually applied down the zones of the foot, the touch is very light and works across from one foot to the other at the same time gradually working down through the zones. This therapy can be extremely useful for hyperactive children. The first approach in a baby or small child is to gently blow on the sole of the foot or hand. In a baby this alone will often evoke a response. Therapy starts on the outer edge of the big toe or thumb on the left and with tiny, slow, light circular movements, executed with the tip of a finger, the therapist works his or her way down from the tip to the base of the fingers or toes, front, sides, then back. This is followed by a U-shaped massage with the tip of the little finger in the groove between the fingers or toes. Next the little finger or toe is held between thumb and index finger, lifted slightly, rotated clockwise then anticlockwise and gently pulled. The other fingers or toes follow. This is an example of holistic multidimensional reflexology. Movements are easier using calendula or vitamin E cream. After a few sessions the older ADHD or autistic children will often mimic the therapy instinctively by treating their own hands when upset. Note that fast moves can wind up a hyperactive child, especially on the thumb. Too much work on the tip of the thumb or great toe, which reflexly links with the brain, will overstimulate rather than calm down the child. As with all therapies, it is best to consult a profession-ally trained reflexol-ogist before embarking on home therapy.

Speech therapy

Speech therapy per se is truly orthodox. However, there are some innovations within the speciality that have not yet been incorporated within mainstream practice.

A number of children with ADHD who have normal intelligence and age-appropriate development in non-verbal skills fail to develop adequate language and communication. Some of these children will have had problems with their hearing due to glue ear, often a result of undiagnosed cow's milk or other intolerance, causing catarrh and lymphatic congestion. Some may have failed to progress through the normal pattern of reflex inhibition and stimulation, which may affect speech (see above). For some, altered perfusion of critical areas of the brain involved with speech (Broca's area), perhaps associated with nutritional factors, may be contributing. Whatever the underlying cause, and other therapy being employed, the contribution of the speech thera-pist is required. Often treatment of these children focuses on the management of their behavioural problems, their attention deficit, motor and co-ordination difficulties and family coping mechanisms, and issues relating to speech, language and communication may be neglected. Yet failure of communication itself may be a significant contributing factor to the syndrome. A study undertaken at the Royal Hospital for Sick Children in Glasgow found that 60% of children referred with ADHD had identifiable speech, language or communication problems. The findings corresponded fairly closely with studies undertaken by Cantwell and Baker and Trautmann, Giddan and Jurs. The main area of deficit seemed to be in the pragmatic use of language. According to Maureen Smillie, who was involved in the Glasgow study, many of the children seem oblivious to situational clues and do not respond to the social context. They fail to assess body language or facial expressions, are likely to be disorganized in communicating information and may well be rejected by their peers because of their limited language skills. Because of these limitations, they are likely to act out or use whole-body responses when angry or frustrated, further reducing their opportunities for successful social interaction. They cannot tolerate frustrated attempts to follow directions or express needs, and develop unwelcome behavioural characteristics.

This type of response is found in children just learning their social skills – the 'terrible twos' – who are also at an early stage in their language development. As their ability to process information and express needs develops, language becomes a substitute for action. Where this language-directed self-control does not develop, there is a risk that a cycle of frustration and psychopathology will result.

Speech and language therapists need to be part of the team involved in the management of children with ADHD, and child-specific intervention plans should be developed to address the needs of each child.

One method to enhance progress in the treatment of language disordered children, which has been found to be helpful for ADHD and dyslexic children, is the use of the ARROW system. The approach has been developed and refined by Dr Colin Lane over the past 20 years, and was based on the observation that in children with impaired hearing, accelerated progress was made in memory, language, literacy and motivation when the teaching programme was delivered by the children's own carefully recorded voices. The approach subsequently has also been found to be effective for children with dyslexia and ADHD. Of course there are training and resource implications for this approach, but ultimately the benefit to the child due to accelerated progress and ability to learn will offset the initial outlay.

Concluding comment

There are many other complementary therapies that have a place in helping children with ADHD including, for example, hypnotherapy, yoga and spiritual healing. I apologize to those practitioners who may feel slighted because their own speciality has been left out. This was certainly not because it is regarded as insignificant.

Reiterating my opening comment in Chapter 7, the aim of these two chapters has been to introduce the concept that there is always more than one way to approach any problem. It is hoped that the information provided will have achieved its goal of whetting the reader's appetite and encourage them to explore all possible avenues when helping children and families afflicted by ADHD.

Further reading

Chancellor PM (1971) Illustrated Handbook of the Bach Flower Remedies. Saffron Waldon, Essex: Daniel.

Davis P (1988) Aromatherapy an A–Z. Saffron Waldon, Essex: Daniel.

Duke M (1973) Acupuncture, The Chinese Art of Healing. London: Constable.

Gimbel T (1993) The Colour Therapy Workbook. Shaftsbury, Dorset: Element Books.

Price S (1994) Practical Aromatherapy, How to Use Essential Oils to Restore Health and Vitality. Hammersmith, London: Thorsons.

Scheffer M (1990) Bach Flower Therapy Theory and Practice. Hammersmith, London: Thorsons.

Sellar W (1992) Directory of Essential Oils. Saffron Walden, Essex: Daniel.

Wheeler FJ (1952/1996) The Bach Remedies Repertory. Saffron Walden, Essex: Daniel.

Wildwood C (1992) Flower Remedies, Natural Healing with Flower Essences. Shaftsbury, Dorset: Element Books.

Wills P (1993) Colour Therapy; The Use of Colour for Health and Healing. Shaftsbury, Dorset: Element Books.

Wormwood VA (1991) The Fragrant Pharmacy, A Complete Guide to Aromatherapy and Essential Oils. London: Bantam.

Useful addresses

1. The Bowen Association, PO Box 182, Witney, Oxon OX8 5YD; Tel./fax 01993 705 769. (Will provide lists of local therapists holding the diploma of and registered with the Bowen Association of Australia, and information about training).

2. The Children's Development Centre, PO Box 32, Manchester M24 6SW; Tel. 0161 654 4104. (Steve Clarke, Developmental Therapist specialising in the 'brushing' technique.)

3. The Edward Bach Centre, Mount Vernon, Sotwell, Wallingford, Oxon OX10 OPZ; Tel. 01491 39489/34678.

4. European College of Bowen Studies (E. C. B. S.). 38 Portway, Frome, Somerset BA11 1QU; Tel./fax: 01373 461 873. (Will provide lists of qualified local therapists on the European Register, and information about Bowen therapy training.)

5. The Institute for Complementary Medicine, PO Box 194, London SE16 1QZ. Tel. 0171 237 5165. (Will provide lists of qualified practitioners by request, on provision of stamped addressed envelope.)

6. The National Federation of Spiritual Healers, Old Manor Farm Studio, Church Street, Sunbury-on-Thames, Middlesex TW16 6RG; Tel. 01932 783164.

7. Osteopathic Children's Centre (OCC), 109, Harley Street, London W1M 1DG; Tel. 0171 486 6160. (A charity. Will also provide lists of qualified practitioners.)

Chapter 9
ADHD and Effective Learning: Principles and Practical Approaches

PAUL COOPER

Introduction and overview

It is neither accurate nor useful to think of ADHD simply in terms of a problem that resides within the individual. It is appropriate, however, to think of ADHD as a problem that stems from the interaction between the characteristics of the individual and the demands of the environment. Effective learning environments are places where just such a view is adopted. Effective schools for children with ADHD are not simply places where the behavioural problems associated with ADHD are controlled, but where students' individual characteristics are harnessed and exploited in positive ways so that opportunities for positive engagement in learning activities are maximized. At this general level the learning needs of children with ADHD are no different from those of all children. Central to this chapter is the view that the specific needs of children with ADHD can and should be met within a teaching and learning framework that is appropriate for all children.

Some basic assumptions

What follows in this chapter is underpinned by the following essentially educational assumptions:

- appropriate responses to ADHD need to go beyond the simple control and management of undesirable behaviour and include measures directed at the promotion of the child's emotional, social and academic development;
- medication may be an important and sometimes necessary component of effective intervention, but it is rarely a sufficient treatment in itself, almost always requiring to be used in conjunction with psychosocial (for example educational) interventions as part of a multi-modal treatment programme;

- the extent to which medication is necessary should be informed by knowledge of how the child responds to psychosocial interventions without medication.

ADHD as a biopsychosocial problem and the importance of non-biological interventions

ADHD is least controversially described as being characterized by the individual's 'inability to maintain effort over time in order to meet task demands' (BPS, 1996).

Crucially, in spite of superficial appearances, the core problems of ADHD are not volitional. The particular cluster and manifestations of behaviours that comprise the various subtypes of the ADHD diagnosis recur with sufficient frequency and to a sufficient degree of severity to make the condition widely accepted by informed medical practitioners and psychologists throughout the world. The biological basis of ADHD, however, is more problematic.

As was noted in Chapter 1, there is a body of research that points to links between ADHD and certain structural and neurochemical dysfunctions in the brain. Furthermore, twin and chemical genetic studies suggest a heritability factor. On the other hand, the ADHD diagnosis is made almost entirely on the assessment of behavioural data. In individual cases there is no known neurological problem, and evidence pointing to genetic transmission is often ambiguous and, at best, speculative owing to the difficulties in controlling experiential influences that are commonly shared by members of the same family.

Therefore, whereas there is sufficient evidence to suggest that some of the children who receive the ADHD diagnosis have the condition in association with biological factors, there is insufficient evidence to allow us to conclude the full extent and nature of the biological influences across the whole population of children with ADHD.

Environment plays a crucial role in determining the nature and course of many conditions in which biology is implicated, including ADHD (Rose, 1997). Even where biological factors are clearly implicated, it is the social and cultural environment that determines whether or not the observed behaviours are perceived to be desirable or undesirable, acceptable or unacceptable, different or deviant. Furthermore, the application of such socially determined judgements itself has an effect on the behaviour and self-image of the individual concerned, as Wolff (1995) has illustrated in her account of the long-term effects of treatment on individuals with schizoid personality disorder.

For example, it is common for children with ADHD to experience social exclusion and peer rejection. The primary cause of this rejection may be the child's impulsive behaviour, which manifests itself in a chronic tendency to interrupt and intrude on other children in social situations. Such behaviour may be related to an abnormality in the neurological mechanisms that are associated with impulse control (Barkley, 1997). However, the rejection may lead to secondary emotional problems, in the form of low self-esteem, which in turn lead to further acting out behaviour of an aggressive or antisocial kind (Goldstein, 1997). We therefore end up with a situation where we have a child with behavioural problems some of which have a biological basis and others of which have a psychosocial basis. Clearly, in these circumstances it is necessary to devise interventions that take full account of the underlying biopsychosocial nature of the presenting problems.

The importance of the environment in the assessment of ADHD

Although in practice it may be all but impossible to separate out the biological from the psychosocial influences on the behaviour of an individual, it is possible to identify the extent to which aspects of the child's environment may be implicated as stressors in relation to his or her problems. For this reason it seems sensible to make assessment of the child's environment an important part of the general assessment process, and to make adjustments to the environment where necessary before opting for pharmacological interventions. Important questions to be asked of the home and the school as part of this assessment are:

- To what extent is positive behaviour seen as a skill to be taught and thus learnt?
- What responsibility are adults taking in the facilitation of positive behaviour?
- What kinds of measures are in place to promote positive behaviour?
- Are positive behavioural expectations being presented in a manner that the child understands?
- Are behavioural expectations reasonable?
- Are efforts being made to educate the child about (a) positive behavioural expectations, and (b) strategies for meeting these expectations?
- What happens when the child fails to meet behavioural expectations? Is the response therapeutic/remedial or punitive?
- What opportunities exist to celebrate the strengths and positive qualities of the child?

Whether or not there is a biological component to the problem behaviour these questions will have to be addressed if the aim is to promote the positive social, emotional and educational development of the child, as opposed to simply seeking to control his or her behaviour.

The role of medication in intervention with ADHD

Where medication is employed it is seen by many specialists in this area as sometimes necessary but never, in itself alone, a sufficient treatment (Hinshaw, 1994). The role of medication, such as methylphenidate (Ritalin), is to facilitate the learning of appropriate behaviour and skills by placing the child in a situation whereby his or her receptiveness is maximized (see Chapter 6). Thus, in the case of methylphenidate the child's ability to concentrate is improved. This creates a window of opportunity through which parents and teachers can begin to help the child develop strategies and habits for effective learning and self-regulation.

The role of psychosocial factors in intervention with ADHD: in the classroom

The child with ADHD presents often as a child with average-to-high ability, but with problems of sustained application, organization and behaviour. This poses the teacher a number of key tasks:

- to help to stretch the child cognitively using the child's existing strengths and preferred ways of learning;
- to help the child to catch up on basic skills (in literacy and numeracy, for example) without making the child feel that his or her lack of these skills makes him or her a failure;
- to recognize and provide for the fact that whereas the child's cognitive development may not depend on literacy and other formal academic abilities, his or her accumulation of credentials and progress in relation to national standards, such as national curriculum attainment targets, will, therefore, depend on his or her acquisition of literacy and other formal skills;
- to boost the child's self-esteem, so as to avoid or reverse the descent into disaffection and poor motivation;
- to meet the educational needs of the child with ADHD in ways that are compatible with meeting the needs of other children in the class or school;
- to help the child become socially integrated and not a disruptive influence in the classroom to the detriment of other children and him or herself.

Dealing with problems: some principles

Many of the classroom problems associated with ADHD present themselves in the form of behavioural problems. These problems will sometimes look like laziness or lack of motivation. The child may often appear not to care, to be uninterested, or wilfully unco-operative. Like everyone else, children with ADHD are sometimes lazy and unwilling to work. Quite a lot of the time, however, for the child with ADHD what looks like laziness or unwillingness to work is a result of the ADHD. This means that it is not a problem that will be solved by the child simply trying harder. In these circumstances the child will have to be helped to learn how to behave in the desired way.

The aim of intervention with the child with ADHD, then, is not simply to control or extinguish the unwanted behaviour, it is to help the child develop cognitive and behavioural patterns that are socially and educationally effective. A necessary by-product of this process is the extinction of negative behaviour patterns.

A valuable way of thinking about behavioural problems is to see them as one of five possible types:

- as resulting from the desire to avoid something;
- as resulting from the desire for attention at inappropriate times and in inappropriate ways;
- as resulting from a misunderstanding, communication difficulty, lack of knowledge or information;
- as an involuntary reaction that has a psychological or physiological cause;
- resulting from a lack of agreed or shared values.
  (Based on Harris et al., 1996)

This typology of interventions can be used as a starting point for the search for solutions, as the following paragraphs show.

Removing reasons why a child might wish to avoid positive engagement in lessons

Children with social, learning and emotional difficulties often avoid engagement in lessons not as a direct result of their primary difficulty but as a secondary response based on experiences of humiliation and failure. The aim of interventions that follow from this principle is to make student involvement as rewarding as possible rather than aversive and discouraging. A rewarding aspect of schooling for many students is the enjoyment of positive relationships with peers and staff (Cooper, 1993). Staff can play a leading role in this process by initiating positive interactions with students, through warmth, friendliness, humour and the showing of empathy and unconditional positive regard (Cronk, 1987). In this way teacher behaviour can help to shape a positive atmosphere in which pupils will imitate the teacher model.

A very important issue here is that of blame. If a teacher is in the habit of emphasizing the source of problems and apportioning blame when things go wrong, then obviously children with difficulties are going to receive a lot of negative feedback. A starting point for overcoming this difficulty is to adopt a solution focus, rather than a problem focus (De Shazer, 1985); to ask 'what can we do to solve this problem?' rather than 'what is the cause of this problem?' This means identifying as precisely as possible what the desirable, positive alternative to the unwanted behaviour looks like (Molnar and Lindquist, 1989).

Creating circumstances in which positive attention is available for legitimate reasons

Any attention is better than no attention at all. Children with learning and behavioural difficulties sometimes learn that it is easier to get noticed by behaving in negative or foolish ways, than by being a 'good student'. The best thing for teachers to do in these circumstances is to minimize the amount of attention given for negative behaviour and to maximize the amount of attention give for desirable and positive behaviour. It is often the case, for example, that teachers will give positive attention for good academic performance, whilst tending to acknowledge students' social behaviour when it is negative. This means that children with learning and behavioural difficulties get plenty of negative attention and can become alienated as a result. A way to combat this is to 'catch them being good' (Smith and Laslett, 1995) by drawing attention to and praising positive social behaviour when it occurs whilst ignoring negative behaviour.

Clearly, it is not always possible to ignore negative behaviour. When this happens, the behaviour should be dealt with as unobtrusively as possible, immediately and decisively, such as through the use of time out (the withdrawal of positive attention). This strategy can be used as a punishment but is perhaps more helpfully seen as positive 'cooling off' period for the student and (sometimes) the teacher and the rest of the class. Whether used as a positive or negative intervention, the application of the time out strategy should always be accompanied by a clear statement of the reasons why it is necessary and a statement of what the desirable alternative behaviour looks like.

Ensuring clear and effective channels of communication

Key issues here are:

- clarity of communication;
- willingness to listen;
- willingness to repeat or paraphrase information and/or instructions as often as it takes, without displaying anger or exasperation.

Misunderstandings and confrontation can often be avoided when teacher expectations are clearly stated and students feel empowered to express their concerns or desire for clarification. Similarly, children are far more likely to accept that they have been wrong, if they are given the opportunity to explain their side of the story (Cronk, 1987). Sometimes, of course, their side of the story indicates that they have not been wrong at all!

Recognizing the importance of language

Language problems of one kind or another are often associated with ADHD, including difficulties with auditory processing and problems with the use of private speech for information processing (self-talk) (Berk and Potts, 1991). This may have a bearing on the often-noted problem that students with ADHD have in conforming to rules, especially when the rules are expressed linguistically and conceptually. There are two important implications that flow from this observation:

* Children with ADHD are likely, to benefit from having rules expressed to them graphically, with visual and or experiential exemplars which allow the pupil to relate the rule to their immediate experience.
* Children with ADHD (like all children) should not be assumed to possess the linguistic skills necessary to understand verbal rules, to discuss ethical issues, or to express and deal with complex emotions. The teaching of these skills should form an important part of the curriculum for all children from an early age (Bennathan and Boxall, 1996). Among other things, pupils should be taught emotional literacy, whereby they are enabled to acquire a sophisticated vocabulary for talking about ethical and emotional issues.

Being aware of individual differences

It is invaluable for the teacher to have an awareness of the specific circumstances in which individual children perform best (Weaver, 1994). It is perhaps tempting to see students with ADHD in terms of what they cannot do, because of the way in which the 'disorder' is often portrayed. However, an educational perspective demands that we should focus on seeking out and capitalizing on the skills and strengths that students already possess. These can then be exploited in order to expand the student's repertoire of skills and attainments.

For example, children with ADHD can often become overwhelmed by the massive overstimulation they experience in a group situation. This problem, coupled with the poor social skills that are associated with hyperactivity, can lead to disruption and mayhem. Sometimes, therefore, it might be advisable to place the child with ADHD in a pair situation, rather than a group (DuPaul and Stoner, 1994). On the other hand, the importance of developing group work skills should not be ignored. If the child with ADHD is to learn group work skills it may be necessary for the teacher to structure his or her group work experiences with particular care, by, for example, ensuring that the child with ADHD is placed in a group with children who are skilled in collaboration and co-operation, and thus unlikely to place undue strain on the child's impaired attentional faculties. This strategy will be further supported if the task that the group is given is one in which the child with ADHD is likely to perform particularly well, and thus be welcomed by other group members as an asset.

Effective classroom teaching for children with ADHD

What follows is an account of the ways in which teachers can make learning tasks accessible to the students with ADHD (see also Cooper and Ideus, 1996). Many of these points are appropriate to *all* children, but they are all especially helpful to the child with ADHD. Key underlying principles are:

- The need for precision and clarity in communicating with the student with ADHD so that whatever it is the teacher wants the child to do is always sharply in focus and not lost in a fog of extraneous detail or ambiguity.
- The need to protect the student from distraction by (a) reducing unwanted stimuli, (b) increasing desired stimuli, and (c) teaching to the child's cognitive and personal strengths.
- The need to protect and nurture the student's sense of self-esteem by (a) maximizing opportunities for success (b) communicating personal warmth and acceptance, and (c) through positive recognition in the form of praise and rewards.

The following are some of the approaches that have been found to be successful with children with ADHD (see DuPaul and Stoner, 1994; Weaver, 1994):

Students with ADHD are often hypersensitive to distraction. It is important, therefore, to ensure that they are seated in the classroom in a place that is (a) relatively free from distraction (away from doors and windows) and (b) in a place where the teacher can readily detect if the student is or is not attending and, if necessary, intervene without embarrassing the child or disrupting the lesson. It is also important that a value be placed on calmness and quietness, when appropriate. This is not the same as saying that a quiet classroom is always a good classroom (Weaver, 1994). There are times, however, when the effectiveness of the teaching and learning processes going on in the classroom depends on an atmosphere of quietness and calmness (when intense individual concentration is required).

Sometimes the child with ADHD may have a greater need for quietness than other children, because of attentional problems. Where this happens it is helpful to have a designated quiet place where the child can go. Some teachers use carrels, or screens in ordinary classrooms, for this purpose. These can be set up in ways that enable the child with ADHD to be screened from the distractions of other students whilst remaining visible to the teacher.

Children with ADHD can also be distracted by their own thoughts, so it is important to ensure that they are stimulated by the required task. This means that the task should be sharply delineated and highly focused. Which is not the same as saying that it should be the only stimulus to which the student is exposed: sensory deprivation is not conducive to effective learning.

Children with ADHD benefit from concise, clear instructions with as few subparts as possible. They should be encouraged to repeat task requirements back to the teacher orally, preferably in their own words. Also, when being given a list of instructions, it is better if each instruction is given and digested before the next instruction is given. Where appropriate, the instructions should be presented in a form that will allow the pupil to retrieve them if he or she forgets – in writing, for example.

All children, and particularly those with ADHD, benefit from clear, predictable, uncomplicated routine and structure. It helps if the day is divided into broad units of time and if this pattern is repeated daily. Within each block of lesson time there should be a similar breaking down of tasks and activities into subtasks/activities. Presenting the student with an enormously detailed list of tasks and subtasks should be avoided. An important goal should be to create a simple overarching daily routine that the student will eventually learn by heart. The number of tasks should be kept small and tight deadlines should be avoided. Complexities of timetabling and working structures merely confuse students with ADHD, because a major difficulty that goes with this condition is a poorly developed ability to differentiate between and organize different bits of information. This clearly makes the formal curriculum difficult enough to manage, without having to struggle with the organisational arrangements that surround the curriculum. Once a workable daily timetable has been established this should be publicly displayed and/or taped to the student's desk/ or inside his or her homework diary.

Avoid repetitive tasks. Whilst the general daily routine should be simple and broadly predictable, the educational content should be as varied and stimulating as possible. If tasks are not stimulating they will allow the child to become easily distracted.

Tasks should be broken down into a small number of short steps. Again, the emphasis should be on reducing complexity and maximizing clarity of focus so that the child and the teacher are both clear about what is expected.

Clearly, the child with ADHD should be encouraged to tackle tasks of increasing complexity. Initially, however, tasks should be relatively short. The length and complexity of tasks should increase only when the student has shown success with shorter assignments. This is important not only from the viewpoint of skill development, it is also a valuable way of enhancing the student's self-confidence and self-esteem.

Academic products and performance (for example, work completion) are nearly always preferred targets for intervention rather than specific behaviours (for example remaining in seat). This stresses the need to focus on positive, desirable outcomes rather than the negative, unwanted behaviour.

If a dead person can carry out the behaviour the teacher requires it is not behaviour (Du Paul and Stoner's 1994 'deadman' test). Negative expectations of this kind are likely to be problematic for all children. Behavioural requirements should involve positive behaviours rather than the absence of behaviour.

Children with ADHD often require more specific and more frequent feedback on their work performance than most pupils. This is partly due to their memory and attention problems as well as being a by-product of low self-esteem.

Praise and rewards should be applied when a child has achieved a desired target. Small and immediate rewards are more effective than long-term or delayed rewards. It is important to remember that students with ADHD are easily distracted, therefore rewards should not be overly elaborate or likely to overshadow the task in any way. Rewards need to be as immediate as possible, since students with ADHD often have problems with thinking outside of the immediate time frame.

Negative consequences, in the form of mild punishment, can sometimes be effective. They should be used sparingly, be clearly focused and highly specific. For example, mild reprimands for being off task will be most effective when they involve a reminder of the task requirement. Thus it is better to say: 'please stop talking and get back to reading page three of your history booklet', rather than, 'please get on with your work'. Their effectiveness will also be enhanced in classrooms where teachers are habitually positive in their behaviour towards children. It is interesting to note that students do not like to be told off by teachers who hold them in high regard; conversely, students often find it difficult to accept praise from teachers who habitually treat them with contempt or disrespect.

Preferred activities (such as working on a computer) are more effective rewards than concrete rewards (such as sweets). It is the student's preference that counts here. For example, not all students see working on the computer as a treat: this may be especially true of a child who makes use of a computer as regular part of his or her learning programme (as is the case for many children with literacy difficulties and ADHD). For this reason, appropriate rewards are likely to be effectively identified through negotiation between teacher and student. This can lead to the development of a 'rewards menu' which contains a variety of possible rewards that can be used to avoid the staleness and boredom that might result from the repetition of the same reward over time.

Previewing and reviewing of tasks helps students to know what is expected of them and to make sense of what they are doing.

'Priming' helps motivate students with ADHD. This involves previewing with the student the task and the likely rewards of successful completion.

Brevity, calmness and quietness should mark interactions with students. Reprimands, where necessary, should be quiet and accompanied by direct eye contact.

Students with attentional problems are more forgetful than most children. Therefore, it is important to avoid signs of exasperation when repeating task requirements to pupils (for example 'if I've told you once I've told you a thousand times'). Always give task requirements as though you are giving them for the first time, in a calm and measured way. The student with ADHD will experience exasperation as unfair. Sarcasm is definitely not appropriate in these circumstances.

Students with ADHD tend to perform best in pairs rather than group situations. This is because there is a tendency for group situations to be overstimulating. In groups there tend to be too many possible distractions and too much strain placed on the child's limited social skills.

Difficulties with sequencing and concentration /distractibility make writing a very difficult task for students with ADHD. Alternative means of presenting knowledge (through tape, use of amanuensis, computer and so forth) can help here. Another important factor is the need for the student to be placed in a calm and quiet place where the often-intense concentration required will not be threatened by noise or other distractions.

Simple behavioural interventions, if applied with great diligence, can be helpful in establishing and reinforcing behavioural requirements and boundaries. For example:

- Time out: a place where the student can be sent for a short, specified period (three to five minutes) when he or she is misbehaving, where he or she will not receive stimulation or attention. It should be clearly explained to the student (a) why it is being done, with direct reference to the offence, and (b) what it is intended to achieve (to give time for reflection, time to cool off). It is also important that when the time out period is over that the teacher responds to the student with warmth and acceptance to indicate that the 'offence' has now been dealt with and can be put in the past in favour of current and more positive pursuits.

- Ignore-rules-praise (Wheldall and Merrett, 1987). In the behavioural sense, ignoring is the removal of attention that might act as reinforcement. It is not an act of rudeness whereby a student's attempts at positive interaction with the teacher are not responded to. Ignoring is always directed at the behaviour rather than the individual and is most effectively employed in the guise of applying attention to a positive act that is taking place simultaneously with the negative act. The intended message here is: 'I am happy and eager to show attention and give praise to a child who is carrying out desirable behaviour. I find this much more valuable than negative behaviour.' If ignoring is carried out in a context where such positive attention is common it may lead to attention-seeking behaviour. Ignoring is only powerful in discouraging behaviour when it is understood by the child to be the absence of positive attention. This technique involves the teacher ignoring rule-breaking behaviour, whilst praising another child who is obeying the rule, in a way that is clear to the misbehaving child. This should always involve a statement of the rule. Similarly, ignoring is only effective if the person whose behaviour is being ignored has experience of their positive behaviour being praised. Clearly this approach depends on the creation of a few simple, realistic, clearly stated rules.
- Behavioural contracts. This is another way of establishing expectations, discussing them with the child and reinforcing them. Here an agreement is made between the teacher and student, or among students, which establishes clear behavioural expectations, states how these are to be achieved and relates their achievement to particular reward. Rewards should be short-term and low-key (see above).
- Token economies. This involve the giving of tokens, in the form of points, stickers or other 'currency', as rewards for positive rule compliant behaviour. These tokens are then exchanged for a more concrete reward (such as a preferred activity or more tangible reward).

Dialogue between teacher and student should be an ongoing aspect of their daily interactions. This dialogue should be carried out in a way that expresses to the student the teacher's empathy and positive regard for the child. It also important that the teacher be honest and avoids misleading the student about the desirability of antisocial or other negative behaviours. It comes naturally to some teachers to show a personal interest in their students by asking them questions or sharing humour with them. Non-sarcastic humour is actually a low-key way of expressing positive regard to another person. This dialogue helps the teacher to:

- monitor the child's mood state and feelings about the success or otherwise of the intervention programme;
- learn about personal, family and social factors that may influence the child's performance;
- detect learning difficulties;
- develop a positive relationship with the child;
- model positive modes of interaction for the child and other children.

Dialogue between teacher and pupil, therefore, provides part of the basis for and one of the best means of meeting the child's needs. It also contributes to the child's sense of being valued and accepted, and his or her personal sense of security.

Thinking positively about ADHD

So much of the phenomenon that we call ADHD is associated with negativity and problems of one kind and another that it is very easy for people to become thoroughly fed up with the condition and the individual who has it. There are no easy answers to this problem. Where this happens, however, the all-important relationship between the teacher and the student suffers. This in turn will often lead to an exacerbation of the student's unwanted behaviours and make the teacher even more fed up. In this section we look at ways in which some of the characteristics associated with ADHD can be construed in more positive ways. The aim here is twofold:

- To offer the teacher strategies for thinking positively when they can see only negativity.
- To offer ways of thinking that can produce solutions to learning and behavioural problems.

The reframing technique

Children with ADHD often come to be locked into cycles of negativity, whereby it seems that everything they do receives a negative response or reprimand. Teachers also can sometimes find themselves trapped into perpetuating these cycles. Reframing is a technique that has many valuable applications, especially when dealing with behavioural problems. It involves finding a new and positive way of thinking about a child's problem behaviour, and has the effect of helping the teacher to break cycles of negativity.

Although the reframing technique may at first appear to defy common sense, it should be pointed out that it is based on practices used by some clinical psychologists to great success with very severe emotional and behavioural disorders. These practices were adapted for educational settings by Molnar and Lindquist (1989) in the US, and were applied to behavioural problems in the UK by Cooper and Upton (1990) and Cooper et al. (1994).

The approach stresses the importance of framing all students' behaviour as positively as possible. This is not the same as condoning unwanted or undesirable behaviour. The purpose of the technique is to help the teacher to develop ideas about the positive ways in which children might use certain of their behavioural characteristics; in particular, those that are seen as a source of problems. The technique also allows the teacher to indicate that although a behaviour may not be appropriate in one situation, there may be situations in which the behaviour is highly or at least more appropriate. This can have important consequences for:

• students' self-esteem;
• the development of co-operative teacher–student relationships in class;
• changing behaviour.

Reframing undesirable behaviours in positive ways helps students to believe that:

• the teacher likes them;
• the teacher cares about them.

In using this technique it is important to avoid communicating approval of undesirable behaviour. It may well be the case that some forms of behaviour, such as those involving violence, may not lend themselves to this reframing. It is important to use the technique where it has a chance of being effective, and where it will be productive and convincing. Sometimes it may be appropriate to use the reframing technique in a way that also indicates a mild disapproval of the current behaviour. This can be done by providing a positive reframing of the unwanted behaviour and then indicating that there are situations, other than the present one, in which these qualities are more appropriately displayed.

For reframing to be successful it must be:

• convincing, in that it fits the facts of the situation as student and teacher see them;
• done in a genuine way (without sarcasm);
• be congruent with your way of behaving towards the student.

Some negative and positive ways of framing characteristics of ADHD (based on Hartmann, 1993) are:

Negative	Positive
Distractible	High level of environmental awareness
Short attention span but with periods of intense focus	Responds well when highly motivated
Poor planner; disorganized; impulsive	Flexible; ready to change strategy quickly
Distorted sense of time	Tireless when motivated
Impatient	Goal-oriented
Difficulty converting words into concepts	Visual/concrete thinker
Has difficulty following directions	Independent
Daydreamer	Bored by mundane tasks/imaginative
Acts without considering consequences	Willing and able to take risks
Lacking in social skills	Single-minded in pursuit of goals

These are some possible positive reframes for common classroom problems:

Being out of seat too frequently	Energetic and lively
Deviating from what the rest of the class is supposed to be doing	Independent, inquisitive, individualistic
Talking out of turn or calling out	Keen to contribute
Being aggressive toward classmate	Sensitive, emotional, passionate
Losing and forgetting equipment	Thoughtful; absorbed in own ideas
Handing in homework late or not at all	Perfectionist; unable to get started because of high standards
Handing in incomplete or sloppy work	Signs of effort in spite of difficulties

Put simply, students with ADHD (like all students) perform most effectively when tasks are tailored to harness positive aspects of their characteristics and so prevent them from becoming dysfunctional. They are also likely to be more motivated when teachers and others behave towards them in ways that are positive and geared to enhancing their self-esteem.

ADHD and cognitive style

Cognitive style refers to the preferred ways individuals have of learning new skills. It is argued by some commentators on the subject that the symptoms of ADHD bear close similarities with the characteristics of high creativity (Crammond, 1994). The danger of adopting this position uncritically are that it can glamorize ADHD inappropriately and inaccurately. If a student's learning difficulties are solely the by-product of an unconventional and highly creative mind, then the child does not have ADHD. However, it is important to recognize that, where there is a mismatch between the demands of a learning situation and the learning characteristics of the student, this is likely to impair the effectiveness of the teaching and lead to learning and, in some cases, behavioural difficulties. Evidence suggests, however, that where teachers create learning environments that enable students to engage in a variety of ways, according to their preferred learning styles, the likelihood of positive learning outcomes, as perceived by teachers and students, is enhanced (Cooper and McIntyre, 1996).

Different learning styles include:

- A preference for learning from *concrete experience*, which emphasizes feeling over thinking; 'here and now complexity' over 'theories and generalizations'; intuitive over systematic.
- A preference for *reflective observation*, which emphasizes understanding over practical application; the ideal over the pragmatic; reflection over action.
- A preference for *abstract conceptualizations*, which emphasizes thinking over feeling; theories over 'here and now complexity'; systematic over intuitive.
- A preference for *active experimentation*, which emphasizes pragmatic over ideal; doing rather than observing.
  (Based on Kolb, 1984, pp. 68–9.)

Children with ADHD tend to favour the concrete experience and active experimentation learning styles (Wallace and Crawford, 1994). These learning styles are most useful in circumstances where tasks are experiential in nature: where the learning emerges from doing. There is still a tendency for schools, however, to focus on tasks that are essentially reflective and abstract, as is demonstrated by the general emphasis on the literary form in the national curriculum in England and Wales and public examinations. Yet, it seems that much curriculum content can be approached by using any of these means (see Cooper and McIntyre, 1996; Cooper and Ideus, 1996).

ADHD and creativity

These are some of the commonalities between traits associated with creativity and ADHD:

- self-centredness
- emotionally hypersensitive
- highly imaginative: 'in a world of their own'
- divergent thinking
- impulsive, spontaneous, unpredictable.
  (Crammond, 1994; Jordan, 1992)

Of course being creative is no excuse for bad behaviour. If, however, a child's negative behaviour is associated with a high level of creativity, it is likely that the student will benefit socially and educationally from opportunities to exercise his or her creativity. Creative students can often be a valuable resource to the classroom teacher in their ability to offer divergent ways of looking at things or novel approaches (and solutions) to problems. Openly acknowledging, and giving status to, a student's abilities in this area can again help to provide the student, in some cases, with a legitimate channel by which he or she can become positively involved in classroom activities.

Effective teaching in context: whole school characteristics to help the child with ADHD

Many of the above items are already in the repertoire of the effective classroom teacher, who combines knowledge of subject matter, teaching techniques, specific pupil characteristics and prevalent conditions to produce lessons that have clearly defined outcomes tailored to the different needs of their pupils. What classroom teachers are able to achieve in the classroom is, of course, constrained by the broader school context. So here, finally, is a list of some of the whole school characteristics that will support these endeavours. Key issues here relate to the extent to which structures exist to identify and address problems as they arise.

- Longer rather than shorter lesson blocks. Efforts should be made to minimize the disruptive effects of too many lesson changes. At the same time the lessons themselves should be carefully structured to provide a variety of activity and focus (as above).

- Attention should be given to environmental distracters in school. The primary function of the school is to enable teaching and to promote learning. If either of these functions is impaired by physical or environmental factors (such as preparations for lunch or maintenance to the building's fabric) then it is necessary to (a) reduce the effect of this impairment, or (b) adjust expectations about teaching and learning quality.

- Balancing physical and cognitive needs. All children behave and attend better under conditions where their needs for physical activity are met. Concentration and application are aided by frequent opportunities for physical exercise. Research on the effects of 'recess deprivation' has pointed to a powerful relation between levels of antisocial and inattentive behaviour during lessons and delayed access to recess (i.e., playtime) (Pellegrini and Horvat, 1995, 1996).

- Concentration of lessons requiring high levels of cognitive engagement earlier rather than later in the day. Timetabling does not always make this possible, but it is important to bear in mind that people tend to be cognitively fresher earlier rather than later in the day. This is one of the benefits of the 'continental day' which may begin at 7.30 am but finish at 2 pm. Similarly, it is important to provide a balance in the educational diet so that whole days are not entirely devoted to cognitive activities or physical activities.

- Teacher consultation on school management and curricular issues is a common feature of well-run schools where channels of communication are open between senior managers and other staff. Without this kind of communication it is difficult for policies to be developed that reflect the everyday realities of classroom life. Of course, for this to be effective requires senior management be proactive in carrying out consultation (Cooper, 1993).

- Pupil consultation on school management and curricular issues echoes many of the points made under the previous heading. It should also be remembered that consultation is not the same as democracy. Consultation is about listening to others and explaining why decisions are made.

- Positive parental involvement requires that parents be made to feel welcome in the school, and that they are kept informed and consulted about school developments.

- The sharing of pastoral and academic responsibilities throughout the staff, rather than having strict demarcation lines between pastoral and academic responsibilities, ensures that these two areas of interest do not conflict. So often do pastoral problems first manifest themselves as academic problems, whilst academic problems can lead to pastoral problems, that it is always necessary for staff to be prepared to deal with any situation as either of these problems or a combination of both (Cooper, 1993).

- All children benefit from effective whole-school policies that (a) celebrate rather than stigmatize individual differences, (b) allow pupils to gain recognition and high self esteem from a wide range of activities (comprehensive reward structure), and (c) provide effective learning and emotional/behavioural support where and when pupils need it.

Conclusion

Effective teaching for students with ADHD, as with effective teaching for students with a wide range of emotional, behavioural and learning difficulties, does not differ in principle from effective teaching for all students. That being said, students with difficulties like ADHD are perhaps more dependent on the skills of their teachers than students without such difficulties. Students who are bored or confused by the set task may become distracted and engage in off-task behaviour. On the other hand some students will persevere, put up with boredom and tackle their confusion in a determined way. It may well be the case that many of our most successful students, in terms of examination grades, fall into the latter group. If this is so, as many writers and researchers have suggested (Silberman, 1971; Barnes, 1975; Schostak, 1982), then we might be tempted to observe that these outcomes are not, primarily, the product of effective teaching, but rather the product of the practice of the 'craft knowledge' of studenthood (Cooper and McIntyre, 1996). Such craft knowledge is developed through the experience of dealing successfully with the obstacles to learning that are commonly placed in the way of students as a result of the constraints that are part and parcel of the 'mass production' approach to the business of learning that is central to our Western education systems. Students with ADHD, who tend not to learn from experience alone, do not, by and large, develop this knowledge base without the kind of help that is described in this chapter.

References

Barkley R (1990) ADHD: A Handbook for Assessment and Treatment. New York: Guilford.

Barnes D (1975) From Communication to Curriculum. Harmondsworth: Penguin.

Bennathan M, Boxall M (1996) Effective Intervention in Primary Schools: Nurture Groups. London: Fulton.

Berk L, Potts M (1991) Development and functional significance of private speech among ADHD and normal boys. Journal of Abnormal Child Psychology 19: 357–71.

British Psychological Society (1996) ADHD: A Psychological Response to an Evolving Concept. Leicester: BPS.

Cooper P (1993) Effective Schools for Disaffected Students. London: Routledge.

Cooper P, Ideus K (1996) ADHD: A Practical Guide for Teachers. London: Fulton.

Cooper P, McIntyre D (1996) Effective Teaching and Learning: Teachers' and Students' Perspectives. Buckingham: Open University Press.

Cooper P, Smith CJ, Upton G (1994) Emotional and Behavioural Difficulties: From Theory to Practice. London: Routledge.

Cooper P, Upton G (1990) An ecosystemic approach to emotional and behavioural difficulties. Educational Psychology 10(4): 301–23.

Crammond B (1994) The Relationship between ADHD and Creativity. Paper presented at the Annual Conference of the American Educational Research Association, New Orleans.

Cronk K (1987) Teacher–Pupil Conflict in Classrooms. Lewes: Falmer.

De Shazer S (1985) Keys to Solution. New York: Guilford.

DuPaul G, Stoner G (1994) ADHD in the Schools: Assessment and Intervention Strategies. New York: Guilford.

Goldstein S (1997) Understanding and assessing ADHD and related educational, behavioural and emotional disorders. In P Cooper, K Ideus, ADHD: Educational, Medical and Cultural Issues, East Sutton, AWCEBD.

Harris J, Cook M, Upton G (1996) Pupils with Severe Learning Disabilities Who Present Challenging Behaviour. Kidderminster: BILD.

Hartmann T (1993) Attention Deficit Disorder: A Different Perception. Novato CA: Underwood-Miller.

Hinshaw S (1994) Attention Deficit Disorders and Hyperactivity in Children. New York/London: Sage.

Jordan D (1992) Attention Deficit Disorder: ADHD and ADD Syndromes. Austin TX: Pro-Ed.

Kolb D (1984) Experience and Learning. Englewood Cliffs NJ: Prentice-Hall.

Molnar A, Lindquist B (1989) Changing Problem Behavior in Schools. San Francisco: Jossey Bass.

Pellegrini A, Davis Huberty P, Jones I (1996) The effects of recess timing on children's playground and classroom behaviors. American Educational Research Journal 32(4): 845–64.

Pellegrini A, Horvat M (1995) A developmental contextualist critique of attention deficit/hyperactivity disorder. Educational Researcher 24(1): 13–20.

Rose S (1997) Lifelines: Biology, Freedom, Determinism. London: Penguin.

Schostak J (1982) Maladjusted Schooling. Lewes: Falmer.

Silberman J (1971) Crisis in the Classroom. New York: Random House.

Smith C, Laslett R (1995) Effective Classroom Management (2 edn). London: Routledge.

Wallace B, Crawford S (1994) Instructional paradigms and the ADHD child. In C Weaver (ed.) Success at Last: Helping Students with AD(H)D Achieve their Potential. Portsmouth NH: Henemann.

Weaver C (ed.) (1994) Success at last: helping students with AD(H)D achieve their potential. Portsmouth NH: Henemann.

Wheldall K, Merrett F (1987) Training teachers to use the behavioural approach to classroom management. In K Wheldall (ed.) The Behaviourist in the Classroom. London: Allen & Unwin.

Wolff S (1995) Loners: The Life Path of Unusual Children. London: Routledge.

Chapter 10
Cognitive Approaches to the Education and Training of Children with ADHD

ÉGIDE ROYER

The use of stimulants and behaviour modification techniques is still considered, particularly in North America, as the treatment of choice for children with attention deficit hyperactivity disorder (ADHD). Nevertheless, the development of cognitive psychology in the past 20 years has created an increased interest in the development of cognitive intervention in association with traditional behavioural techniques. Usually referred to as cognitive behaviour modification (CBM), this new set of intervention techniques focuses generally on the development of self-control by the ADHD student. CBM has a strong appeal for clinicians but even more for educators. The possibility of ADHD students learning how to control their own behaviour is something that makes sense to educators, parents, peers and others in the school environment.

This chapter presents a resumé of the actual state of knowledge regarding the use of CBM with hyperactive children. After a brief history of the development of CBM, we propose a definition of CBM and the premises that support its use with ADHD children. We then describe some widely used CBM interventions and programmes and a summary of research regarding the efficacy of CBM as an intervention of its own and in comparison with the use of stimulant medication. Considering the mixed results of the studies on CBM effectiveness, the future of cognitive interventions with ADHD children, as a component of an integrated intervention package, is addressed in the conclusion.

A brief history of cognitive behaviour modification

Gordon and Asher (1994) trace the history of CBM to the 1920s when Vygotsky observed the early stages of language development in children. He then developed a theory concerning the relationship between overt behaviour and covert language (talking to oneself) used by children to mediate their behaviour and to solve their problems. The influence of

Vygotsky's thinking has become important in recent years, more particularly in academic circles preoccupied by learning and behaviour self-control. The socio-constructivist approach, as it is now known, is prevalent in the educational research community and has made its impact on the behavioural intervention with behaviourally disordered students in supporting the cognitive aspects of behaviour management and self-control. All these developments grew from the realization that we must focus our clinical and educational interventions on covert behaviours, as thoughts and feelings, and not only on observable behaviour.

Cognitive behaviour modification techniques were first used with ADHD children having deficits regarding the ability to 'stop, look and listen' (Douglas, 1972). At the same time, the development of CBM as a strategy that combines behavioural techniques with cognitive strategies was based on the work of Meichenbaum and Goodman (1971). As proposed by these authors, CBM consists of teaching students strategies for modifying and controlling their own behaviour and addresses, as we will see, some of the most important problems facing ADHD children (Fiore et al., 1993). The increased attention given to social skill training by the school community and by researchers studying behaviour disorders in children has also contributed to the emergence of CBM as an intervention with great potential to help ADHD children. As noted by Kaplan (1991), CBM has been around for a number of years, but only recently, with the popularity of social skill training, has it become more widely used by teachers.

What is cognitive behaviour modification?

Essentially CBM consists of teaching students to guide themselves by using an internal language (dialogue) and to control their self-verbalization. Cognitive behavioural modification programmes are also aimed at making children learn self-instruction and self-reinforcement skills to help guide their behaviour. Some of these programmes teach them how to analyse the components and requirements of a given task, how to develop problem-solving skills, and how to choose and modify their behaviour in order to apply the strategy chosen (Camp and Bash, 1981).

These interventions have a prima facie appeal because they guide students to become actors to solve their own problems. They teach them portable strategies that they can use in many different situations, allowing them independence from an external agent like medication or rewards from teachers or parents.

According to Kaplan (1991), CBM has five characteristics:

- the subjects themselves rather than external agents are the primary change agent, if not at the beginning of the programme, certainly by the end;

- verbalization, at first on an overt level, then on a covert level, is the primary component; CBM requires that the student talk to him or herself, first out loud, then silently;
- students are taught to identify and use a series of steps to solve their problems;
- modelling is used as an instructional procedure;
- CBM is about helping the individual to gain self-control.

Why using cognitive behaviour modification with ADHD is so appealing to educators and clinicians?

CBM may be conceptualized as a logical development of behaviour modification. Its use in teaching ADHD students self-control skills with cognitive and behavioural procedures is considered by many researchers and educators as well suited to the needs of ADHD students (Kendall and Braswell, 1993; Whalen and Henker, 1987). It is an intuitively appealing intervention to help ADHD children because it combines behavioural techniques with cognitive strategies designed to directly address core problems of impulse control, higher order problem-solving and self-regulation (Fiore et al., 1993). These are cardinal ADHD problems.

Gordon and Asher (1994: 133) summarize the position of CBM proponents as follows:

> the difficulty regulating behaviour seen in the child with ADD stems from a flaw in the development of the child self-talk skills. Predictably, cognitive behaviour therapy (CBT) is designed to foster self-regulatory skills through the use of self-talk or self-statements.

According to Whalen and Henker (1984: 420) cognitive programmes that teach students self-instruction and self-reinforcement skills that help them guide their behaviours are promising and attractive because 'they encourage children to become active agents of change in their own treatment program'.

Another aspect that is relevant for the CBM proponent is the question of locus of control and of the emanative effect of medication. ADHD children tend to have an external locus of control (Linn and Hodge, 1982) that may be reinforced by the use of medication. The emanative effect of medication, as it is called, leads children to attribute their problems to biological causes, rather than personal or social factors and, in accordance, positive change in their behaviour as the effect of medication and not of their abilities (Dulcan, 1986). Whalen and Henker (1984) suggest that a cognitive inoculation programme, such as self-control, may be given prior to or simultaneously with medication to develop some kind of positive self-appropriation of the control of their behaviours.

Types of cognitive behaviour modification interventions

Terminology differs from author to author on how to classify CBM interventions. Usually, most researchers and educators make a broad distinction between self-monitoring, associated with self-assessment, self-observation and self-reinforcement, and self-instruction, usually associated with self-talk and problem-solving strategies.

Self-monitoring

Self-monitoring refers to the training of children to observe their own behaviour and to record their observations. In general, self-monitoring refers to three types of activities: self-observation, self-assessment and self-reinforcement.

Self-observation is the recording by a child of his or her own behaviour. For example, a child may be trained to observe when he is asking a question without raising his hand and to record each time he does so (Parker, 1992). This intervention is well known by behavioural scientists and practitioners and is usually used in conjunction with self-assessment. It has been established that when a child observes his or her own behaviour, it tends to improve, even though this improvement may be temporary. Self-observation is the first step of most self-control programmes because knowing the frequency and intensity of one's behaviour is crucial to the use of self-evaluation and self-reinforcement. The following steps are usually prescribed:

- specify the behaviour in operational terms to help the individual observe its frequency;
- present the child with an easy recording instrument (Figure 10.1);
- make sure that the recording method gives appropriate feedback to the child concerning improvement or deterioration of his or her behaviour.

Self-assessment consists of selecting, with the student, a target behaviour that is causing some problem and identifying also the replacement behaviour. This behaviour must be selected following a discussion with the student concerning the problem and the positive consequences of using the replacement behaviour. It is important that the behaviours be defined as operationally as possible and be easily recognizable by teachers and students. In the second step the student is taught how to evaluate his or her own behaviour in a way that is practical and comprehensible to the student. Finally a form is used to record the self-evaluation (Figure 10.2). Usually the chart is, at first, filled out by both teacher and student; any difference in ratings is discussed and the adult reinforces the level of agreement.

DATE _____

Was I paying attention?

1	yes	no
2		
3		
4		
5		
6		
7		
8		
9		
10		

11	yes	no
12		
13		
14		
15		
16		
17		
18		
19		
20		

Figure 10.1: Self-observation form.

How did you do today?

Your rating	1	2	3	4	5
	Not so hot	OK	Good	Very good	Super
Teacher rating	1	2	3	4	5

Do the ratings agree (within one point)?
If they do, you get 2 points!

Figure 10.2: Self-evaluation form (from Kendall and Braswell, 1993).

Self-reinforcement refers to the use of positive consequences following the occurrence of the desired behaviour. The procedure requires the child to give himself or herself rewards when the desired behaviour is executed. The procedure is age-dependent. With young schoolchildren, the teacher will help the child to identify the target behaviour to be reinforced and the type of reinforcement to be used. This procedure implies that the child engage himself or herself in self-observation in order to decide if the target behaviour is at the desired level or not. The individual may, in this way, increase or decrease by the frequency of his or her own behaviour by giving himself or herself adequate consequences.

Self-instruction and problem solving

Self-instructional training is based on the works of Luria (1961) and Vygotsky (1962) and has been developed as an intervention programme by Meichenbaum (1977) who used self-instruction to help ADHD children bring their behaviour under their own control. Self-instructional training is now a relatively well-established intervention, which is always used in conjunction with problem-solving skills. Problem solving may be defined as 'a behavioural process . . . which a) makes available a variety of potentially effective response alternatives for dealing with the problematic situation and b) increases the probability of selecting the most effective response from among these various alternatives' (D'Zurrilla and Goldfried, 1971: 108).

Consequently in self-instructional problem solving, students learn, through training and rehearsal, to control their own learning. They are taught to follow a series of steps to guide them in their actions (Camp and Bash, 1981; Kendall and Braswell, 1993) similar to those proposed by Lerner et al. (1995):

1. Repeat the instruction.
2. Describe the task.
3. Verbalize an approach to the task.
4. Think about the consequences of the approach.
5. Decide how to proceed.
6. Perform the task.
7. Evaluate the success of the approach.
8. Replace verbalizations with self-instruction.

Among the programmes that exist regarding the use of problem-solving strategies with children, the Think Aloud Programme (Camp and Bash, 1981) is one of the best known. The Think Aloud Programme is about verbal mediation: 'the use of language as an internal regulator and tool of rational thought and logic' (p. 3). The main objective of this programme is to teach children from Grades One to Six the use of verbal mediation (talking to oneself to guide one's own behaviour) and of self-management skills (self-evaluation, self-control and self-monitoring). This programme combines training in both cognitive and social problem solving through verbal mediation. Camp and Bash give the following examples of some of the kinds of learning that took place as a result of the application of this programme:

> A second-grade teacher overheard the following dialogue during an art lesson: Alex: This stitchery is boring! Ellen: What's wrong with it? Alex: It's too hard. Ellen: You planned your own thing. Maybe you need a new plan. What's a different idea?
> The same teacher was excited by the empathy and attention to feeling that Ruth expresses in the following hall scene: Mark to Suzan: I don't like you! Ruth to Mark: Does that make her feel good? Mark: It's true Ruth: Yes, but there's something better you could say. You didn't have to make her feel bad. (Camp and Bash, 1981: 19)

Braswell and Bloomquist (1991) have also developed a programme for teaching problem-solving and self-talk skills to ADHD children. They use a five-step intervention:

1. Stop! What is the problem?
2. What are some plans?
3. What is the best plan?
4. Execute the plan.
5. Did the plan work?

This is an example of the process as presented by the authors:

> In this situation, you are sitting behind me in class and you are kicking my chair. OK, start kicking my chair. (The child pretends to kick the chair.) Stop! What is the problem? The problem is that he is kicking my chair and I am getting mad. What are some plans? I could turn around and kick his chair, I could tell the teacher, or I could ignore him. What is the best plan? If I turn around and kick him, he might get very mad at me but or (if I tell the teacher) he might call me a tattletale. If I ignore him, he may stop kicking me. I think I'll try ignoring him. (The therapist models ignoring while the child kicks his chair.). Did my plan work? Yes, it did. I thought about it; came up with some plans; did the best one, which was to ignore him; and he stopped kicking my chair. (Braswell and Bloomquist, 1991: 151)

The effectiveness of cognitive behaviour modification

Inconsistent findings characterize the research literature on CBM. Some evidence, but not clearly demonstrated, suggests that CBM may produce positive changes in attention, impulse control and hyperactivity.

In a review of self-management outcome research conducted not only with ADHD children but more broadly with children and youths exhibiting behavioural disorders, Nelsonet al. (1991) concluded that self-management procedures can be used to enhance social and academic behaviour of behaviourally disordered students. The studies they reviewed showed moderate to large durable treatment effects that, according to the authors, support the view that self-management may be a viable alternative to externally managed procedures. The fuzzy side of the story is that self-management intervention will not generalize spontaneously, unless generalization is systematically programmed.

It seems that the situation is not so bright with ADHD children. When we examine the literature regarding the efficacy of CBM with ADHD children, we must conclude that CBM is probably an important, but not a sufficient, intervention. Mixed results in terms of children's academic achievement, as well as teacher and parent ratings of behaviour and social functioning, are usually reported

Lloyd and Landrum (1990) reviewed studies using self-monitoring to increase attention to task and showed that it could improve attention to the task even when students did not record their behaviours accurately. Whalen and Henker (1986) indicated that self-monitoring and self-reinforcement are effective methods of improving social and academic behaviours of students with ADHD, even superior to external reinforcement and monitoring.

Reviewing cognitive training (CT) studies that have been carried out with children with attention deficit hyperactivity disorders in the 1980s, Abikoff (1991) found little empirical support for its clinical utility with ADHD children on cognitive, academic and behavioural aspects of their functioning:

> In the treatment of children with ADHD, cognitive training has more face validity than perhaps any other therapeutic modality. However, as this review has indicated, the belief, especially in early studies, that the development of internalized self-regulation skills would facilitate generalization and maintenance effects has not been realized . . . Notwithstanding CT's inherent appeal, the expectation of its clinical utility in children with ADHD has now been tempered by a decade of research. Moreover, none of the studies has generated results to indicate, or even suggest, that cognitive training is a competitor to stimulants, or that it enhances their beneficial effects. (Abikoff, 1991: 208)

Many research studies were aimed at evaluating the treatment of choice to address the ADHD children's needs and to compare the respective effectiveness of behaviour modification and medication. CBM has often been part of these comparative studies. In a study on the behaviours of ADHD boys in anger-provoking situations, Hinshaw et al. (1984a) evaluated the respective effect on anger control of a CBM intervention and of medication. They concluded that medication decreased the boys' behavioural intensity but did not increase their self-control skills. CBM was able to increase self-control and helped them to use functional adaptive strategies. In another study, the same authors (Hinshaw et al., 1984b) demonstrated that medication with self-evaluation was superior to medication alone and interpreted that the use of medication helped the child to make a more precise self-evaluation of his behaviour. Brown et al. (1985), in a study of hyperactive boys, evaluated the effect of three treatments: CBM, stimulant medication and a combination of the two. They found that medication plus CBM was not more efficient than medication alone. Horn et al. (1983), using a control group, found that medication (Dexedrine) and a self-control training were more efficient together than when used alone to increase attention to school tasks and diminish hyperactivity.

Hall and Kataria (1992) investigated the relative effectiveness of behaviour modification and cognitive therapy implemented with and without medication. Cognitive therapy with medication was the only intervention that significantly improved a subject's abilities to reduce impulsive responses. In a review of studies that evaluated the respective effectiveness of drugs and CBM, Fiore et al. (1993) found that only the medication condition produced significant improvements in attention, impulsivity and school achievement. Cognitive behaviour modification alone or CBM plus medication never produced results superior to medication alone. Whalen and Henker (1984) stated that CBM was more promising than productive with ADHD children. Cognitive raining enhanced self-control and coping strategies without reducing behavioural intensity. Methylphenidate reduces behavioural intensity but has no impact on coping strategies.

So, results about the effectiveness of CBM are, at the best, mixed. Lerner et al. (1995: 142–3) summarize the state of the question by proposing the following generalizations about CBM:

> 1- Self-instruction and self-monitoring can reduce such symptoms of ADHD as inattention, distractibility, impulsivity, difficulty in following rules, and poor social skills. 2- When students learn to regulate their own behaviour, they may no longer require external reinforcement and external behaviour control by teachers. 3- When children develop their own strategies to improve their behaviour in one setting, they must learn to generalize the strategies to other settings.

Furthermore, CBM is a refinement of behaviour modification and is used in conjunction with other behavioural techniques. In practice, response cost and positive reinforcement are often added to increase the effect of the intervention. Environmental control or manipulation of environmental contingencies are essential to the success of CBM because of the low motivation of ADHD students (children) to be engaged in problem-solving tasks. To maintain gains, the teacher will have to continue to prompt the child to use the new skills, using hand signals, a poster on the walls or a note card on the student's desk (Gordon and Asher, 1994).

Conclusion: what lies ahead

The weight of the empirical evidence does not clearly support the efficacy of CBM or CBT. It has not consistently demonstrated positive effects and cost effectiveness. Although promising, the overall picture of the effectiveness of CBM is far from clear. It is not helpful with young children (under seven) who don't seem to have the cognitive development necessary to use problem-solving strategies effectively and to generalize them in other settings (Kendall and Wilcox, 1980). The efficacy of CBM with ADHD children is not better or even equivalent to the use of medication or traditional behaviour modification techniques. In this regard, study must continue on CBM, but as a component of an efficient intervention package to address ADHD students' needs. Most researchers agree with the fact that CBM remains an attractive adjunct to any comprehensive intervention package with ADHD students and must be the subject of further research, because it addresses primary deficits of ADHD students (Dulcan, 1986).

It is also clear, as noted by Whalen and Henker (1987), that CBM will not be useful in all situations and with every ADHD child and that it must be an individualized intervention. Generalization remains an important question in CBM as with any teaching or learning activity. Generalization should be programmed and children must learn in various environments when to use the self-management skills they have learned. In this respect, we must put aside the 'train and hope' attitude and be proactive agents of the generalization process.

But the most relevant question to address may still be the variety of needs of the ADHD children themselves. ADHD is not an empirically well-defined syndrome (Royer, 1989). In fact, the variety and magnitude of the problems confronting ADHD children in a developmental perspective are impressive. The needs of a five-year-old ADHD child are different from those of other children of the same age and different from his or her own future needs at 10, 15 or 20 year of age. It seems obvious that a comprehensive intervention package is necessary and that this package must be individualized.

Even though, in most cases, the research supports the efficacy of stimulant medication, this intervention appears to be necessary but not sufficient. ADHD children show learning and social problems that cannot be addressed by medication alone. Social skill training, remedial education and behavioural management are also essential components of a comprehensive intervention and must be suited to the child's needs. CBM, in this context is essential, in particular concerning attribution of positive change in behaviour. This question can only be addressed by the development, by the ADHD child, of a sense of control and responsibility for his or her own behaviour, which is at the core centre of CBM intervention programmes. Even though self-monitoring and self-instruction may not be sufficient interventions in themselves to reduce impulsivity, inattention or hyperactivity, we must, in accord with most of the researchers in the field, conclude that CBM remains an essential component of an educational intervention with ADHD students, as the development of self-management and self-control will stay an essential objective of schools and teachers.

References

Abikoff H (1991) Cognitive training in ADHD children: Less to it than meets the eye. Journal of Learning Disabilities 24: 205–9.

Braswell L, Bloomquist ML (1991) Cognitive-Behavioral Therapy with ADHD Children: Child, Family and School Interventions. New York: Guilford Press.

Brown RT, Wynne ME, Medenis R (1985). Methylphenidate and cognitive therapy: a comparison of treatment approaches with hyperactive boys. Journal of Abnormal Child Psychology 13: 69–87.

Camp BW, Bash MA (1981) Think Aloud. Increasing Social and Cognitive Skills: A Problem-Solving Program for Children. Champain IL: Research Press.

Douglas VI (1972) Stop, look and listen: The problem of sustained attention and impulse control in hyperactive and normal children. Canadian Journal of Behavior Science 4: 259–82.

Dulcan MK (1986) Comprehensive treatment of children and adolescents with ADD: The state of the art. Clinical Psychology Review 6: 539–69.

D'Zurrilla TJ, Goldfried, MR (1971) Problem-solving and behaviour modification. Journal of Abnormal Psychology 78: 107–26.

Fiore TA, Becker EA, Nero RC (1993) Educational interventions for students with attention deficit disorder. Exceptional Children 60: 163–73.

Gordon SB, Asher MJ (1994) Meeting the ADD challenge: A practical guide for teachers. Champain IL: Research Press.

Hall CW, Kataria S (1992). Effects of two treatment techniques on delay and vigilance tasks with attention deficit hyperactive disorder (ADHD) children. The Journal of Psychology 126: 17–25.

Hinshaw SP, Henker B, Whalen CK (1984a) Self-control in hyperactive boys in anger-reducing situations: Effects of cognitive-behavioural training and of methylphenidate. Journal of Abnormal Child Psychology 12: 55–77.

Hinshaw SP, Henker B, Whalen CK (1984b) Cognitive-behavioural and pharmacologic interventions for hyperactive boys: Comparative and combined effects. Journal of Consulting and Clinical Psychology 52: 739–749.

Horn WF, Chatoor I, Conners KC (1983) Additive effects of Dexedrine and self-control training: a multiple assessment. Behavior Modification 7: 383–92.

Kaplan SK (1991) Beyond Behavior Modification: A Cognitive-Behavioral Approach to Behavior Management in the School. Austin TX: Pro-Ed.

Kendall PC, Braswell L (1993) Cognitive-Behavioral Therapy for Impulsive Children (2 edn). New York: Guilford.

Kendall PC, Wilcox LE (1980) Cognitive behavioural treatment for impulsivity: Concrete versus conceptual training in non self-controlled problem children. Journal of Consulting and Clinical Psychology 48: 80–91.

Lerner JW, Lowenthal B, Lerner SR (1995) Attention Deficit Disorders: Assessment and Teaching. New York: Brooks-Cole.

Linn RT, Hodge GK (1982) Locus of control in childhood hyperactivity. Journal of Consulting and Clinical Psychology 50: 592–3.

Lloyd JW, Landrum TJ (1990) Self-recording of attending to task: treatment components and generalization of effects. In T Scruggs, BYL Wong (eds) Intervention Research in Learning Disabilities. New York: Springer-Verlag.

Luria AR (1961) The Role of Speech in the Reulation of Normal and Abnormal Behaviours. New York: Liveright.

Meichenbaum D (1977) Cognitive Behaviour Modification: An Integrative Approach. New York: Plenum Press.

Meichenbaum D, Goodman J (1971) Training impulsive children talk to themselves: A means of developing self-control. Journal of Abnormal Psychology 77: 115–26.

Nelson JR, Smith DJ, Young RK, Dodd JM (1991). A review of self-management outcome research conducted with students who exhibit behaviour disorders. Behavioral Disorders 16: 169–79.

Parker HC (1992) The ADD Hyperactivity Handbook for Schools: Effective Strategies for Identifying and Teaching Students with Attention Deficit Disorders in Elementary and Secondary Schools. Plantation FL: Impact Publications.

Royer E (1989) Ecole et hyperactivite: Une etude des services educatifs quebecois. Doctoral dissertation, Université Laval: Quebec.

Vygotsky L (1962) Thought and Language. New York: Wiley.

Whalen CK, Henker B (1984) Hyperactivity and the attention deficit disorders: Expanding frontiers. Pediatric Clinics of North America 31: 397–427.

Whalen CK, Henker B (1986) Cognitive behaviour therapy for hyperactive children: What do we know? Journal of Children in Contemporary Society 19: 123–41.

Whalen CK, Henker B (1987) Cognitive behaviour therapy and hyperactive children: What do we know? In J. Lonet (ed.) The Young Hyperactive Child. New York: Haworth Press, pp. 123–41.

Chapter 11
ADHD in the Classroom:
A Teacher's Account

JANE LOVEY

Introduction

During 1993, whilst working as a support teacher of children with special educational needs in secondary school classrooms, a colleague asked me if I had heard of 'the new dyslexia'. She drew my attention to an article in the *Times Educational Supplement* (21 October 1994). The children described in the article reminded me so much of many of the children whom I had encountered in a fairly long and varied career.

I recalled Kafiswe, a small girl in Zambia in the 1970s, who seemed bright but was impossible to teach in Grade 1 as she never settled for long enough to complete any work. She barged into the games of others and often endangered herself by acting before thinking. When she accompanied her parents to the USA for a year we breathed a collective sigh of relief and wondered how on earth a school would cope with her in a confined space, without all the nannies and others who were always at hand to give some individual attention in Zambia. She returned still lively, but teachable and focused. We were told that she suffered from hyperkinetic syndrome but was being treated.

Some years later, when I was teacher in charge of an off-site unit for disruptive pupils who had been excluded from school, there were a number of children and adolescents who seemed really depressed at their inability to behave. Their parents came in total despair. These were often the children of families who had made and tried to keep contracts with the school. Often other children in the family were doing very well at school. Older siblings were sometimes at university. I was frequently told that this child had been a difficult baby, a demanding toddler who had to be taken to casualty several times because he (just occasionally she) had had no sense of danger, and the parents had been constantly called into school. They sometimes mentioned another member of the family, an uncle, aunt or cousin, who was also like this. Sometimes they mentioned a sibling who gave them cause for concern because she (usually she) was so quiet and sometimes seemed to live on another planet.

I realized, as soon as I started to read about ADHD (Train, 1996; Cooper and Ideus, 1995, 1996; Du Paul and Stoner, 1994; Hinshaw, 1994; Hallowell and Ratey, 1994; Barkley, 1990) that this could provide an explanation for some of the unhappy children whose uncontrollable behaviour gave them such a bad time at home and at school. By the time they reached secondary school they had often almost stopped trying and were already displaying the kind of defences, and sometimes oppositional behaviour, that made it difficult for teachers to be patient with their demands.

Importance of the teacher's role in the child's life

Having worked for many years with children with special educational needs, I have long been convinced of the vital role of multidisciplinary teams in monitoring the treatment and progress of the child with ADHD. Unfortunately, as consciousness of ADHD rose in the UK, many lay people and professionals latched on to the fact that some of these children were being given psychostimulant medication to change their behaviour. These valid concerns were picked up by the press and popular journals and sensationalized by them (Mould, 1993; Sharron, 1995). The result of this was that readers, many teachers among them, became polarized in their perception of the disorder (Cooper and Ideus, 1996). Since the Warnock report (DES, 1978) there had been emphasis on looking at the curriculum and the environment, rather than within the child for the problem. Now it seemed that we were being asked to recognize the problem as being totally within the child.

Parents, who had been run ragged by the demands of children whom they described as 'whirling dervishes', welcomed the change in behaviour that was often quite dramatic once drug therapy was started. As they went along to their children's schools and asked for the school to co-operate in administering the lunchtime top-up dose, problems often arose. There were a number of teachers who were, understandably, opposed to 'drugging' children in order to make them behave. Some heads refused to have the medication in school but would allow the parent to come at lunchtime to give it. Some secondary schools were very unhappy about pupils carrying their own pills but did not want to have them in the school office.

In the early days of diagnosis in the UK often the first the teacher knew about the syndrome was when a child in his or her class was diagnosed and being treated with Ritalin. The situation is improving in some areas, with teachers now sometimes being involved from the earliest stages. Since the behaviour must be pervasive in order for ADHD to be diagnosed, it is very important to have a teacher's report at a very early stage (Cooper and Ideus, 1996).

The teacher has a tremendously important role in monitoring the medication. Often the child leaves for school before the first dose of the day begins to take effect. The second dose might well be wearing off by the time the child arrives home. The teacher will be able to say whether the medication is lasting through, and whether there is a 'rebound' effect as the first dose wears off and before the second dose kicks in. The teacher will know if the child suffers side effects such as a feeling of nausea or stomach cramps. If the dose is changed the teacher will be important in detecting if real advantage is being achieved.

The teacher will also be important in helping a sensitive child to cope with the questions and comments of other children in the class. Now that the child is being helped to focus it will be important for the teacher to make sure that his or her accessibility to learning is maximized. It will still be important to encourage and keep the child on task. The optimum seating is usually near the middle of the front three rows in the classroom. A seat near a door or a low window is not a good idea because of the difficulty the child has in shutting out distractions. The aural stimuli that distract the child with ADHD are often described as coming into his mind like programmes from a badly tuned radio. He might, primarily, be tuned into the class teacher but, as the 'disc' slips and other sounds enter the airspace, his aural focus might tune him in to the other 'programme', especially if it is more interesting or less demanding.

The best place is also beside a good role model. This can be difficult because often children who take their work seriously will be anxious about having someone they know to be distractible beside them. However, if the diligent child is reassured that the teacher will be monitoring the situation, this is often seen to be an advantage. When the class is divided up into groups for practical work it is usually best for the child with ADHD to work in a pair as that way he or she can retain focus. If the child is very distractible, it is safest and better for both if, initially, the lab technician can be the third member of the group. I say this because the child with ADHD might want to dominate whatever is being done so that his or her partner can end up with little experience of the process.

The medicine is not 'magic' but the intervention of the teacher can make it seem that way. There might easily be pupils with ADHD symptoms who can be helped with structured interventions at school and at home, and who do not need to have medication. It is important, whether medication is given or not, that the child, once diagnosed, is helped to learn good habits of behaviour and of learning.

There is a strong likelihood that there is a child in nearly every classroom (on average) whose behaviour and achievement is affected to some extent by attention deficit disorder. Even if the condition has been diagnosed and the child is already receiving medication, the intervention of the teacher(s) who deal with him or her every day will be important for the child and for the rest of the class. If he or she is already receiving appropriate medication he or she will be more receptive to the teacher's efforts but might still need careful monitoring and help in order to reach his or her potential. It will be helpful here to look at a few pupils known to have been diagnosed as having ADHD.

Bobby

Bobby was a boy of above-average ability. However, when he arrived at his south London school at the age of six it was almost impossible to teach him. He arrived at this school already ahead of his age group in reading skills but, according to his record, the family had moved to London because Bobby's parents had split up and his mother wished to be nearer to her family. Bobby had returned to the school where his mother had spent her early years. When the headteacher rang the Midland infant school from where he had come, she was told that Bobby's mother was an epileptic and they knew of at least two occasions, since his father had left home, when Bobby had had to ring for an ambulance because she had lost consciousness. There were also two younger children.

It was assumed that this was the reason why this child was unable to sit still, talked incessantly, often upset other children's games and frequently sobbed with frustration because he could not finish his work. Even when the teacher helped him to start and the work seemed to be going well, Bobby often tore it up because of some small mistake.

Bobby's mother's life seemed to be sorting out nicely. Not only was she near her family but she seemed to have a stable relationship with a man who had moved in with the family and of whom the children were clearly fond. However, Bobby's problems were not improving at all and not only had he no friends but other children did not want to sit near him as he disturbed them. The psychologist felt that he was very damaged by his earlier experiences and suggested that he should attend the nearby hospital once a week to see a play therapist. Bobby enjoyed this when he had the therapist to himself but could not bear to be with other children. It was then decided that he was articulate enough to benefit from psychotherapy and this might help him to come to terms with his past experiences, which were holding him back socially and emotionally. At this time, at the age of nine, he was still an enthusiastic reader who often read two or three books at the same time but was underachieving since he had never completed a piece of written work or number work. Even with him out for two sessions a week the school was finding it increasingly difficult to deal with his behaviour. He was upsetting other children as he was losing his temper and hitting out in frustration several times a day. His mother was finding it difficult to cope with him at home, especially when the school started excluding him for a few days at a time.

Eventually it was agreed that he would have to be excluded and found a place in a special school. This was during the first term of his final year at primary school. The statementing process was already well under way. Meanwhile it was decided to send Bobby to the hospital school for four days a week. In their INSET training the hospital teachers were beginning to hear more and more about ADHD. They suggested that, although Bobby had been through a number of family traumas, it was possible that his problems could have other origins. An assessment was arranged at the department of child psychiatry. All those who had been involved with Bobby were asked for input and, initially, 5 mg of Ritalin was prescribed three times a day.

The effect was immediate. Bobby managed, within the first week, with the support of his teacher, to finish several pieces of work. He managed to stay in his seat for longer periods and no longer interfered with the other children so much. However, the effect wore off fairly quickly and there was a time in the late morning when Bobby was vulnerable to suddenly erupting.

I met Bobby when he started at a mainstream secondary school. Although a place in a residential special school had been found, Bobby's mother now found him so much easier she wanted him to stay at home and go to school locally. St Richards was a fairly formal Catholic school and had some misgivings about accepting this child. His statement was issued with a whole day's support allocated so it was decided that I should decide how best to use this. Initially I went in for a full day and followed Bobby's class. The idea was that no one should know that I was there for him. However, he asked outright whether I was his special helper almost as soon as I appeared! He clearly found it easier to deal with adults than his peer group. Since the school was streamed, I was pleased that he was put in the second class as he was with a group of boys who would be good role models. It was much quieter than the other two classes and teachers were eager to make life as easy as possible to enable Bobby to do his best.

There still seemed to be a bad patch towards the end of the morning when Bobby would change from being an eager pupil who was making a real effort to keep the classroom code, to a tearful anxious little boy who would throw his book across the room or dig his neighbour with a pencil if he made the slightest mistake or had his raised hand ignored. Bobby has always had great difficulty in accepting that even if his hand is raised another child might be asked to answer the question. Because of this pattern of behaviour I arranged to go in on three days a week during the last two periods of the long morning. I also attended an afternoon technology lesson on one day a week and visited his home alternate weeks.

In the classroom my support was often to talk Bobby out of his impulses and monitor the situation when he worked with his peers. Technology and science were particularly problematic, especially as Bobby found it quite difficult to co-operate with others on practical projects. It was clear that I could not offer all the help Bobby needed but I was able to negotiate with the science and technology technicians to make sure that they would be available for Bobby at times in the lesson when he might have difficulties in conforming with the rest of the class. I had Bobby's mother's permission to explain the problem to anyone who needed to know in order to make his life at school easier. During the lunchtimes, when I was in school, I managed to work with teachers who were sympathetic to Bobby and bent over backwards to adapt their work. In English, he was totally daunted by having a long exercise to do but if a plan was prepared and he could tackle it bit by bit he could cope. He needed frequent feedback because he had very low self-esteem. This was not helped by the fact that peers tended not to choose Bobby to be their partner in any activity as he always wanted to dominate and relate with the teacher. In most lessons the teachers decided to tell pupils whom they were to work with and Bobby was with a different child every time.

Most of the staff were very sympathetic but there were two or three who felt it important that all children had to meet the same criteria whatever their special need. Unfortunately Bobby's form teacher, a teacher of long experience, was one of these. Homework was a very big problem with Bobby and at the end of the first term a decision was made to place Bobby in a lower form purely because his homework was not completed for each lesson. I first knew about this decision when I arrived and found Bobby walking around the school crying and screaming aloud. His form-mates came to tell me what had happened. They were also indignant. Much to my surprise they had a very good understanding of Bobby's difficulties and felt that he should not have been punished in this way just because he sometimes could not do things as they could.

There was less academic pressure in his new class, but for Bobby it was a disaster. It was an extremely noisy class with a number of students with similar difficulties. There were no good role models and for a child who already has difficulty in prioritizing the aural stimuli coming in, the constant noise sometimes made Bobby aggressive with the class. I tried to sit him away from a group who made sport of trying to provoke him into a tantrum and I shamelessly 'bought' the co-operation of some of the quieter, more diligent boys by always making sure I had an ample supply of whatever bits and pieces it was they needed for their next project.

A student from the higher education institute where I also taught wanted to do a project on ADHD so I obtained permission from Bobby's family and from the school for Andrea to support Bobby and his friends in some of their lessons and to help Bobby with his homework at home two nights a week. The student worked well with the boys and for that term all the boys were eager to work with Bobby. Bobby also experienced the advantages of coming to school with a bagful of completed homework. This coincided with an appointment at the hospital to see the consultant. The family suggested that I should come along since I knew what went on in school. It was agreed that the pattern of medication needed to change so that Bobby did not have this bad hour at the end of the morning. Initially there had been reluctance to give Bobby a dose of Ritalin after school in case it kept him awake all night. However since homework was assuming such importance it was agreed to try this. In fact the new pattern of medication seemed to solve both problems and Bobby actually seemed to sleep better. We had found out that his mother had been making him go to bed at 8 pm with his younger brother and suggested that she should give him an extra hour to read or relax before bed.

No-one had expected Bobby to survive in the mainstream school and there had been difficulties, but at the end of the year only one teacher felt that he would be better off elsewhere (and she did not teach him). He was difficult at times, even exasperating, but staff were pleased that they had taken up the challenge and were eager to continue. I was planning to move on during the first term of his second year and so met the senior management team, including his year head, to discuss how the money allocated might be used during the following year. Since the student had been so successful with Bobby it was decided to employ two students for a session three times a week to run a homework club in the school library. This would serve not only Bobby but would be offered to a small group of boys who came from homes where it was difficult to do homework and who had also fallen behind because of this. This meant that Bobby had a small friendship group with whom he would have juice and biscuits before the session and walk to the bus stop after the session. I was allowed to go into each of the sets for science and technology and say which one would best match Bobby's needs since the whole year had these subjects at the same time. Regardless of the subject taught, I recommended the teaching group where there were good role models, a technician available and a teacher who had a well-established routine at beginning and end of lessons.

Bobby is nearly at the end of his third year in mainstream and is looking forward to the next year. It has not always been easy for the school or for Bobby and he has needed a great deal of support because he was only diagnosed five months before he transferred to secondary school. He also is very severely affected with the disorder. Some of the staff have served others in their classes better because they have been alert to his needs. All the students now understand that it is distressing for Bobby when there is a lot of noise as he cannot concentrate. Some have commented that a quiet room is easier for them too and so there has been peer pressure to keep noise down. The homework club is doing well. Another boy has been diagnosed with ADHD and one of the new intake also has it, but the staff are confident.

David

David was another boy whose self-esteem was already badly damaged by the time he was diagnosed. Like so many boys whose self-esteem is low, he had become oppositional both in school and at home so that getting dressed in the morning, doing homework, co-operating with a group and doing anything he was asked to do became a battle of wills. His mother was a colleague of mine and I had been aware for some time that she had a son who caused her a great deal of distress. He was the second of two boys. The eldest boy played chess for the county and had won a scholarship to a fee-paying school, and was a great joy to his parents. His younger brother was also a formidable chess player, but here the similarity ended. This was a boy who, at nine, was still unable to read a book for pleasure, who rarely completed his work at school and now had been excluded from school for dangerous behaviour. As the head said, he really did not seem to think about the consequences of his actions and, although afterwards he was always contrite, she was afraid someone would be badly hurt if something was not done. His mother knew that I had trained as a screener for scotopic sensitivity syndrome (Irlen, 1991) and thought that this might be what was delaying his reading. She was a dyslexia specialist and so found his inability to benefit from her help extremely frustrating.

He may well have been scotopic. He certainly claimed to be helped by having such a dark overlay over his book that I could barely read the print, whereas he suddenly read a page fluently. What I did notice was that he was incapable of sitting still. I did not manage to achieve the whole battery of tests in an hour because he fell off the seat beside me several times, cavorted under the table until he banged his head, overturned a pot plant and spilled my coffee. When his parents came in I tentatively broached the subject of ADHD and, instead of being defensive, they showed relief that he might have something that could be treated. Apparently he had been a baby who never slept, he had had countless accidents as a toddler and they could no longer visit grandparents because of the chaos he caused. They had agreed to attend different services at the local church as he was no longer welcome there. Apparently he caused such a distraction that other parents said that they could not expect their children to behave when this older boy was badly behaved.

Their general practitioner, who was a NHS fundholder, and had seen the father through a nervous breakdown and prescribed Valium for the

mother for years, agreed to pay for a full assessment at the Learning
Assessment Centre in Sussex. David responded quickly to the Ritalin. It
was not an easy decision for his parents to accept that he should take this
as they were very concerned about side effects, especially stunted
growth. David had always been a fussy eater and was small for his age.
However, they decided to try it. They then came up against the school's
resistance. They would readmit David as something had been done for
him but they could or would not agree to have anything to do with the
medication. His mother had to reschedule her work in order to travel to
his school each lunchtime with the midday dose. However, before long
the school could see the difference it made and by the beginning of
David's final year stated themselves willing to handle the medication.

David made rapid progress academically and also obtained a scholarship to go to the same fee-paying school as his brother. He still has
problems socially and finds it difficult to make friends.

Peter

Peter was nine when his mother rang me up. She had spoken to a
mutual friend who had told her about my interest in the classroom
problems of pupils with ADHD and suggested she should talk to me
about her son. Peter's father had left her when he was a baby, a baby who
seemed never to sleep and spent much of his time crying. He was a difficult toddler and troubles began as soon as he started infant school. He
refused to settle down and do anything. His behaviour was immature. By
some miracle he learned to read but he never settled long enough to do
any written work. His mother was constantly stressed because she was
unable to change things. He made constant demands and would not
take 'no' for an answer. He was unable to get on with other children. She
went back to teaching but found it difficult to find a minder for Peter
after school because of the way he behaved with other children. When
she spoke to me she was in despair because she realized how very
unhappy Peter was and he had actually said that he wished he were dead
rather than in trouble all the time. He knew how unhappy he made her.

She remembered an occasion when, on a train journey, she had
apologized to a fellow passenger for Peter's behaviour during the
journey and this woman had explained that she was a psychologist in
Canada and suggested that Peter be checked out for attention deficit
disorder. Just in the last few weeks she had seen this mentioned in the
educational press and was eager to know more. I gave her the details of
the Learning Assessment Centre in Sussex. Her general practitioner was
unconvinced and did not feel able to refer Peter. However, her family
helped her to raise the money to take Peter there. After a day of intensive
tests Peter was diagnosed as having the disorder and prescribed the
medication. He responded quickly and was soon able to finish written

work and have better control of his behaviour. He still has to be reminded from time to time but he is able to respond to normal discipline and teaching. He is relieved to have help with his problems and his mother says that, although she has always loved Peter, she never felt she would be able to enjoy him as she does now.

Peter's mother has a friend who acts as a mentor for Peter. She feels that it has been important to Peter's progress that this friend, a social worker, has spent a little time with him each week talking about whatever is on his mind and is available if he has a problem at another time. Her general practitioner has since learned more about ADHD and is happy to prescribe the medication. However, the family take a pride in returning the 180 miles to the Learning Assessment Centre to show Dr Kewley how well Peter is progressing.

Wasted years

All three of these boys showed problems from before they were seven but were not diagnosed until after they were nine. With Bobby it was thought for a long time it was because of earlier traumas. The same conclusion might well have been made with Peter, but with David it was easier to see it as being a problem of the child. All of the parents involved were made to feel that their child's problems were because of their poor parenting skills.

Anna

Anna is a beautiful little girl of six. She and her four-year-old sister have recently been adopted by loving foster parents with whom they have lived for nearly two years. I first met Anna in the group of small children who are taken out of Mass for a separate children's liturgy. I quickly realized that her hand went up whether she knew the answer or not. I knew that she could not stay still to listen but squirmed in her seat or on the floor throughout the story. However, she is only six and she is not much worse in that respect than the other three to six-year-olds in the group. I was surprised when I told them that the pictures they had made were for their mothers and Anna dashed straight into the church to present hers there and then. The others were taken aback with this behaviour. Later there was debate among the other helpers about whether we could actually cope with Anna in this group.

By chance, I met her mother out shopping and she told me of the problems they were having with Anna. She also told me of the neglect and abuse that Anna, and to a lesser extent, her sister, had endured before being permanently removed from their very disturbed natural mother. She was relieved that Anna had been given a place in an assessment unit for a year as the school was not able to cope with her behaviour. Anna has been to my house for tea. She went through a colouring book, magic painting, Plasticine and gummed shapes within the first half-hour. She rearranged every ornament in the house and even managed to take large pictures off the walls. She was like a whirlwind around the house. I could not keep up with her or predict what she would do next. She jumped off the landing at the top of five stairs before trying to climb up my airer. Her mother was close to tears and needed reassurance that I was interested in Anna's behaviour, but not angry.

Anna is a sweet and loving little girl whose behaviour is testing her new parents to the limit. They dare not even visit the relatives who are so happy for them to have the little girls. I mentioned ADHD to their mother and the psychiatrist agreed that this could well be the case. However, I am glad that, at six, Anna is going to have a full assessment that will, I presume, include an opportunity for skilled psychotherapy, as she will have problems to resolve that are the result of a disrupted infancy. She had two sets of short-term foster parents before the ones who have now adopted her.

It is important not to assume that this label can be applied to every case of behaviour that displays these characteristics. Since there are very good reasons for not giving children under the age of seven drug therapy (Hinshaw, 1994), other interventions can be tried first. Sometimes programmes to help the parents to handle their child can be provided.

Underdiagnosis?

Nevertheless we have reasons to believe that ADHD is still very under-diagnosed in this country and there are children in secondary school classrooms who may well have benefited from much earlier intervention. Here I am thinking of a boy who, at 14, is isolated and under-achieving. He is quiet and rarely noticed in his class except that his homework is nearly always missing, his biology is often in his history or maths book and the PE master often has to leave Martin to lock up the changing room because it takes him so long to change after PE. The other children call him 'the space traveller' because of his air of always being elsewhere. The staff dismiss any concern with a chuckle and say 'Oh, Martin is just a dreamer. He drives his parents mad because he never knows where anything is.' Martin has no friends and is seriously underachieving.

I suspect that he has attention deficit without hyperactivity and there-fore does not disrupt the class he is in. Boys and girls like Martin can so easily go all through their school life not realizing that their problems are because of their poor short-term memory and their lack of internal motivation. Attention deficit without hyperactivity is as detrimental to a child's education and subsequent mental health as the type with hyper-activity but it is less likely to be referred for diagnosis. It has been suggested that some teenagers with ADD without hyperactivity become so depressed at realizing that there is something holding them back from achieving that they are a grave suicide risk (Brown, 1992). Teenagers who are put on Ritalin for this disorder often describe its effects as 'a mist clearing' or 'a net curtain around them suddenly lifting'.

Because of increased awareness of ADHD, parents are more and more likely to suggest to teachers that their child has it. Teachers may also be the ones who wonder if a child who is unable to settle has it and wonder what they can do to decide whether there is a cause for concern. There is an observation schedule that is described by Dr Sam Goldstein (1990) that I find very useful for this purpose. I have adapted this for use by teachers, or any second adult in the classroom. I have found it can be done by students or technicians as the behaviours are easily defined. The acronym TOAD stands for:

- Talking
- Out of seat behaviour
- Attention problems (demanding attention or not paying attention)
- Disruptive behaviour.

I divide a piece of A4 in two down the middle, and divide each half further into four columns. I head each column with the letters: T O A D. On the left-hand side I record the behaviour of the child who is causing concern. On the right I record that of any other child in the class whom I select as a control.

Subject _Pupil A_				Control _Pupil B_			
T	O	A	D	T	O	A	D
1. ✓							

Figure 11.1: Goldstein's observation schedule.

Both pupils are observed for 10–15 minutes after the initial settling down period in the lesson and the behaviours are recorded every 30 seconds for10 minutes in three lessons. At the end of the 10–15 minutes it is usually possible to see whether the subject does display notably more of these behaviours than normal. However, it is still useful to do it in three lessons, especially for secondary pupils. I usually choose three sessions where the demands and the setting are different, for example English, maths and a science or technology.

If a pattern of talking, out of seat, attention problems and disruption is evident from the assessment it is useful to sit down with the pupil and discuss what you have found and together agree on a target for improving the behaviour before this is done again. If this is done and the pupil can work on improving the behaviour and be rewarded by recognition for doing this, it will have been a useful exercise and might well be used as a Stage 1 strategy. If after two or three observation sessions the behaviour has not improved, the next step might be to seek a wider assessment of the pupil's difficulties, such as a multi-modal assessment for ADHD.

After this kind of monitoring, children without ADHD might have benefited so much from the extra positive attention that their problem is alleviated.

If the observations are done in response to a concern voiced by parents, it is useful to discuss the findings with the parents. It is evidence that you have begun to act on their concerns. The fact that the school is methodically monitoring the situation may well prevent a parent from rushing off to demand drug therapy from a general practitioner. Although drug therapy might later be prescribed, it is important that this is not seen as the only intervention. Parents whose concerns are ignored might just later sue the teacher for subsequent poor examination results!

In the Classroom

As well as suitable positioning in the classroom and the proximity of good role models, there are other strategies that will help the child with ADHD, and also others in the class:

- make sure the child is in a position where there will be a minimum of distractions;
- break complicated tasks down into manageable segments;
- prime the child before starting an exercise (talk about how he or she will start, what will come next, what will be included);
- after giving instructions ask the child to repeat them back;
- give very clear, concise instructions;
- have an uncomplicated, reliable routine in the classroom;
- identify a quiet place where the child can go to work when he or she cannot cope with the distractions of the classroom (for example, it might be possible to sit in the laboratory prep room with the technician, to do an end-of-module science test);
- tasks should be stimulating and not repetitive;
- focus on the academic task rather than the behaviour when calling the child back on to the task;
- give frequent feedback;
- small, short-term rewards should be available rather than larger long-term ones;
- these rewards should be varied from time to time;

- behavioural expectations should be realistic;
- avoid signs of exasperation when reprimanding the child for something that has been forgotten or mislaid – treat each occasion as if it is the first, as these children are more forgetful than others;
- do not wait until homework becomes a problem but discuss possible difficulties with the parent or carer and try to negotiate the best solution possible as tasks may have to be adapted;
- there might be times when it is helpful to have a safe place for the child to be sent to have a few minutes' 'time out'.

'Remember!'

Finally, I would like to describe a strategy used by a SENCO in a mainstream high school. Gayle spent time at the beginning of term sitting in lessons with John, in order to define his main needs. She then made a set of laminated cards, the size of a credit card, bearing one word, REMEMBER! The cards were green, amber and red. Staff were asked to leave a brief note in Gayle's pigeonhole if they had experienced problems with John that day. According to this he would be given a green, amber or red card to take home. If the red card came home, John's mother knew there had been considerable difficulties and she should contact the school quickly. If the card was amber, there had been some difficulties which she would discuss with John and then might contact the school. Sometimes when the red was brought home she realized that she had forgotten to give John his Ritalin before school.

As well as achieving home–school liaison in a simple and creative way it could also be used to remind staff of the boy's difficulties. The card placed discretely on the desk not only reminded the boy that he must concentrate and check each piece of work and remember not to shout out, it also reminded the teacher to keep and eye on him and cue him from time to time. In a large secondary school where a teacher only sees particular children once or twice a week, a gentle reminder, carried by the child, can help avoid misunderstandings.

Experienced teachers will find their own strategies to help pupils with ADHD once they understand the difficulties of these children. The need for continuing teacher education in this area is of paramount importance. Skill and insight in catering for the needs of pupils with ADHD in the classroom will serve the needs of all children with emotional and behavioural difficulties.

References

Barkley RA (1990) Attention Deficit Hyperactive Disorder; A Handbook for Diagnosis and Treatment. New York: Guilford.

Brown T (1992) Attention-Activation Disorder in HI IQ Underachievers. Paper given at the 145th Annual Meeting of the American Psychiatric Association in Washington DC.

Cooper P, Ideus K (eds) (1995) Attention Deficit/ Hyperactive Disorder: Educational, Medical and Cultural Issues. East Sutton, Kent: The Association of Workers for Children with Emotional and Behavioural Difficulties.

Cooper P, Ideus K (1996) Attention Deficit/Hyperactive Disorder: A Practical Guide for Teachers. London: David Fulton.

DES (1978) Special Educational Needs: The Warnock Report. London: HMSO.

DuPaul GJ, Stoner G (1995) AD/HD in the Schools: Assessment and Intervention Strategies. New York: Guilford.

Goldstein S (1990) Understanding and Managing Children's Classroom Behaviour. New York: Wiley.

Hallowell EM, Ratey JJ (1994) Driven to Distraction. Recognising and Coping with Attention Deficit Disorder from Childhood through Adulthood: London: Touchstone Books (Simon & Schuster).

Hinshaw SP (1994) Attention Deficits and Hyperactivity in Children. London: Sage.

Irlen H (1991) Reading by the Colours. New York: Avery Publishing Group Inc.

Mould S (1993) Chaos in the classroom. Special Children 66: 8–12.

Sharron H (1995) Behaviour drugs –headteachers speak out. Special Children 83: 10–13.

Train A (1996) AD/HD: How to Deal with Very Difficult Children. Oxford: Blackwell.

Part III
ADHD in Practice

Chapter 12
How Professionals
Perceive ADHD

LESLEY HUGHES

This chapter forms part of a larger study that explores the child's perspective on ADHD. It was thought necessary to begin the research by obtaining an understanding of how the various professions view ADHD as they are the ones responsible for diagnosing and proposing appropriate intervention strategies for these children. I then suggest that effective team working is an essential prerequisite for managing children that suffer from ADHD and suggest a framework for good practice.

Introduction

The behaviour traits associated with ADHD have been well-documented over the years with theorists attempting to define the etiology and origins of the syndrome. Still, in 1902, noted that children's behavioural problems stemmed from their inability to control their moral behaviour, the trait of which he believed was inherited. Recently the emphasis has been placed on children having problems with attention and impulsivity, with or without hyperactivity, the origins of which are still not conclusive in that causal agents swing from a biological perspective to social learning theory and a psychodynamic perspective (Hinshaw, 1994). Despite the fact that there is prolonged inconsistency over which behaviour is predominant in ADHD, there is now new evidence from Barkley to suggest that the prominent behaviour is disinhibition (Barkley, 1997). However, inconsistency remains regarding what constitutes the causal factors behind the manifestation of ADHD characteristics. The continued uncertainty surrounding the syndrome has resulted in changes being made to the diagnostic criteria. Currently the Diagnostic and Statistical Manual of Mental Disorders, fourth edition (DSM IV) (American Psychiatric Association, (APA) 1994) describes symptoms that identify three distinct types of ADHD, a predominantly inattentive type, a hyperactive-impulsive type and a combined type. The diagnostic criteria stipulate that symptoms must be developmentally extreme relative to the child's age and gender, must have persisted for the last six months, that the onset must have occurred before seven years of age and that symptoms must be pervasive (Hinshaw, 1994).

A multidimensional model

If we consider ADHD in the light of the most recent body of research, we are looking at a multidimensional model that applies a holistic perspective to our understanding of etiology and origins (BPS, 1996). The inference from the causal model (Frith, 1995) is that ADHD has a biological origin but that this may or may not have a neurological link. It suggests that children have an innate biological predisposition to react to environmental influences, and consequently the quality of the environment is a precursor for influencing behaviour. Regardless of the causal factor, there results an indirect assault on normal psychological mechanisms and this in turn is manifested in behaviour. Such a broad causal link model influences the assessment and intervention process, and provides us with a strong argument for establishing a collaborative inter-professional approach for dealing with ADHD in children.

Teamwork: a medical perspective

Teamwork has long been advocated as the way forward for providing quality healthcare for patients, but the message was not always made explicit and the climate not always suitable for collaborative growth. In the publication *Better Services for the Mentally Handicapped* (DHSS, 1971) it was advocated that collaboration should be sought between professions, and in 1976 the Court Report pursued integrated services for children; in 1986 the Cumberlege Report advocated comprehensive care. Underlying these reports is the recognition that individual and community needs must be met, with some reports being more specific than others about how this could best be achieved. As early as 1973, the NHS Act set out four categories of collaboration: sharing of services, co-ordination of service delivery, joint planing and joint prevention (DHSS, 1973).

In 1984 the DHSS Report of the joint working group on collaboration between family practitioner committees and district health authorities called for collaboration between local family practitioner committees and departments of health as a means of serving the interests of the local community. This report was the first to identify the principles of collaboration as being:

> Mutual understanding and respect for each other's role and responsibility, identification of areas of common interest and concern, the establishment and pursuit of common goals, policies and programmes.

The ability to communicate and therefore share information was an apparent requisite for achieving effective collaboration. This was further endorsed by the government in 1990 with the NHS and Community Care Act expecting not only collaboration of services, but mutual exchange of information if the assessment and provision involved different agencies. These reports were advocating collaboration between agencies, with the assumption that the message was implicit.

Despite the government's obvious move in advocating collaborative teamwork as a means of achieving a healthier nation through the recognition of individual and community needs, the economic climate was not formidable. According to Loxley (1997), the concept of collaboration was viewed with suspicion, its term ambiguous, and the culture in the health profession not aligned to fostering healthy collaborative aims; rather it fostered professional isolation. In the 1990s the culture amongst health professions was one of a competitive internal and external market for resources, with accountability of expenditure high, and quality and efficiency of services targeted as incentives for financial rewards. Competition was the priority, not collaboration.

It is now the priority of the new government to provide us with a 'new NHS' that will replace the internal market and provide the opportunity to cultivate a collaborative approach to meeting the health needs of the individual and the community. The 'new NHS' document (HMSO, 1997) suggests 'integrated teamwork' involving primary and community services to include social care together with joint planning and that the needs of the patient form the centre of the care process.

The policy endorses a move towards 'bridging' services more closely together so that 'services such as child health where responsibilities have been split within the health service and where liaison with Local Authorities is often poor, will particularly benefit'. (The policy clearly has positive implications for ADHD.) In addition, the 1997 report on the roles of mental health staff, *Pulling Together* (Sainsbury Report, 1997) suggests that staff working with patients who have mental health problems need to develop the skills, knowledge and positive attitude necessary for working in a multidisciplinary team. The report is mindful of the need for practitioners to audit their work and provide evidence for therapeutic effectiveness, suggesting that staff working as part of a multidisciplinary team should be able to 'adapt their roles and practice to achieve the better outcomes for service users and carers'.

The latest government health policy document, *Our Healthier Nation* (HMSO, 1998), leads on from the *New NHS* White Paper (HMSO, 1997). It prioritizes child health and wants to see an improvement in the school environment. As one means of achieving this priority whilst remaining sensitive to the escalating numbers of children with educational needs, the paper strongly advocates the need for these children to remain in mainstream schools. The paper refers to health being not only freedom from disease but quality of life. It stipulates the need to consider social and economic, environmental and lifestyle factors as much as genetic factors in affecting our health, and recognizes 'that poor mental health is a risk factor for physical health' (HMSO, 1998).

In addition to advocating that professions must work collaboratively, this government paper refers to a more informed public informing health professions of their health needs.

There has been a move forward with the document proposals, from collaboration to listening to the voice of the client, but will altering the cultural climate by removing competitive markets be sufficient to motivate collaboration?

Tribalism

Crossing professional boundaries in order to achieve collaboration is not easy as professions are taught in isolation with little or no concept of the role of the other profession they are to work with, and are not competent in teamwork (Davidson, 1993). As early as 1962, Strauss argued that the very nature of professionals taught in isolation means that they have claim to a specialist point of view that fosters dispute rather than co-operation between the professions. Leathard (1994) suggests that, in order to achieve effective teamwork, professional barriers must be removed. The Sainsbury Report (1997) recognized that the nature of multidisciplinary working would cause confusion, resulting from the overlapping functions, skills and knowledge, added to which practitioners would be working outside traditional support structures.

Despite teamwork being advocated and the difficulties of implementation recognized, there is little evidence that teamwork is occurring (Bond et al., 1991; Butler Sloss, 1988). Training in isolation is only one explanation. West and Slater (1997) suggest that there is a misunderstanding amongst the professions on what is meant by working in a team, and they identify a major gap between the rhetoric and reality. However, there are a few positive examples of successful teamwork. Health promotion programmes have been innovative in trying to develop collaboration between the different services, the Healthy City and Healthy Schools initiatives (DOE, 1992) being two such programmes. The success of such programmes was as a result of strategic planning with clear aims and objectives and an appropriate evaluation protocol built into the original proposal. Clearly such initiatives required the contribution of a number of key players whose co-ordination and collaboration were pivotal to the outcome; an example of good practice which could be adopted by other agencies.

Davidson and Lucas (1994) suggest preventing the development of professional barriers and developing skills for effective teamwork through training undergraduate healthcare students together, using an interactive curriculum framework to promote interprofessional communication and the understanding and respect of professional roles. (For further details see Hughes and Lucas 1996, 1997.)

Teamwork: an educational perspective

Children with behaviour problems and learning difficulties who are educated in mainstream schools have requirements over and above those of children without these difficulties. Similar to the health service, the educational system cannot make provision in isolation when the problems are multifactorial and the needs are multidisciplinary. The government Green Paper on education, *Excellence for all Children* (DFEE, 1997), prioritizes the need for collaboration between agencies at local and national levels as a means of detecting behaviour problems early, and the setting of targets for managing children with difficult behaviour. From September 1998 schools will assess all children at the beginning of their primary education to identify where a child needs help, and local education authorities will be responsible for providing support and resources to meet local educational needs. The paper favours schools collaborating with parents, and supports training for teachers to strengthen their skills in managing behaviour problems in the classroom, with the involvement of other agencies (especially educational psychologists) to support teachers in meeting the needs of the child.

There is a strong emphasis placed on parents receiving help from both statutory and voluntary services in order to support their child. This is primarily a move to empower parents, who in return will be more able to interact with the schools' requests, enabling prepared targets to be achieved. Overall, the paper advocates meeting the needs of the child, but there is also an emphasis on the need for collaboration between and within agencies, and a need for these agencies to be accountable for their actions. This paper coupled with the 1989 Children Act, advocating the need for the child's voice to be heard, has similar goals to the government's health papers, which advocate inter-agency collaboration and listening to the client's needs.

Collaboration

Both the medical and educational services are advocating collaborative teamwork as a means of achieving the best interests of their users, but is this expected to occur spontaneously from agencies that have previously worked in isolation? I turn now to the word 'collaboration' and to look at the skills required for effective teamwork. I use the recommendations laid down by Guzzo and Shea (1992) that effective teamwork needs to recognize individuals and their organization. Individuals need to feel that they are important to the success of the team; roles should be meaningful and intrinsically rewarding; individual contributions should be identifiable and subject to evaluation; there should be clear team goals with built-in performance feedback, but in recent empirical work by West and Slater (1997) the suggestion is that these recommendations will only be possible if clear objectives are developed to guide work activities and co-ordination among team members. West and Poulton (1995) identified four significant indicators in the quest for achieving effective teamwork:

- agreed aims, goals and objectives;
- effective communication,
- patients receiving the best possible care;
- individual roles defined and understood.

With these indicators in mind, the availability of the biopsychosocial model to aid our understanding of ADHD, and government health and education policy supporting the voice of the client, I turn to the findings from my study on the professional's perspective of ADHD.

Interviews with the medical and education professions

My study was in the form of face-to-face interviews with nine professionals from the fields of psychiatry, neuropsychiatry, paediatrics and educational psychology. The interviewees were all practitioners with experience of working with children with ADHD. The interview themes were centred around the following research questions:

- What is your understanding of the origins of ADHD?
- What do you believe to be the main behaviour characteristic of ADHD?
- Which diagnostic criteria do you use?
- What is your preferred treatment and management strategy?
- How do you confer with the children?
- With whom do you collaborate in order to assess and evaluate children?

There follows a report of the findings, and a discussion of the similarities and differences in the respondents' perspectives.

Findings

Table 12.1: Beliefs concerning origins of ADHD

Respondent	1	2	3	4	5	6	7	8	9
Biological	/		/	/	/	/	/	/	/
Genetic	/		/	/	/	/			/
Env/School		/		/			/		/
Env/Home		/	/	/	/	/		/	/
Diet	/		/						
Does not believe	/				/				/

Eight of the nine respondents believe that ADHD has a biological origin, with only five of these eight suggesting that there is a genetic link to the condition. There is only one respondent taking a completely biological stance, but seven stress the influence of the home environment as a causal factor, with only four mentioning the school environment as a contributing factor to the condition. The findings support Frith's causal model, which suggests ADHD has a biological origin, which causes behaviour to be susceptible to environmental influences. Two respondents emphasize diet as a contributing factor, but not in isolation to other factors, however, three respondents thought that ADHD was not a separate entity from other behavioural problems.

Table 12.2: Behaviour characteristics

Respondent	1	2	3	4	5	6	7	8	9
Attention	/	/			/	/	/	/	/
Inhibition			/	/	/	/		/	
Hyperactivity	/	/	/	/	/	/	/	/	/
Non-hyperactivity					/	/		/	/
Impulsivity	/		/	/					/
Low motivation	/								
Low self-esteen	/			/	/				
Outgrow behaviour	/			/			/	/	
Not outgrow						/			/

When comparing the DSM IV criteria with the behaviour characteristic respondents looked for in diagnosing ADHD, the statistical data suggest that hyperactivity is the prominent behaviour, with four respondents mentioning impulsivity and hyperactivity as a combined behaviour trait. Two respondents reported on the hyperactive-impulsive type, and four respondents recognized that, in the absence of hyperactivity, inattention was a feature of the condition. Whether or not these statistical data are aligned to meeting the DSM IV criteria is not clear and requires an analysis of the narrative data.

Table 12.3: Diagnostic criteria

Respondent	1	2	3	4	5	6	7	8	9
ICD10		/							
DSM III		/	/					/	
DSM IV		/		/	/		/	/	/
None	/					/			
Pervasive		/		/		/	/		/
Non-pervasive	/		/		/	/			
								/	
Gut feeling	/								
Observation	/			/					/
History					/	/	/		
Performance test				/	/				

Having explored the behaviour characteristics required to confirm a diagnosis of ADHD, it is evident that the professions are using different diagnostic criteria. Some are using more than one, and two respondents would not comment on the use of any particular criteria. The DSM IV criteria highlights the importance of pervasive behaviour in the diagnosis, but four respondents do not look for this. Despite the fact that pervasive behaviour was not a feature of the DSM III criteria, one respondent still uses the criteria and seeks confirmation of pervasive behaviour. There is no mention of using performance tests in the DSM IV criteria, but two respondents use these, one of whom also uses observation of behaviour in the clinical setting. In addition, two other respondents rely on their own observation when assessing the child.

Table 12.4: Treatment and management

Respondent	1	2	3	4	5	6	7	8	9
Medication	/		/	/	/	/	/	/	/
Behav/man in school				/	/			/	/
Behav/man at home									
Self-control				/					
Diet				/					
Council parents	/			/	/	/			

All respondents agreed that medication was an important form of treatment for ADHD in that it helped the child concentrate, and some believed that it helped the child to conform to behavioural rules. Four respondents advocated the need for schools to manage behaviour but no-one identified the home environment as contributing to behaviour change. However, four respondents thought it sufficient to counsel parents on the benefits of medication for changing behaviour.

Table 12.5: Informing the child

Respondent	1	2	3	4	5	6	7	8	9
Attention problem ADHD	/	/	/			/		/	
Nothing		/			/		/	/	/
Self-control				/					
Brain dysfunction				/				/	

On the basis of respondents' claims, it seems that the dialogue between the professions and the child was poor. Although no-one explained to the child that they had ADHD, two respondents explained their behaviour in terms of a brain dysfunction. One of the respondents suggested to the child that they were responsible for controlling their behaviour, advocating that empowerment through knowledge and medication would bring about behaviour change. Five respondents informed the child that they had a problem in attending to tasks and that medication would help them to focus on their work. Three respondents said nothing to the child about the diagnosis, whereas two contradicted themselves during interview by offering conflicting responses to this question.

Table 12.6: Working in a team

Respondent	1	2	3	4	5	6	7	8	9
Work alone	/	/	/	/	/	/	/	/	/
Work with other professions									
Parents	/								
Teachers				/					

All respondents worked alone, they did not consider themselves to be part of a team even when they had to inform other professions of the diagnosis, or obtain information from parents and teaching staff. There is no evidence of a collaborative approach to managing ADHD; rather there is evidence that professions are working in isolation despite the fact that the nature of the condition is multifactorial and pervasive.

Analysis

ADHD origins and behaviour

Three respondents were sceptical as to whether ADHD existed, one suggested that it was 'a concept that people have invented to aid communication'. He described how diet, multiple carers, a lack of parental attachment and different parenting styles can cause behaviour similar to ADHD and that the word was just a fad. Another response was that if such a condition existed then it must have 'some neurological basis to result in behaviour symptoms that approximate to what is called ADHD'. Three informants were confused with the symptoms of ADHD and the symptoms of child abuse, seeing them as one and the same. Two sceptics suggested the symptoms resulted from biopsychosocial factors, and one respondent said that it was essentially a psychosocial problem. I suspect that scepticism mirrors feelings of confusion in their understanding of the condition.

Eight respondents believed ADHD to have a biological origin, 'a brain dysfunction with a genetic input, certainly not a psychosocial condition caused by bad parenting or a bad early environment', but a condition that children grew out of as the brain developed. One respondent thought that a biological dysfunction in these children was due to 'heavy smoking by the mother in pregnancy, causing placental insufficiency stunting the foetal brain development' and suggested that 'we are buying time [with medication] until the child grows up'. This represents a contradiction in the prognosis of ADHD, but does not appear to influence the choice of treatment.

Low self-esteem was reported by three respondents to be a symptom of ADHD, but one suggestion was that children with ADHD obtained self-esteem in a negative way by 'going into class clown mode with their shirt hanging out'. In other words, they behaved in a socially unacceptable way in order to attract attention, therefore reinforcing unacceptable behaviour. Such a statement made me wonder if this informant perceived ADHD behaviour as 'attention seeking' and that the children could control how they behaved, a perspective that would contradict Barkley's theory on inhibition.

ADHD was perceived by some as resulting from a combination of biopsychosocial factors. One clinician gave three perspectives about the origin of ADHD. Originally he stated 'it was a brain chemical imbalance', then blamed a poor rearing environment and finally stated that 'if you change the rearing environment then you can sometimes change the symptoms', suggesting that environmental influences could be manipulated to alter behaviour, and supporting Frith's theory. Interestingly, his choice of treatment was medication, with no evidence of a behavioural change programme to alter environmental influences. This move from a biopsychosocial perspective in favour of a biological origin became clear when he said 'ADHD is a health problem rather than an educational or social problem'.

This apparent contradiction was not atypical from respondents and could be construed as evidence that exploring a topic through interview encouraged respondents to reflect and make changes to their perspectives on ADHD based on discussion of the questions. However, it could also suggest that respondents view ADHD as an enigma.

At first glance the profession's perspectives on the etiology of ADHD support Frith's causal model. They recognize a biological origin but that this is not necessarily neurological; rather there is a blueprint for sensitivity to environmental influences. There is some uncertainty as to whether the school or home environment has equal parity, with most respondents erring on the side of one or the other. Hyperactivity is recognized as the predominant behaviour characteristic, associated with either inattention or inhibition, or all three may be present. However, there is some scepticism about whether the behavioural characteristics should be given the specific term ADHD or left to stand as behavioural problems per se.

Diagnostic criteria, treatment and management

A variety of criteria are being used to diagnose ADHD, some respondents are not using any, and despite using a specific criteria, a few are failing to meet the necessary criteria for diagnosis. For example pervasive behaviour was not thought to be necessary for confirming a diagnosis:

> Pervasiveness is overworked.

> Pervasive behaviour is important but only if pervasiveness is not a result of environmental factors.

There was also some ridicule of the necessity for a diagnosis:

> A diagnosis isn't very helpful.

> Nobody can make absolutely certain [when making a diagnosis], certainties were the problem of religious bigots rather than clinicians.

> The behavioural symptoms [of ADHD] are so common that they are just extensions of normal behaviour.

> Labelling is just a way of explaining bad behaviour.

The findings did reveal a correlation between perspectives on environmental influence on behaviour, and attitude to pervasive behaviour. Those criticizing the home environment made negative comments and tended to favour information from the school:

> Sometimes it is just the school having problems, parents think this is acceptable behaviour.

> Many children said to have attention problems are normal.

> Parents play less games with their kids.

Those critical of the school environment favoured the parent's explanation of the child's behaviour:

> The increased stroppiness of teachers in not being tolerant to children.

> Teachers sometimes don't report features of ADHD at school because they are prejudiced against anything other than a naughty child explanation, so ADHD features just go unreported.

It was interesting how perspectives on environmental influences affected whether a clinician was loyal to pervasive behaviour as a diagnostic criteria for ADHD.

In the light of a distrust of pervasive criteria, there was a suggestion of misdiagnosis. One respondent identified that some schoolchildren were being prescribed medication for ADHD when there was no evidence of them having behavioural problems at school. This not only questions the rigour of the DSM IV criteria, it also suggests that a biological perspective on the etiology of ADHD is perceived to require pharmacological intervention. The value of using diagnostic criteria was dependent on what, and for whom the clinician was diagnosing:

> If I want to diagnose ADHD then the only way to do it is to use a criterion, but the criterion may be a mistake. It is constantly changing.

> The problem with diagnosing is that it puts the onus on us the professionals to treat the child when in fact what should happen is the parents need to get their act together.

> Parents come to us wanting a diagnosis of ADHD and if we don't give them this they get very angry.

> Parents come with their own agenda wanting a trial medication.

> Medication makes it easier for the school and parents to manage the child in an effective way.

Respondents appeared to be under pressure to medicate. There was an overall agreement that medication was effective in helping the child concentrate but this did not necessarily alleviate their behaviour problems. One respondent declared that medication focuses attention, but on existing negative behaviour. Another respondent voiced his reservation on the use of medication: 'we are medicating biological and social problems'.

Although medication was a priority in treating behavioural problems, the reasons for its choice over and above behavioural management programmes varied:

If the diagnosis is right then the taking of the tablet will prove it's own evidence of improvement.

Two other respondents suggested that as this was a hereditary problem:

Some of our parents haven't got the intelligence to put a behaviour programme together.

Behaviour programmes are difficult to implement in the home because parents tend to be impulsive and demanding.

Where there were examples of schools implementing behaviour management strategy, respondents criticized the parent's ability to compliment behaviour change in the home environment. Whereas another respondent suggested that parents did not need help with behaviour management programmes, 'what they need is the opportunity to use their natural parenting skills': This was a contradiction to an earlier statement made by the same respondent who declared that ADHD was a result of poor parenting skills.

A number of issues arose to suggest that clinicians are giving 'lip service' to environmental influences, that their professional training based on the medical perspective prevails and dominates their thinking in terms of diagnosis, treatment and management of ADHD.

Informing the child and interacting with others

In the light of evidence that clinicians have different perspectives about the etiology and treatment for ADHD, it is of no surprise that their perspectives also differ on their explanation to the child regarding the diagnosis and treatment. Two respondents focused on the child's concentration improving with the use of medication, despite admitting to not asking the child if there was a problem with concentration. Others focus on the need for medication in order to improve performance in school. One explanation was: ' I try to put across to the child that they have a brain disorder, basically that one part of the brain hasn't quite grown up with the rest of it.' This explanation was in the hope that knowledge would empower the child to take control of their own behaviour, which differed only slightly from another perspective on the power of knowledge, 'we are buying time with this tablet until you grow up'. No further explanation was given to these children. One respondent said nothing to the child but recognized that it was bad practice to discuss the child's negative behaviour with the child present, and on the strength of this recognition was going to change his approach. It was clear that respondents avoided asking the children their perspective about their behaviour. If a child was informed at all, the focus was on medication as a means of controlling behaviour and as means of gaining parental and school approval. The latter has implications for self-esteem in that the child's perspective on obtaining approval is based on the effectiveness of medication, not on the ability of the self. There was no mention of the environment having an effect on the child, only of the medication having an effect on the environment. What will happen to the child's behaviour when the medication doesn't work or ceases to be effective?

Not only is there a reluctance of respondents to liaise with children about their behaviour, there is a similar reluctance to liaise with members of other professions. Despite government papers recommending closer collaboration from health and education services as a means of meeting the needs of the individual and the community, there is a distinct lack of any collaboration between the professions involved with children identified as having ADHD. Such evidence is conflicting with the causal model proposed by Frith in 1995 where it identifies a multi-modal causal relationship to ADHD and the BPS and the Green Paper (1997) suggest a multidisciplinary approach to addressing such issues.

The respondents work alone, they recognize themselves as clinicians whose role is to diagnose, inform and prescribe, not to be part of a team; that is the responsibility of others. There is ignorance as to who these others should be, their role and responsibilities; and respondents criticize (in ignorance) roles of other professions that they admit to knowing very little about. One respondent said of social workers: 'they don't recognize ADHD, they put [such] children into care'. Another respondent admitted to different goals attributing to poor teamwork: 'there is a big dichotomy between the teaching staff and the care teams wanting different things, and there was no co-ordination between the services'. Others focused blame on the lack of resources for creating poor collaboration between the agencies. Working in isolation with children whose behavioural problems are multifactorial, requiring interagency support for both child and parents, suggests that either there is a poor understanding about the condition and its requirements or that respondents' perspectives dictate an isolated approach. On the basis of the evidence presented in this study, there is a general agreement that ADHD has a biological origin and that the resulting behaviour can be arrested through medication. This medical perspective prevails under disguised veils, and fails to address the wider environmental issues associated with ADHD.

Proposed collaborative problem-solving approach to ADHD – an evolving model: "DEF"

The proposed model has to be flexible to align itself with the evolving needs of the child:

1. *Define* areas of concern for the child, family and school. Identify needs and specific professions involved.
2. *Explore* needs in the context of the environment.

3. *Framework* – set objectives with appropriate evaluation instrument.
4. *Define* areas of concern (as in 1.).

Conclusion

There is evidence that the professions' perspectives on the etiology of ADHD influence their approach to diagnosis, treatment and attitude in the management of children, resulting in a very turbulent foundation from which clinicians are diagnosing.

At first glance respondents do appear to support the work of Frith. However, further analysis on the use of diagnostic criteria and attitude to environmental factors, plus the chosen method of intervention, highlight a shift in their perspective to a biological stance.

There are ethical implications. They are treating lifelong symptoms with medication alone, yet it is recognized that the effects of medication cease to be effective in adulthood. What coping strategies will be open to the young adult who has come to rely on a drug to control behaviour? Are the professions helping these children, only to see them fail in later life?

What do the findings suggest in the light of current cultural and political policy? An application of Frith's model defines ADHD as having neurological origin influenced by environmental factors. Government papers claim that the way forward in addressing complex health and education issues (such as that of ADHD) is for professions to work collaboratively together whilst taking into account the voice of the child. Traditionally, professions have undergone training aligned to a medical model, where communication and teamworking skills were not part of the curriculum. Today there is a move away from training in isolation to a curriculum that incorporates interprofessional education and skills of collaboration. Such training needs to be available to professions in the clinical field to remove professional barriers and to promote collaborative working. The pro-fessional bodies need to devise a model that can be used by clinicians as guidelines on how to meet the requirements set out by government papers. They need to recognize how to meet individual needs and the community's needs, identifying common goals and set attainable targets. Only through the development of a strategic work plan can professions work effectively as a team and assist the needs of children with ADHD.

References

American Psychiatric Association (1994) Diagnostic and Statistical Manual of Mental Disorders (4 edn). Washington DC: APA.

Barkley RA (1997) ADHD and the Nature of Self Control. New York: Guilford.

Bond J, Gregson BA, Cartlidgel A (1991) Interprofessional Collaboration in Primary Health Care Organisations. Occasional paper. London: Royal College of General Practitioners.

British Psychological Society (1996) Attention Deficit Hyperactivity Disorder (ADHD): A Psychological Response to an Evolving Concept. Leicester: BPS.

Butler Sloss E (1988) Report of the Inquiry into Child Abuse in Cleveland 1987. Cm. 413. London: HMSO.

Davidson LA (1993) An evaluation of 'shared learning' for undergraduate paramedic students. A dissertation submitted in partial fulfulment of the requirements of the degree of MA in health research, University of Lancaster.

Davidson LA, Lucas J (1994) Multiprofessional Education in the Undergraduate Curriculum: A Turbulent Journey. A paper presented at the European Network for the Development of Multiprofessional Education in Health Sciences at the University of Tromsø, Norway.

DFEE (1997) Excellence for all Children. London: DFEE.

DHSS (1971) Better Services for the Mentally Handicapped. Cmnd. 4683. London: HMSO.

DHSS (1973) Report of the Working Party on Collaboration between the NHS and Local Government. London: HMSO.

DHSS (1984) Report of the Joint Working Group on Collaboration between Family Practitioner Committees and District Health Authorities. London: HMSO.

DoH (Department of Health) and DoE (Department of the Environment) (1992) Housing and Community Care. London: HMSO.

Frith U (1995) Dyslexia: can we have a shared theoretical framework? Educational and Child Psychology 12(1): 6–17.

Guzzo RA, Shea GP (1992) In MA West, J Slater (1997) Teamworking in Primary Health Care: A Review of its Effectiveness. Research report prepared for the Health Education Authority.

Hinshaw SP (1994) Attention Deficits and Hyperactivity in Children. London and New York: Sage.

HMSO (1997) The New NHS. London: HMSO.

HMSO (1998) Our Healthier Nation. London: HMSO.

Hughes LA, Lucas J (1996) An evaluation of problem-based learning in the multiprofessional education curriculum for the health professions. Journal of Interprofessional Care 11(I): 77–88.

Hughes LA, Lucas J (1997) Interprofessional Education: Does it Work? Observations from Evaluations of an IPE Curriculum Using Problem-Based Learning. Paper presented at an international conference sponsored by the NHS Executive, University of Liverpool.

Leathard L (1994) Going Inter-Professional: Working Together for Health and Welfare. London: Routledge.

Loxley A (1997) Collaboration in Health and Welfare. London.: Jessica Kingsley.

Sainsbury Report (1997) Pulling Together: The Future Role and Training of Mental Health Staff. London: Sainsbury Centre for Mental Health.

Strauss (1962) In L Leathard (1994) Going Interprofessional: Working Together for Health and Welfare. London: Routledge.

West MA, Slater JB (1997) Teamworking in Primary Health Care: A Review of its Effectiveness. Report prepared for the Health Education Authority.

West MA, Poulton BC (1995) In MA West, J Slater (1997) Teamworking in Primary Health Care: A Review of its Effectiveness. Report prepared for the Health Education Authority.

Chapter 13
Teachers' Classroom Strategies for Dealing with Students with ADHD: An Empirical Study

SAMUEL DANIEL AND PAUL COOPER

Introduction

This chapter describes a study that was carried out on teachers' class-room strategies for dealing with children with ADHD. The study took place in 1997 and was conducted in a special school for children with learning and behavioural difficulties in the UK (this is the same school that is referred to in Chapter 14). This is an important contribution to this field as existing literature on this topic tends to rely heavily on research carried out in the US (e.g. DuPaul and Stoner, 1995).

The study set out to answer the following questions:

- What strategies do teachers employ in response to the behaviours associated with ADHD in their classrooms?
- What reasons do teachers give for employing these strategies?
- How effective are these strategies in managing inappropriate behaviour?

The school chosen for the study offered an excellent site for three main reasons.

First, the institution has an assessment centre with a team skilled in clinical psychology, counselling and psychometric testing, with partic-ular experience and expertise in the assessment of ADHD and learning difficulties. This team works closely with a consultant paediatrician who has extensive experience of diagnosing ADHD and related childhood problems. This maximizes the probability that children bearing the ADHD diagnosis in this setting are appropriately diagnosed.

Second, the institution has an educational programme that incor-porates a lower school (ages 5–10), a middle school (ages 11–13) and an upper school (ages 14–18+). The middle and upper schools are operated like a secondary school, offering the full curriculum that one would expect to find in UK and US mainstream secondary schools. This was of particular relevance to the current investigation because it gave us the opportunity to explore possible relationships between school subjects, student behaviour and teachers' strategies. Existing research and writing suggest that students with ADHD may favour certain kinds of academic experience, whilst finding others less congenial (e.g. Crammond, 1994; DuPaul and Stoner, 1995).

Third, the institution promotes itself as having a long and successful history in the education and management of students exhibiting maladaptive behaviour, including ADHD. Further, the school's promotional literature emphasizes the positive nature of teaching approaches employed in the school, and places an emphasis on therapeutic rather than coercive approaches. This suggested to us that the school's professed ethos was in line with dominant thinking about appropriate ways of meeting the needs of children with learning and behavioural problems (see, for example, DFEE, 1997).

The participants

The children and teachers in this investigation were from the middle school of this institution and aged 11–13. The study focused on students of mixed gender (five girls and ten boys) who formed small group classes for various subjects. Four of these class subjects – maths, English, history and music – and their teachers were chosen solely on the basis of feasibility in relation to the ways in which the school timetable fitted in with the researcher's programme for observations. The group represented a variety of social and cultural backgrounds (with six Americans, six English, two Canadians and one Dutch student). The four teachers shared similar international backgrounds, two originating from America, one from Africa and the other from England.

Data-gathering methods

Data were gathered using a combination of systematic observation and interviews. These took the form of:

- an observation schedule, which was developed by the researchers to provide systematic data on the frequency of students' dysfunctional behaviour and teacher management techniques;
- two semi-structured interview schedules (one contextualized, the other decontextualized) designed to elicit teachers' perceptions of the nature and effectiveness of their management techniques.

The observation schedule

The observation schedule employed the *antecedents, behaviour and consequences* (ABC) approach to observing and analysing behaviour

(Braswell and Bloomquist, 1991; Ayers ey al., 1996). This approach involves observing behavioural sequences in terms of:

- Antecedents: the setting in which the behaviour occurs, including the event or events that happen immediately before the behaviour.
- Behaviour: the behaviour itself described in very clear and precise behavioural terms.
- Consequences: what happens afterwards, and especially what seems to reinforce the behaviour.

Included in the antecedents section were observations of the teacher's mode of delivery or role (e.g. lecture, group work), and the required student activity (e.g. listening, discussing). In addition, consideration was given to evidence that suggests that students with ADHD are easily distracted by visual and auditory stimuli or by the behaviour of other students (DuPaul and Stoner, 1994; Cooper and Ideus, 1996), therefore, 'physical classroom distracters' were included in this section. The behaviour section was designed to record the 'hallmark symptoms of ADHD' (Barkley, 1995) – inattention, hyperactivity and impulsivity – which were likely to be the types of negative behaviours students would display. These were coded as numbers 1, 2 and 3 respectively for the convenience of their inclusion on the instrument as well as for the ease of identification. These behavioural categories were defined according to the DSM IV criteria for ADHD (American Psychiatric Association, 1994) and were modified as follows:

- Inattention: lack of attention to specified task/failure to sustain attention to a specified task. Inattention was determined by the direction of the child's gaze (Pellegrini et al., 1995) and was coded if the child was looking away from the specified task.
- Hyperactivity: high levels of verbal and motoric activity. For example, being 'over-talkative', fidgeting with hands or feet in seat, leaving seat when remaining seated is expected.
- Impulsivity: difficulty in withholding active responses (e.g. blurting out statements, grabbing materials); often interrupting or intruding on others (e.g. butting in while others are speaking). (Adapted from the DSM IV) (APA, 1994: 83–5.)

In order to decide on the teacher strategies to be included in the observation schedule, a list was drawn up based on existing literature (DuPaul and Stoner, 1994; Cooper and Ideus, 1996), and then this was discussed with the participating teachers. As a result of this process the following items were established as being appropriate for inclusion in the schedule:

(a) *Positive reinforcement (PR)* – a strategy that seeks to strengthen desirable or positive behaviour in students, such as in the form of:
   • frequent, specific, positive feedback;
   • immediate praise or reward

(b) *Mild punishment (MP)* – the explicit application of negative consequences in response to undesirable behaviour.

(c) *Seating arrangement (SA)* – the adjustment of student seating in the classroom.

(d) *Student instruction (SI)* – the use of clear and concise instructions to focus or refocus student attention.

(e) *Pedagogical strategy (PED)* – the modification of instructional methodology and mode of presentation of educational stimuli, such as:
   • adjustment to organization and timing of lesson structure;
   • selection of learning activities;
   • segmentation of tasks into small(er) steps;
   • time out from positive reinforcement (TO) – removal of student from the classroom setting to a designated place for a specific period.

(f) *Ignoring undesirable behaviour (I)* – the withholding attention from a student who is infringing a class rule.

(g) *Pupil grouping (GRP)* – the placing of students in groups according to specific criteria.

The next section of the instrument, *behavioural outcome*, was designed to capture the consequences of the behavioural strategies. Four possible outcomes of the application of such strategies are (Skinner, 1953; Bandura, 1969):

• the undesirable behaviour is extinguished (Ext.);
• the undesirable behaviour is modified (Mod.);
• the undesirable behaviour is continued (Cont.);
• the undesirable behaviour is intensified (Inten.).

Student performance was included at the bottom of the observation schedule as a final category to be identified during classroom observations. This consisted of two sections: on-task and off-task performance. Miller (1996) argues against the inclusion of 'on-task'/'off-task' categories in favour of categories like 'academic work output' and other skills when focusing on students' behaviour. However, the use of these subcategories seemed justified for two reasons. First, they served the purpose of easily identifying a positive or negative student outcome, which was the immediate visible result of a teacher's strategy. Second, the inclusion of 'on-task'/'off-task' categories as part of the social coding systems for the behaviour of students with ADHD and has been supported by other researchers. For example, DuPaul and Stoner (1994:

59) describe 'on-task' as a positive student behaviour and define it as 'visual orientation towards assigned task materials or activities for entire interval'. They describe 'off-task' behaviour as negative and define it as 'visual non-attention to one's task or assigned behaviour' (p. 60).

These definitions help to underscore the arguments made by researchers like Hinshaw (1994) that intervention for ADHD should be designed with a positive focus. In including these two subcategories, both positive and negative student performance contingent upon teacher approaches could be easily identified. Therefore, both definitions were adapted and 'on/off-task' subcategories used for the purposes of this observation schedule, as a means of identifying student performance.

The final section of the observation schedule is the notes section. This was included to provide a means of recording other categories of teacher strategies that were not catered for in the other areas of the instrument as well as other observations of interest.

Reliability

The reliability of the observational instrument was established by the use of a videotape of classroom behaviour. Two raters independently carried out observations of the same tape. All Spearman rank-order correlations were above the level of 0.70. Reliability in the 0.70 to 0.90 range would be sufficient in dealing with instrumentation invalidity in coding. The instrument was therefore considered reliable for acquiring the requisite data.

Interview schedules

Two semi-structured interview schedules were developed for probing teachers' perceptions of the effectiveness of the strategies that they used. One was designed to be used before classroom observations were made. The other was designed to be used immediately following each classroom observation. These were so designed as to assess whether what teachers thought, in a general sense, in relation to the classroom strategies to be used with students with ADHD, was reflective of what they actually thought and did in the classroom. It also provided a form of triangulation for the investigation. The schedules were therefore labelled 'decontextualized' and 'contextualized' and the questions were chosen to reflect this difference.

Procedure

The agreed times in which information could be sought for the research project was six days (over two school weeks). The first four periods of the day were used for classroom observations. This allowed for the four chosen subjects – English, maths, history and music – to be observed as they were presented during these times respectively.

Findings

Which strategies do teachers employ in response to manifestations of ADHD in their classroom?

Before the above question could be answered it seems obvious that the frequency of strategies used by teachers during the period of observation had to be influenced by the occurrence of negative student behaviour. Table 13.1 presents the frequency of inattention, hyperactive and impulsive behaviour of students for the four subjects observed.

Table 13.1: The frequency of student behaviour for the four subjects

Behaviour	English	Maths	History	Music
Inattention	12	3	13	1
Hyperactivity	59	54	20	15
Impulsivity	54	14	50	12
Total	125	71	83	28

From Table 13.1 it can be seen that most of the disruptive acts occurred during the English periods (a total of 125). Of these negative acts, just less than half (59 exactly) were behaviours of hyperactivity. This recording was the highest frequency occurrence for any single category of behaviour across all the subjects observed. Acts of hyperactivity also yielded the highest scores for maths and music (54 and 15 respectively). In history, more than half of the recorded acts were behaviours of impulsivity, although the highest recording of this behaviour category for all subjects was 54 in English. Behaviours of inattention seem to feature at the lowest level across subjects with the lowest overall recording of 1 in music.

With respect to the finding that most disruptive acts occurred during the English period, the following may have accounted for this. Pellegrini and Landers-Pott (1996) affirm that certain activities and academic subjects, like reading and spelling, may exacerbate behavioural differences among children with ADHD. They assert that it may be that maths and related spatial activities, compared to reading/spelling, are less problematic for boys with ADHD because mathematics and spatial activities are male preferred.

Their explanation seems to fit in with the study's findings. The class gender ratio was 2:1 (male to female) and this could have accounted for the increase of negative behavioural acts during English as opposed to maths, for example. In addition Teacher 'H' – the teacher of maths – seems to support this theory during the decontextualized interview when she states that 'I am more concerned with the girls who are usually quiet and withdrawn but easily distracted. These tend to get neglected.'

From this statement it can be gleaned that the boys are usually more involved or attentive during the maths periods than girls, as Pellegrini and Landers-Pott suggest.

Even though this research question did not specifically solicit information with respect to student behaviour over time, it also became apparent that this information was nevertheless available. This derived from gauging the incidence of student negative behaviours (inattention, hyperactivity and impulsivity) in relation to the chronological subject periods 1–4 (of English, maths, history and music) over the course of the observation. This information is represented in Figure 13.1. From Figure 13.1 it can be seen that student behaviour of inattention, hyperactivity and impulsivity featured at irregular levels for different subject periods. The behavioural level of inattention was lowest across all subject periods but featured at its overall lowest in music (period 4). The highest frequency of behaviour recorded overall was hyperactivity during the English sessions (period 1). The highest level of impulsivity was also recorded during this subject period although the recording of this behaviour was slightly lower in history (period 3). In mathematics (period 2), acts of hyperactivity accounted for more than half of the recorded behavioural categories of that subject.

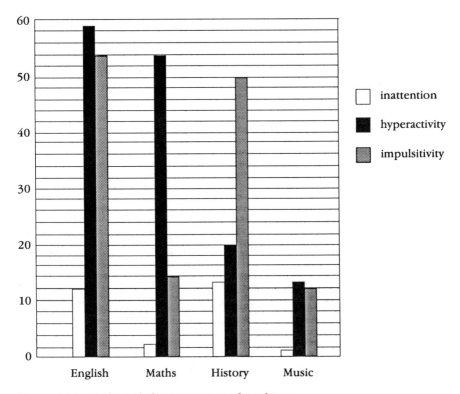

Figure 13.1: Students' behaviour patterns by subject.

The results obtained here and findings of other researchers in this area have not been consistent. For instance, the findings of Pellegrini et al. (1995) that inattention rates of children involved in field experiments were higher before recess than after, or Pellegrini and Landers-Pott's (1996) claim that 'all children should become less attentive to seat work as a function of time preceding a break' were not confirmed in this investigation. The highest recorded level of overall misbehaviour was recorded during the English period (period 1 – before break) and this level included the second highest recording of inattention across subjects. The maths lessons (period 2) preceded break and had the second lowest recording for inattention; but the period immediately following break (history, period 3) recorded the highest level of inattentive behaviour of subjects. Accordingly, a likely explanation here is that differences in the level of misbehaviour among students may be related to differences in subject period content, lesson antecedents or student interest instead of an increase in time or the break placement. This could be supported by the fact that the lowest recordings of negative behaviours were made during the music lessons (period 4) – after break (almost before lunch). This lesson was consistently the least 'academic' of the four subjects throughout the study period, with the lesson invariably involving substantial opportunities for students to listen and perform music under the guidance of the teacher. It therefore could have been that the lesson content was stimulating and helped to foster student attention as well as other positive behaviours. Zentall (1993) supports this view that students with ADHD selectively attend and strong stimuli captivate their attention. Content of the other subject lessons tended to involve less practical and active tasks than the music lessons. English, in particular, was notable for the emphasis that was placed on literacy skills in the form of writing and reading. These tended to be aspects of maths and history lessons, but generally maths tended to focus on mechanical computation, whereas history was marked by the generation of lively discussions and the use of video and other visually stimulating materials.

With regard to the strategies that teachers employed when undesirable behaviour occurred, the raw tallies obtained from observations of the teacher approaches were summarized. This information is presented in Table 13.2.

From the table it can be seen that the eight teacher strategies that were included on the observation schedule were used by teachers over the period of observation. However, subject teachers differed in the frequency and the types of strategies that they used. For example, the teacher of English made use of the highest number of interventions (120 overall) and was also responsible for the only use that was made of positive reinforcement (PR). This was in contrast to the teacher of music for whom was recorded the least frequency use of strategies overall (27), and who only used two types of strategies – mild punishment and ignoring (1 and 11 respectively) – in response to student misbehaviour.

Overall, subject teachers appear to have used mild punishment (MP) and ignore (I) more than the other strategies for controlling student behaviour but the teacher of history seemed more inclined to use MP (a total of 53) than other teachers. Similarly, ignoring was used most frequently by the teacher of English than any other subject teacher. Interestingly, for the teacher of music, the highest frequency of overall strategies used was MP, but this was the lowest overall recorded frequency for the use of this strategy across subjects.

Mild punishment most often took the form of a verbal reprimand coupled with a direction to get on-task. Other punishments included requiring the student to move to another seat and the rare use of after-class detentions.

Teacher-decontextualized interviews yielded some interesting trends with respect to this research question. Generally, teachers agreed on their reporting that they use all eight strategies that were included as part of the observation schedule as well as others.

Table 13.2: Teacher strategies used for each subject

Strategies	Maths	English	History	Music
PR	–	1	–	–
SI	10	35	8	–
MP	24	28	53	16
SA	1	–	1	–
GRP	2	1	–	–
PED	12	12	1	–
TO	1	1	–	–
IRP	17	42	15	11
TOTAL	57	120	78	27

Key: (teacher strategies) PR – positive reinforcement, SI – student instruction, MP – mild punishment, SA – seating arrangement, GRP – grouping, PED – pedagogical, TO – time out (from positive reinforcement), I – ignore, IRP – ignore rules praise.

There was a general sense in which all the teachers expressed the positive intentions behind their interventions, with the stress always being placed on the intention to maintain a purposeful classroom atmosphere and encourage student engagement, even when punishment is the chosen strategy. This is illustrated by Teacher 'D', the teacher of history who had the highest frequency of recording for the use of mild punishment (MP) (in Table 3.2), who accounted for his use of MP for managing student behaviour in terms of a signal for stopping the negative behaviour; not for affecting the individual ego.

Teachers also agreed in their reporting that strategies like seating arrangement (SA), grouping (GRP) and positive reinforcement (PR) are organized in advanced as preventative means as well as part of classroom antecedents. For example, Teacher 'H' stated that 'a lot of thought is given to seating beforehand as a preventative measure'. This was confirmed by Teacher 'D' who said that 'our use of cubicles minimizes distractions . . . proper seating arrangement also affect peer assistance'.

Overall, three of the four teachers interviewed out of the classroom context (Teachers 'H', 'M' and 'D') agree that seating arrangement is considered beforehand and is important for setting the atmosphere and thus preventing student misbehaviour. In another interview, a senior administrator also affirmed this idea and stated that 'teachers should be proactive and not wait to remediate classroom problems they experience'.

Existing research and theory support the views of these teachers. For example, DuPaul and Stoner (1994) emphasize 'effective educational strategies' as a preventative means. They argue that teachers should consider arrangements that will ensure student participation in class activities and not restrict opportunities to learn and benefit from instruction. They contend that those arrangements should limit proximity to potential distractions inherent in classrooms. In addition, they submit that 'a child identified with ADHD probably will not do well when seated beside a frequently used classroom activity centre for example' (p. 126).

Teacher 'H' also reported that PR formed a major part of teacher approaches for the management of student behaviour but that this was incorporated in a token economy system organized in advance of classroom lessons. This could be a partial explanation for the low frequency of its use as a teacher strategy (shown in Table 13.2).

Why do teachers employ these strategies?

Information relating to this question was sought by means of the contextualized teacher interviews. These were held soon after lessons were observed, as the situation allowed, and were aided by the use of the semi-structured interview schedule. Interviews lasted for about 10 minutes. Generally, teachers gave a variety of explanations as a means of justifying the choices they made of behavioural management strategies. These explanations were triggered by the use of leading statements that specifically referred to incidents of student behaviour and the corresponding teacher's approaches that were used during the observed lesson. A pause enabled teachers to further comment on the incident. Teachers were then questioned as to why specific chosen approaches were used. What appeared to be the general trends, as was revealed by more than one teacher on the interview transcripts, will be highlighted.

Teachers who used student instruction (SI) as a means of managing student behaviour tend to use this strategy for redirecting students to their set task. For example, during an interview, Teacher 'M', who used this strategy most often during the English periods (see Table 13.2), affirmed: 'I find this approach useful for reminding students of their task. I used this a lot since your initial presence probably affected their attention somewhat, and they are still very excited from their trip [to Disneyland].'

Teacher 'H' (the teacher of maths) gave a similar explanation for the use of SI. She said: 'I find that gentle reminders and clarifications help to keep students on their working path.' The use of mild punishment (MP) for controlling student behaviour was perceived by teachers as a strategy that brought quick positive results. In justifying her use of this approach during the music lessons, Teacher 'X', who usually used simply a verbal reprimand coupled with direction to get on-task, declared: 'This is what I know . . . that works.' The teacher of history, Teacher 'D', expressed similar sentiments: 'Students understand what this signal [the use of a verbal reprimand in a slightly raised voice] means and therefore respond to it positively.'

Braswell and Bloomquist (1991) support the views expressed by these teachers. They contend that although such approaches vary in their comprehensiveness and/or intensity, they have been found to produce at least moderate, positive change in children with ADHD. They maintain that such an approach seems to work as children with ADHD require more frequent and immediate feedback about the acceptability of their behaviour. This latter point is also supported by Fowler (1992).

The use of grouping (GRP) as a teacher strategy for managing student behaviour was thought to minimize distractions while allowing for peer assistance. This strategy was commonly justified in pedagogical as well as disciplinary terms. For instance, on speaking about the reason for the use of grouping during mathematics, Teacher 'H' said:

> Grouping helps to minimize distractions by having those who are studious sit next together . . . Those who don't work well in groups can be allowed to work in cubicles.

The teacher for English (Teacher 'M') stated that 'placing students next to their peers helps to foster student understanding of some concepts'.

Researchers also support the use of GRP as a strategy for managing students with ADHD. For example, DuPaul and Stoner (1994: 130) advocate the use of small groups in the form of peer tutoring as 'a good example of an effective instructional strategy' that has gathered powerful empirical support'. Their review of research in the area confirms its effectiveness in subjects like maths and English as a means of improving students' on-task behaviour, activity level and academic performance.

The explanation given by teachers for the use of time out (TO) as a strategy in student behaviour control seems to be that it helps to reduce pupil aggression and the likelihood of pupil–teacher confrontations, while expressing strong disapproval of disruptive acts. Two teachers (maths and English) each used this approach once. English teacher 'M' reported:

> he [a pupil] gets overly wound up and uses these expletives which are totally inappropriate . . . He knows that this is just unacceptable.

Teacher 'H' affirmed:

> I'll never argue with them. I use time out. I have them use the room. I have them back when they are ready to work.

Researchers (for example, Hinshaw, 1994) recommend the use of time out. DuPaul and Stoner (1994) also agree that the strategy should be applied 'swiftly, following a rule infraction'; that a short period of calm, non-disruptive behaviour should be required before its termination and that the child should express a willingness to correct, amend or compensate for the misbehaviour. This seems to accord with the teachers' views. Moreover, Fowler (1992) support the use of the approach for reducing aggression. The teachers of English and maths were the only teachers who made explicit use of 'pedagogical strategies'. Teachers were able to explain that the approach helped to provide students with a consistent structure, clarify issues that were confusing or remind students of their tasks. Teacher 'M' reported:

> As a teacher, I try to be firm, fair and consistent. But students should be made responsible for their behaviour. Medication only works with the help of structure.

Teacher 'H' said:

> Structuring and consistency is key for using any of the strategies . . . Students have poor memory therefore understanding principles is key . . . theoretical explanations must be reinforced by principles that guide understanding and practise from actual work. The additional explanations help to get students back on task.

Explanations given by DuPaul and Stoner (1994) and Cooper and Ideus (1996) of the components that constituted the formulation of the term 'pedagogical strategy' seem to support the reasons teachers gave for its use. The approach is also endorsed by Train (1996).

All teachers used ignoring (I) in response to student misbehaviour. However, they gave different explanations for using it. For instance, Teacher 'X' (music), seemingly used it as a pedagogical aid for the encouragement of desirable forms of classroom engagement: 'I guess I used this approach since the students did not seem to enjoy other musical styles other than those from Britain and the US and this seemingly was causing the distractions.'

Teacher 'D' reported using it for the extinction of unwanted behaviour:

> Very often too much attention helps to reinforce student negative behaviours. When behaviours are not too serious, providing eye contact is made, they can be ignored. Most of the time they tend to stop.

Though in this case the use of eye contact makes the strategy appear to be more akin to 'signal interference' (Kounin, 1997), which refers to the use of a sign or gesture intended to re-engage the student.

Teacher 'H' justified her ignoring of some disruptive acts thus:

> sometimes students need to see the teacher as more than a disciplinary figure.

Teacher 'M' seemed to use ignoring for negative reinforcement. She said:

> students like to know that teachers react to what they do . . . they enjoy feedback. Withholding feedback seems to help them to think about what they did.

Many researchers support the use of ignoring (for example, Fowler et al., 1992; DuPaul and Stoner, 1994; Taylor, 1996) but only for reasons expressed by Teachers 'D' and 'M' – as a form of negative reinforcement.

As was mentioned before, the use of positive reinforcement (PR) and seating arrangement (SA) were organized in advance as measures to prevent student misbehaviour. The use of these strategies during the observation period was therefore minimal but the teachers who used them agreed that SA helps with minimizing distractions. This view is endorsed by Hallowell and Ratey (1994) who recommend that many arrangements be tried.

How effective do teachers perceive these strategies as in managing students' behaviour?

From the contextualized teacher interviews it was discovered that all teachers thought that the approaches they used for managing student behaviour were very effective. However, an attempt was made to ascertain whether teachers' perceptions matched their classroom practice. In order to do this, a comparison of teachers' perceptions of the effectiveness of their strategies with respect to the behavioural outcome and the performance of students had to be made. Table 13.3 presents the behavioural outcome of the total number of teacher strategies used over the observation period.

From the graph it can be seen that most negative student behaviours of inattention, hyperactivity and impulsivity were extinguished by the teacher approaches used. Less than a quarter of these negative behaviours continued or intensified following teacher responses. This pictorial presentation of the student behavioural outcome as a result of teacher strategies seems to support teachers' perception that their strategies were effective. Clearly (like Hinshaw, 1994; Miller, 1996) the most desirable outcomes of educational interventions are best judged in terms of academic achievement and not simply in terms of reductions in classroom disruption. It is difficult to ascertain academic outcomes from observation alone, but it is possible to ascertain from observation the extent to which individuals appear to be complying with task demands, which is an issue of particular significance to the study of students with ADHD, as rule compliance appears to be a major problem for such students. Table 13.3 below presents the percentage frequency of student performance for the total teacher strategies used in terms of on-task and off-task behaviour.

Table 13.3: The frequency of student behaviour for the four subjects (N = 282)

Subjects	Strategies*	Percentage on-task	Percentage off-task
Maths	57	19	1
English	120	41	2
History	78	26	2
Music	27	7	3
Average	71	23	2

* Number of teacher interventions.

From Table 13.3 it can be observed that most strategies used by teachers in response to student misbehaviour resulted in students going back 'on-task'. The highest frequency percentage of student on-task performance was recorded for English lessons (41%) whereas the least was recorded for music (7%), although it must be emphasized that the measures of on- and off-task behaviour were associated directly with the level of deviant behaviour observed in each subject area. However, since deviant behaviour, by definition, is directly equated with off-task behaviour, the fact that off-task behaviour across the four subject areas is roughly equivalent indicates that the four teachers were equally successful in promoting on-task behaviour, though some had to work harder than others to achieve this through the use of remedial strategies. Overall, an average frequency of 23% for student on-task performance was recorded, as opposed to 2% for off-task behaviour. This evidence seems to support individual teachers' perceptions that the strategies they used for managing student behaviours were effective, and to suggest, in addition, that as individuals in a group of teachers they were generally equally effective.

Medication

The teacher strategies were almost always used in conjunction with medication, with 14 of the 15 students studied being prescribed medication, mostly in the form of the psychostimulant methylphenidate (Ritalin). This illustrates the point that appropriately prescribed medication does not in itself control students' behaviour, but rather enables compliance within an appropriately structured environment (Pelham and Murphy, 1986). The fact that these students are responsive to teachers' behavioural strategies in terms of modifying their off-task behaviour suggests that they might be equally susceptible to reinforcers for their negative behaviour. This illustrates the crucial importance of appropriate educational strategies in meeting the needs of students with ADHD.

Summary and conclusion

Teacher approaches to behaviours associated with ADHD

Teachers use a variety of approaches in response to the misbehaviour of students with ADHD. Among the teacher approaches used are positive reinforcement, student instruction, mild reprimand, seating arrangement, grouping, pedagogical strategies, time out and ignoring. Different subject teachers differed in the frequency of behavioural problems they experience and, as a consequence, in the frequency and type of strategies that they used. Positive reinforcement and seating arrangement strategies were organized in advance as preventative strategies. The lowest frequency of misbehaviour occurred during the music lessons. This teacher therefore used the least number of strategies for managing students' behaviour. Mild punishment was the teacher strategy most used by the four teachers overall. The teacher of history used mild punishment more than the other subject teachers. There appears to be a high level of consistency between what teachers say and what they do in response to student misbehaviour. That is, teachers' perceptions (out of class context) and their in-class practice, with respect to strategy use, seem to agree. Inattention, hyperactivity and impulsivity occurred at irregular levels across the four progressive periods observed. Increases in time (or subject periods) did not result in increases in the level of student misbehaviour. The level of student misbehaviour seemed to vary with individual subject teachers, antecedents, subject content and learning activities. There is a possible association between lesson content and the level of behavioural problems, which has important consequences for the design and planning of learning environments.

Why do teachers employ these strategies? Teachers had a variety of reasons for their choice of strategies. Most of these explanations appeared to be supported by research and/or theory. Teachers' explanations for their choice of strategies were as follows. They tend to use: student instruction (SI) as a means of redirecting students to their set task; mild punishment (MP) because it brought quick positive results in that negative behaviours were extinguished and students went back on task; grouping (GRP) as it was thought to minimize distractions and enable peer tutoring; time out (TO) as it seemed to reduce pupil aggression and pupil–teacher confrontations, and signalled the teacher's strong disapproval of disruptive acts; pedagogical strategies (PED) to provide students with a consistent structure, to clarify issues of confusion or for reminding students of their set tasks; ignoring (I) as a means of negative reinforcement of students' behaviour and for negative feedback; seating arrangement (SA) was organized in advance of lessons as a means of minimizing student distractions; positive reinforcement (PR), for the most part, as an aspect of a token economy system.

How effective were these strategies in managing students' behaviour? All teachers felt that the strategies they used for managing student misbehaviour were very effective. Teachers' positive perception of the effectiveness of their strategies and the evidence gathered from observing their performance were in agreement. Most teacher strategies resulted in negative behaviours becoming extinguished and students getting back on-task. The study also shows that medication alone is an insufficient treatment to extinguish undesirable behaviour in children with ADHD.

Conclusions

This study demonstrates the successful use of basic behavioural strategies with students with ADHD. The study also illustrates the important point that the use of medication alone is not an adequate treatment for controlling the symptoms of ADHD or for promoting the educational engagement of students with ADHD, although it may create circumstances in which students are more responsive to behavioural strategies and effective teaching. This is not a novel finding. Experts such as Barkley (1990) and Hinshaw (1994) have asserted this insight forcefully, by emphasizing the need for medication always to be used as a part of a multi-modal treatment programme that will always involve educational interventions where school students are concerned. Yet, there remains a popular misconception that ADHD is a simple biological condition that is treated solely through the use of stimulant medication (Rose, 1997). As Chapter 14 of this book indicates, there are ADHD sufferers who experience this same mistaken perception.

With regard to the kinds of strategies that teachers employed, whereas a wide range of strategies were used, there seems to be a disproportionate use of what might be termed the 'negative' strategy of 'mild punishment'. For three of the four teachers mild punishment was the single most commonly used strategy (maths: 42% of recorded interventions; history: 67%; music: 59%). The English teacher was the only teacher who used other strategies more frequently than mild punishment (mild punishment was used in 23% of recorded interventions; student instruction was used in 29% of cases and ignoring was used in 3% of cases). Interestingly, although the English class was the site of the greatest number of recorded incidents of disruptive behaviour (40% of the total number of interventions observed, N = 307) (see Table 13.1), it is also, however, the site of the second lowest percentage of off-task behaviours (see Table 13.3). This could be taken to indicate that the English teacher's use of remedial behavioural strategies is at least as effective in promoting on-task behaviour as that of the other teachers. Other evidence points to the possibility that the higher level of disruptive behaviours in this subject area might be related to antecedent issues.

We can speculate that the greater level of behavioural disturbances in the English lessons might be related to the nature of the lesson subject matter, which the students experience as being less congenial than that of other subjects. This might be due to the fact that there is often a strong relationship between ADHD and literacy difficulties of one kind or another (Hinshaw, 1994). If this is so, then the teacher's achievement in maintaining a level of on-task behaviour is impressive, because it indicates this teacher's success in controlling a greater tendency among the class to go off-task than the other teachers experience. The use of non-punitive approaches in these circumstances is likely to be a significant factor (Wheldall and Glynn, 1989), as it will be necessary to compensate for the aversive nature of the subject content by causing it to be associated with positive outcomes in the form of teacher support and positive reinforcement. The high level of the use of the student instruction strategy would support this hypothesis, by suggesting that the students experience a higher level of difficulty in these lessons than in the other lessons.

A tentative conclusion from this study is that lessons and tasks that involved reflective and analytical skills were sites of considerably greater levels of dysfunctional behaviour than those involving sensory and kinaesthetic skills. We might also observe that this is consistent with existing theory relating ADHD and cognitive style (Cooper and Ideus, 1996). However, having said this, it is important to note that the small scale of the current study does not allow us to differentiate between the effects of the subject on student behaviour and the effects of the differences between individual teachers' professional skills and personal characteristics.

Whether or not these speculations have any substance in relation to the current study setting remains at the level of informed speculation. In the meantime we must return to the issue of the effectiveness of behavioural methods with students with ADHD. An important point to make here is that whereas behavioural methods are widely understood within the teaching professions of the USA and the UK (Ayers et al., 1996; Goldstein and Goldstein, 1990), it would seem that there is still powerful evidence to support the view that these approaches are not widely practised (or practised effectively). Evidence from studies of the correlates of behavioural problems in schools tends to indicate that students who are most in need of positive reinforcement for pro-school and pro-educational behaviour are inclined to be met with punitive sanctions culminating, to an increasing extent, in the ultimate sanction of exclusion from school (Castle and Parsons, 1997; Hayden, 1997). This is not to say that there are not many schools where good behavioural management is practised. What can be said is that the presence of such good practice cannot be taken for granted. The point being made here is that the absence or presence of such good practice should be established before a student can be confidently diagnosed as having ADHD. Where such practice is not in place it should be introduced before concluding that the student's behaviour arises as a consequence of an internal disorder. Even where the individual is found to have ADHD it is clearly appropriate to explore ways in which the educational environment can be made more effective before medication is applied. Given that ADHD is often defined as a chronic and debilitating problem with meeting behavioural expectations (Barkley, 1990; Hinshaw, 1994), it is surely a matter of simple logic to ensure that appropriate expectations and compliance strategies are in place as a starting point of the assessment process.

A similar point needs to be made in relation to the learning environment. By 'learning environment' we refer not only the physical environment in which the student is required to operate, but also issues of lesson content, pedagogical style and learning tasks. It is clear from existing research and scholarship that the performance of students with ADHD is likely to be affected in specific ways by variations in these factors. As was noted, it is possible that these might have been factors to account for the different levels of disruptive behaviour across the different subject environments. Clearly, it is possible that the severity of the ADHD symptoms might be exacerbated by inappropriate learning environments that exploit the weaknesses of students with ADHD. A further starting point for the assessment/diagnostic process should therefore be an evaluation of the learning environment.

References

American Psychiatric Association (1994) Diagnostic and Statistical Manual of Mental Disorders (4 edn). Washington DC: APA.

Ayers H, Clarke D, Ross A (1996) Assessing Individual Needs – A Practical Approach (2 edn) London: David Fulton.

Bandura A (1969) Principle of Behaviour Modification. New York: Holt, Rinehart & Winston.

Barkley R (1990) Attention Deficit Hyperactivity Disorder: A Handbook of Diagnosis and Treatment. New York: Guilford.

Barkley R (1995) Taking Charge of ADHD – The Complete Authoritative Guide for Parents. New York: Guilford.

Braswell L, Bloomquist ML (1991) Cognitive-Behavioural Therapy with ADHD Children. New York: Guilford.

Castle F, Parsons C (1997) Disruptive behaviour and exclusion from school. Emotional and Behavioural Difficulties 2(3): 4–11.

Cooper P, Ideus K (1996) Attention Deficit/Hyperactivity Disorder: A Practical Guide for Teachers. London: David Fulton

Crammond B (1994) The relationship between ADHD and creativity. Paper presented at the Annual Meeting of the American Educational Research Association, New Orleans.

Department for Education and Employment (1997) Excellence For All Children: Meeting Special Educational Needs. London: The Stationery Office.

Du Paul GJ, Stoner G (1994) ADHD in the Schools: Assessment and Intervention Strategies. New York: Guilford.

Fowler M (1992) Educators Manual – Attention Deficit Disorders. Virginia: CHADD.

Goldstein S, Goldstein M (1990) Managing Attention Disorders in Children – A Guide for Practitioners. New York: Wiley.

Hallowell EM, Ratey JJ (1994) Driven to Distraction – Recognising and Coping with Attention Deficit Disorder from Childhood through Adulthood. New York: Touchstone.

Hayden C (1997) Exclusion from primary school: children in need and children with special educational need. Emotional and Behavioural Difficulties 2(3): 36–44.

Hinshaw SP (1994) Attention Deficits and Hyperactivity in Children. London and New York: Sage.

Kounin J (1997) Discipline and Group Management in Classrooms. Huntington NY: Robert E Krieger.

Miller, A (1996) Pupil Behaviour and Teacher Culture. London: Cassell.

Pelham WE, Murphy HA (1986) Attention deficit and conduct disorders. In M Hersen (ed.) Pharmacological and Behavioural Treatment: An Integrative Approach. New York: Wiley.

Pellegrini AD, Davis-Huberty T, Jones I (1995) The effects of recess timing on children's playground and classroom behaviours. American Educational Research Journal 32(4): 845–64.

Pellegrini AD, Landers-Pott M (1996) Children, classroom context and activity and attention to tasks. Journal of Emotional and Behavioural Difficulties 1(3): 29–35.

Rose S (1997) Lifelines: Biology, Freedom and Determinism. London: Allen Lane/Penguin.

Skinner BF (1953) Science and Human Behaviour. New York: Macmillan.

Taylor, E (1996) The 1996 David Wills Memorial Lecture: attention deficit/hyperactivity at school and home: a developmental psychopathological approach. Emotional and Behavioural Difficulties 1(3): 3–10.

Train A (1996) ADHD: How to Deal with Difficult Children. London: Souvenir Press.

Wheldall K, Glynn T (1989) Effective Classroom Learning. Oxford: Blackwell.

Zentall, SS (1993) Research on the educational implications of attention deficit hyperactivity disorder. Exceptional Children 60(2): 143–53.

Chapter 14
ADHD from the Inside: An Empirical Study of Young People's Perceptions of the Experience of ADHD

PAUL COOPER AND TREVOR SHEA

Introduction: in search of the missing voice in the ADHD debate

Objections to the concept of ADHD include:

- it individualizes behavioural problems and, therefore, underplays the importance of the educational and broader social environment in causing and remedying these problems (Slee, 1995);
- the use of medication in the treatment of ADHD serves a social control function by keeping potentially disruptive and troublesome individuals docile (Slee, 1995; O'Brien, 1996);
- it allows both bearers of the label and their carers to abdicate from their responsibility to take charge of the problems associated with ADHD by allowing them to blame the condition on causes that are outside their sphere of influence (Prior, 1997).

These are powerful criticisms that cannot be ignored or easily dismissed by persons concerned with young people who may be diagnosed with the condition. They amount to a fairly widely held view that, by its very nature, the ADHD concept is in itself debilitating and thus harmful. That is, regardless of the characteristic behavioural problems of hyperactivity, impulsiveness and/or inattentiveness that are associated with the ADHD diagnosis, the diagnostic label itself creates particular problems for individuals who bear it, is undesirable and, therefore, to be avoided.

These criticisms are often made in the context of arguments about the need to protect children and young people from the negative consequences of pathological labels. It is also true to say, however, that these criticisms are made almost always without any direct reference to empirical evidence for these presumed effects of the ADHD diagnosis. They are also always made without any direct reference to the first-hand accounts of individuals who bear the diagnosis. This last point is one of particular concern when considered in the light of recent and current thinking about the rights of children and young people and the importance of their unique perspective on the circumstances of their lives.

There are now strong moral, legal and pragmatic reasons for listening to 'the voice of the child' (see Cooper, 1993a; Lloyd-Smith and Dwyfor-Davies, 1995; Davie et al., 1996) which can be briefly summarized in the following terms.

- Children and young people are increasingly seen as representing a disenfranchised group in society. It was not until the 1989 Children Act in the UK that children and young persons were granted a series of specific 'rights' and, therefore, direct protection under the law. In particular, this legislation placed a duty on the carers for children under the care of local authorities to consult the children on matters affecting their care and placement, and to pay heed to their wishes and preferences in making decisions affecting them. This development is echoed in legislation affecting children with special educational needs in the UK. The non-statutory SEN Code of Practice (DFE, 1994: para. 2.35) stresses the principle that 'children have a right to be heard. They should be encouraged to participate in decision-making about provision to meet their special educational needs'.
- Children and young people are increasingly seen as 'expert witnesses' who may have valuable insights to offer that might be useful to those responsible for delivering and developing services for children and young people, such as teachers in schools (Cooper, 1993b; Davie et al., 1996).

In addition to these major contemporary concerns it should also be stressed that there is a powerful tradition of broadly humanistic educational practice with children and young people who experience EBD that stresses the importance of the child's/young person's voice to the therapeutic process. Workers and carers such as David Wills, George Lyward, AS Neill and Bruno Bettelheim stressed the importance of listening to the children and young people in their care and were very concerned to stress the need for mutual respect between carer/educator/therapist and client (Bridgeland, 1971; Laslett, 1999). An important outcome of this mutual respect is the growth of a sense of self-worth and, along with this, a sense of competence and a willingness to engage positively with the challenges that enable Emotional and Behavioural Difficulties (EBDs) to be overcome.

It is also interesting to note the way in which similar concerns are reflected in developments in cognitive theories of learning, such as those proposed by Lev Vygotsky (1978) and Jerome Bruner (Bruner and Haste, 1987). Their theories place considerable stress on the active role of the learner in the teaching–learning process, not only at the cognitive level but also at the social level. These sociocultural theories of learning increasingly point us towards a view of effective teaching and learning environments as places where students are encouraged to bring their existing individual and idiosyncratic knowledge and understandings to bear on learning tasks (Cooper and McIntyre, 1996). This in turn requires forms of social relationships that place a higher status on the voice and intentions of students than is traditionally the case in teaching establishments that have adhered to outdated teaching and learning theories that have relied on 'transmission'–'reception' metaphors (e.g. Hirst, 1974).

All of this preamble amounts to a powerful case for placing the voice of children and young people at the centre of debates about their education and treatment (in all of the meanings of this word). They are invaluable sources of information about the issues in which we are interested and they perform an active role in shaping the social realities that surrounding issues of concern to us. This view has been embraced by special educational researchers, particularly in the UK (see for example, Cooper, 1993a, b; Lloyd-Smith and Dwyfor-Davies, 1995; Bowers, 1997; Norwich, 1997). The rest of this chapter is devoted to what we believe to be (at the time of writing) the first published empirical study of the perceptions and attitudes of children with ADHD to their condition, its effects and their 'treatment'.

Study: participants and methodology

The current chapter provides an account of a study that was carried out with 16 young people attending a day special school for students with learning and behavioural problems. All of the students in the study were formally diagnosed as having ADHD. There were ten boys and six girls. Five students (four boys and one girl) were in the 13–16 age (upper schools) range; the remaining 11 were in the 11–13 (middle school) age range.

The school catered for an international clientele of some 48 students, offering twin tracks of GCSE and American High School Diploma routes to upper school students. The students come from a variety of international backgrounds including: the USA, Canada, Germany and the UK. The average class size was 12 students. The school was also a private school, with the parents of children being responsible for tuition fees. These factors make the group of students and their circumstances untypical of the UK context, but there are good reasons for focusing on this group. First, the school concerned has a relatively long history, beginning in the early 1980s, of working with children with the ADHD diagnosis in the UK context. Second, the school operates a rigorous and uniform multi-modal assessment process that applies to all students. The same paediatrician, who has long experience of working with the

ADHD diagnosis, has assessed all of the students in this group. The disadvantage of unrepresentativeness is, therefore, balanced by the claim that these students, having been diagnosed by the same physican and having undergone a uniform assessment process, are likely to bear reliable diagnoses.

The status of the current study is that of a preliminary investigation, which is currently being developed in a larger-scale study in mainstream schools in the UK and Canada. The findings of the preliminary study are of urgent significance to current debates about the possible nature and effects of the experience of bearing the ADHD diagnosis. This urgency is made all the more compelling by the current absence of data of this kind. It should by stressed, however, that for reasons outlined above, the generalizability of the current findings cannot be assumed.

The study was set up in order to provide answers to the following questions:

- What are students' perceptions of the effects of the ADHD symptoms on their lives?
- How do students construe the ADHD diagnostic label and its effects on their lives?
- What are students' views of and attitudes towards treatment and management approaches that are associated with ADHD (including medication) and how do they construe the purposes and effectiveness of these interventions?

The method of data gathering was that of one-to-one informant-style interviewing (Powney and Watts, 1987). Central to this approach is the emphasis on the interviewee's individual manner of recalling and construing issues and events of concern. The interviewer's role in this process is to facilitate and gently guide the focus of the interviewee's thinking through the use of a loose interview structure, which is experienced by interviewer and interviewee as a conversation rather than an interrogation. To facilitate this the interviewer enters the interview with a mental plan of the areas that are to be covered in the interview, but avoids the use of pre-formed questions. It is suggested that this approach makes for greater 'authenticity' of interviewee response than the more traditional 'respondent' style of interviewing (whereby an unchanging schedule of questions is applied to different interviewees) and is, therefore, better suited to exploratory research of the type intended here. For a fuller account of this methodological approach see Cooper (1993c) and Cooper and McIntyre (1996).

In this study all the students were interviewed twice, with a period of several days between the first and second interviews. Each interview lasted for between 30 and 45 minutes.

Findings: the experience of ADHD

Behaviours associated with ADHD

Examination of the students' records revealed that, as a group, they represented the different subtypes of ADHD, with some being diagnosed with the 'combined type', others with the mainly hyperactive-impulsive subtype and others, often the girls, being diagnosed with the mainly inattentive type. There was also a smattering of co-morbid conditions, including dyslexia. What was clear from all the interviews was that all the students claimed to have experienced some form of what Wakefield (1992) terms 'harmful dysfunction' in behavioural terms. That is, patterns of behaviour that are associated with significant social and or educational difficulties.

It is interesting to note the way in which they often volunteer accounts of such behaviours without being prompted by the interviewer to talk about their behavioural history. The most common stimulus for these responses is a question about how they came to be students at their current school. This suggests that for one reason or another these behaviours are deemed by them to be significant aspects of their personal histories and, possibly, therefore, important features in their personal constructions of their own identities.

Being disruptive

A strong theme among some of the boys who are deemed hyperactive is a tendency towards loudness and anger, which are both difficult to control:

> [I used to] talk loud in class, shout, get angry, talk with my friends –
> there's many things [. . .] I got kicked out of school. (Liam, 14)

James (14) describes his own sense of being out of control:

> [. . .] I don't think I had any control, because when I got into a temper I
> could try and talk not loud, but then I thought, 'Ughhhh!' And I would
> get all stressed out.
>
> [. . .]
>
> [. . .] sometimes at home [. . .] I would like – I wouldn't mean it – but
> sometimes I would just like shout. You know, like I would think people
> were shouting, but they're not. And when I was talking, it would sound
> like I was talking really loud. [. . .] and sometimes I wouldn't notice I was
> talking really loud [. . .]; my mom would say: 'you're shouting!' And I
> would say, 'no I'm not!'

James also refers to what appear to be communication and literacy difficulties that created additional problems for him in terms of conflict and a sense of incompetence:

[. . .] sometimes at the end of school it would be quite difficult, 'cause like they would have homework out on the board. Then they would say to me an' Daniel (this boy), 'write it out!' And it would take us quite a while to write the thing out. And we never used to do any homework. I used to say, 'I can't do this!' And then he [the teacher] used to go: 'well you go and write it out now!' And in the end I just didn't do it. [. . .] if I can't learn at school, how am I supposed to do homework? You know!

In another anecdote James describes his experience of difficulties with oral communication:

[. . .] Normally I talk really fast sometimes. [...] when I used to talk fast and I was thinking about something, I forgot [what I was talking about]! It would be hard to explain what you were talking about. Yeah?

[. . .]

And my mum would say, 'what are you talking about?' And I would go: 'I just told you!' And I would say it again. And she wouldn't understand sometimes.

He goes on to describe a specific incident in which he became frustrated and angry at his apparent inability to express himself as clearly as he would wish:

[. . .] sometimes I would try and explain something, but I couldn't explain where it was. Like, you know Crawford? [. . .] Well, it's the other side of Wilmington Castle, and my brother goes to the pub there sometimes. And I said to my mother: 'what's over the other side of Wilmington Castle?' And she said: 'Frampton.' And I said, 'No, it's not Frampton! You've got it wrong.' And I couldn't think of 'The Wilmington Arms'. And I was just like getting quite a temper. And I was saying: 'You're wrong! You're wrong!' I wouldn't believe her. And she was saying that's the only place there. But I couldn't think of it! [. . .] But then when I went into a temper, I would sometimes shout. It's hard to control!

The sense of being prone to frustration and anger is a strong theme throughout the transcripts, particularly among boys who are considered to be hyperactive-impulsive.

Impulsive oppositionality

Oppositionality figures in several accounts, with many students describing a tendency to be persistently argumentative with teachers (e.g. James, Liam, Herbert, Joan). Sometimes this is associated with impulsiveness:

Sometimes I can't help saying what I feel! (Herbert, 13)

[. . .] I never think. 'Cause like, before I do something. Sometimes [it] happens – If I'm like thinking: 'if I do this, I'm going to get into trouble'. But I never normally do that. I'll do it, and [. . .] until afterwards, it's OK. So I do something bad and afterwards I realise that I've done something bad, and that I shouldn't have done it. (Jeff, 12)

Equally often oppositionality towards and conflict with peers is also mentioned. In Ian's (13) case, as with many other of the students, this problem is combined with other school problems:

I never did my homework at that school, and I got in a whole bunch of fights with some kids. And, they didn't let me back [to the school he attended previously].

For Ian this was all part of a pattern that began quite early in his child-hood:

Ian: Well [at first] I was always good at home, and at school. When I got up to first grade things started to change. I was kind of good in school. And I built up a lot of steam at school and I would take it out at home – like on my mom, my sister or my dad. Mostly my mom or my sister. And in the end it started to change. I would be good at home, and I would take my steam out at school. That's when I started getting into fights and stuff.

[. . .]

I have a bad temper. If someone starts me off and they go a little too far, I have a go at them.

TS: OK. So it doesn't take much to set you off?

Ian: No.

Again, where oppositionality and aggression are mentioned they are often talked about in ways that indicate a sense of lack of self-control. Ian believes that he becomes involved in conflict situations with little provocation, and that it is his need to 'let off steam' that underpins this, but he has no power over this need. Sometimes this lack of self-control is described in more dramatic and graphic terms, as Liam illustrates:

I get very angry easily. And I get so angry I can knock somebody's head off. It's like – that's how I got kicked out of school [. . .] Ummm. Before I got kicked out of school – we go on the bus, you know [to] [. . .] the sports place, you know. Ummm, this boy called Paul – you know, Paul. [. . .] we're just going on the bus and my head was so whizzz, buzzz. Just like that [motions around his head]. My head was so banged!

[...]

I was totally, like, I could not stand it! I got so angry!

[...]

So I turned around. He [Paul] thought I was going to hit him. He grabbed my hand. And I got so angry, I went toyoyoy! in the middle of his head here [gestures to forehead and gives a head-butting gesture].

Both Ian and Liam illustrate ways in which many of the students in this study describe their behavioural outbursts essentially as involuntary reactions to internal stressors. In Ian's case the stressor is seen as a build-up of energy in the form of 'steam'. For Liam it is a buzzing in his head. This can be related to instances when students speak of their tendency to fidget and other physical 'tics' (i.e. repetitive, involuntary physical movements), such as finger tapping, which they believe irritate others, and in some cases find irritating themselves.

Dangerousness

Others describe the ways in which their impulsive behaviour not only cause them social difficulties but, sometimes, put them in physical danger:

I used to be mad!

[. . .]

I just used to do stupid things.

[. . .]

I used to fight a lot and stuff. Being rude to teachers and all that. Doing stupid things like trying to jump off ten foot walls and stuff. That sort of thing. Ugh! I remember I went on the train tracks once! Things like that!

[. . .]

The trains were running at the time. They weren't actually there at the time. It's sort of electric as well. And the trains go about 70 miles an hour.

[. . .]

Someone threw my skateboard on the railway tracks and that's why I went over. (Joe, 14)

Joan (13) describes two incidents from her early childhood that she sees as significant, both of which seem to encapsulate qualities of impulsivity and dangerousness:

> One time when I was living in a bungalow, and we had a fire in the fireplace, [I remember] taking the hot ashes out of the fireplace and [I] put them in the garage on paper. Two minutes later: fire!

> [. . .]

> I remember my mother telling me: my dad was in the toilet; I was trying to play horsey on Homer's [a pet dog] back, and I ripped out two big bundles of fur. And he turned round, and he snapped at me, right here [just below one eye].

> [. . .]

> I ripped out bundles of his fur. It was an accident – he didn't mean to hurt me, 'cause he was really a lovely dog.

Interestingly, she seems more concerned to defend Homer's behaviour than her own: the dog scars her accidentally, and it is her behaviour that is the cause of the problem.

Concentration problems

Problems of concentration are also commonly referred to. Hope (13) describes a common scenario that illustrates the way in which distractibility can lead to interpersonal conflict. In her case this is in the family situation:

> [. . .] when my mom asks me to do stuff, like say empty the dishwasher. And then I would get distracted or something. And I wouldn't do the dishwasher, because I would forget about it. And then she would come and yell at me because I didn't do it.

Christian (16) describes the effect of this problem in the school setting:

> I've always had a problem with concentration and attention. [. . .] Well, sometimes in class, I wouldn't be able to concentrate. And I'd be talking to other people. And I wouldn't be concentrating on my work. And part of that was because I was at a young age. And I've matured a lot since then. I've actually got much much better. In the last year and a half. But there's always that little concentration thing, of me not being able to concentrate. And me not being able to settle down and get on with a piece of work. Which I feel is a drawback.

Christian goes on to describe his particular difficulty with a piece of English work that he is attempting to complete at the time of the interview. There is a hint of frustration here that echoes the more overt feelings of James:

> I've had a hard time starting that [essay on *The Merchant of Venice*]. And it's not because I don't want to do it; it's because I find it hard to concentrate on it.

Twelve-year-old Kate gives a similar account. It is interesting, however, to note that she sees her attention problems as being discovered by a third party, unlike Christian, who implies that he discovered his problems for himself:

> They found that I had difficulties paying attention in my old school. I always used to talk to my friend. I used to never pay attention.

> [. . .]

> Some of my friends are hyper; some have difficulty in reading and spelling. But I don't have those. I have difficulty with paying attention.

Academic issues

Academic disappointment is a common theme throughout the transcripts. Many students refer to literacy problems, and there are several references to 'dyslexia' as a problem that has inhibited educational progress. Commonly students express a sense of failure and sometimes bewilderment at their failure to master basic educational skills, such as reading.

On the other hand there are students who claim to have literacy problems but also claim to possess skills in other subject areas, particularly art. One student, Christian (16), who claims to have 'concentration problems' that are a 'drawback' (see above) also provides information that suggests that he may be unusually gifted in English:

> I've never had any problems in English [. . .]. I've always been told that I'm very, very good in English, and last year I started writing a book of my own. I only got to the – it's supposed to be ten chapters – but I only got to the, you know, sixth one.

> [. . .]

> It's waiting to be re-erected when I have more time. My mother actually took it to a friend of hers, who is a publisher, and she said it was very, very good. They actually published part of the book in a WH Smith young writers' competition.

[. . .]

[. . .] which made me feel good about it. I've always been a very, very keen writer. And I always write stories. [. . .] My short stories – actually, I think I've done [pauses for thought] three romances – they would both be about 100 to 150 pages each. So, you know, three romances, two adventure ones. Most of my ones have been thrillers.

Interestingly, Christian links this apparently not inconsiderable gift with what he has earlier described as one of his major dysfunctions: his distractibility:

[. . .] a lot of my writing comes straight from my head. People think – people say, I have a gift, because a lot of the time – that's another reason why I don't concentrate, because I'm always thinking about things.

[. . .]

[. . .] it's strange, but I think about writing these life and death situations. There was one boy with leukaemia, and he went to America actually. And he tried to raise money to get an operation. He raised this money, and there was another plot. Because something else had happened. I can remember somebody else was dying, and he actually gave the money to this other person, instead of having it for his own operation.

[. . .]

It's just a tale of how he stayed around his friends, and how his friends reacted to him. And how he eventually died. But I never actually got to write it. It's up here [indicates head] and there's a lot more of them up here.

[. . .]

I'm always thinking about stories – one of my major distractions is – I'll get distracted and I always think about, like, stories.

[. . .]

[. . .] for some reason it's either something to do with what I'm writing, or it's just like what's popped into my head, and I, I just imagine these situations. And I make them into stories in my head. So that is a problem that I have.

Christian's distractibility interferes with his engagement in lessons, and this remains 'a problem' and source of dissatisfaction in spite of its apparent positive side.

The majority of students do not consider themselves to be gifted in the way that Christian clearly does. Janine's (13) self-deprecating comment on her academic shortcomings is typical:

> I'm always the type of person who struggles, 'cause that's just me.

This succinct self-dismissal is indicative of the low self-esteem that many of these students appear to experience in relation to beliefs they hold about their lack of academic ability.

Commentary on harmful dysfunction

Clearly, the accounts of these youngsters reflect many of the behavioural problems that are described in the DSM (American Psychiatric Association, 1994) diagnostic criteria for ADHD. For these youngsters the traits of inattentiveness, impulsiveness and hyperactivity are significant aspects of their personal histories, which in turn are associated with negative social and educational experiences. However, it is also important to consider, social contexts in which these accounts are rooted. Accounts of early childhood experiences, such as Joan's account of her experience playing 'horsey' with her dog, are often presented in ways that indicate that personal recollection is mixed with the accounts of other people such as parents. Many of these young people have grown up, it would seem, in family and school circumstances in which their behaviour has been a source of concern and comment to parents and other adults. It is impossible for us, on the basis of data such as this, to assess the effects of adults' influence on the ways in which these young people see themselves and their 'problems'. What we can assert with some confidence is that these young people express concern about what they perceive to be their attentional and behavioural shortcomings. Furthermore, they express an almost palpable sense of disappointment and negative self-image in relation to their problems. This is illustrated most vividly by Christian's account of his attention problems. In spite of the fact that his ability to construct stories is celebrated as an unusually well developed 'gift' for someone of his age, he still describes the process by which he mentally rehearses these stories as a problem. On the one hand this might be taken to illustrate the sometimes observed association between ADHD and creativity (Crammond, 1994), but it also points to the destructive power of individual deficit explanations of learning and behavioural problems (Slee, 1995).

What do they think about the diagnosis?

Acceptability and stigma

All of these students showed an awareness of the ADHD diagnosis as a concept. Fourteen out of the 16 considered themselves to be bearers of the diagnosis. Two claimed not to be diagnosed with ADHD. Interestingly, many of the students made a clear distinction between ADHD and ADD, the indication being that ADHD was the more stigmatizing of the two subtypes. Frequent references were made during the interviews to other pupils in the school who were described as being 'hyper'. To be hyper was clearly seen by the majority of these students as being associated with extreme and unpredictable behaviour that makes the bearer of the label unpredictable and disruptive:

> [he's] quite good at it [schoolwork], but he has ADHD problems as well. [. . .] H stands for 'hyper' [. . .]. Well, if he's around a lot of people, if he's in schools and he didn't take his pills, he would be like crazy! (Janine)

> he gets too hyper. [. . .] what shall I say? He's really happy most of the time. I, I don't really know how to describe it, but he gets on my nerves. He just [. . .] does stupid things sometimes. (Herbert, 16)

In contrast ADD is defined in much more benign terms, as Ian (13) illustrates:

> Ian: It just means that I don't pay attention in class, and when things get boring, I just block the teacher out and just ignore 'em. [. . .] [then] I get in trouble. [. . .] It makes learning hard.

> TS: At school?

> Ian: Yeah.

> TS: How about in other places?

> Ian: As long as it's fun and hands on – like watching my dad build things. Like he's an excellent engineer. He's excellent with cars. And I've seen him do things one time, and I can do the exact same thing. I love doing things like that.

Ian's account reflects distinctions that are commonly made by this group of students. ADD is defined in terms of a failure to meet expectations in certain circumstances, whilst ADHD is a more proactive problem in the sense that it involves inappropriate and disruptive behaviour. The association between ADHD and social incompetence seems to make this the more stigmatizing of the two subtypes, so far as these students are concerned. This observation is underlined by the fact that ADHD is spoken of by those who claim to experience it, and is identified as being displayed by others; ADD, on the other hand, is only spoken of by those who claim to experience it.

The students' feelings about the diagnosis are at best neutral and more generally somewhat negative. Prominent among their concerns about the diagnosis (ADHD or ADD) is its potentially stigmatizing effect outside of the school setting. Christian, for example, is wary about telling people outside of the school about his ADD for fear that it might make him the subject of unwanted attention in the form of people 'looking out for me'. His plans for the future involve going to college, where he will 'pretend I am a normal person'. Janine also is very direct about her discomfort with the condition:

> [. . .] I don't like it. [. . .] Well I don't like having it. Well, I was born with it. [. . .] Well most of the time people are born with it, or something evolves in their blood, or something. I don't know. Most of the time people are born with it. [. . .] I think it's just passed from generation to generation. I don't know. I thought that I just lost a couple of screws in the head.

Janine's lost screws metaphor points to the sense of damage and incompleteness that is expressed by many of the students in this group. At another point Janine picks up this theme again, and shows how ADHD is associated with a deep sense of hurt. This quotation relates to her early experience of her behavioural problems and the diagnosis (which she received in first grade):

> TS: [. . .] What does ADD mean for you?

> Janine: That I have a problem with me that really I cannot solve myself [. . .] Sometimes, when I was little, I thought that I was an alien; that I was different from others. Because if I walked down the street everyone's normal and I'm like an alien really; going down the street and everyone's like, really weird.

> TS: What made you think that, do you think?

> Janine: I don't know, because I thought that I was different from the others, and I didn't really care about me because – well like, I cared about me – but I didn't care about me much, because I just thought that I was really different. And that I wasn't the type of person I should be.

This quotation sums up vividly the sense of isolation, helplessness, low self-esteem and stigma that she believes ADHD has caused for her.

It is important to note that Christian's and Janine's accounts suggest that they see the behavioural problems they experience and the ADHD diagnostic label as synonymous. Other students view the behavioural characteristics (symptoms) and the diagnostic label as not necessarily connected to one another. For these students the behavioural symptoms are often experienced as setting them apart from other students, whereas the diagnostic label is viewed as an additional aspect of their individual identities. So while many students are able to speak in detailed terms about what they see as their behavioural difficulties, when it comes to talking about the ADHD diagnosis they are often vague in terms of their understanding of it.

The perceived value of the diagnosis

Some students declare little obvious interest in the diagnosis itself, though even for these students the diagnostic label is often described as providing an explanation for difficulties that they have experienced. Kate, for example, describes the ADD diagnosis as providing her with 'the meaning of why I was having difficulties'. When asked if this explanation was important to her, she replied in the negative, describing her reaction to the explanation in a matter of fact way:

> Kate: [. . .] I hardly ever concentrated in my other school. So I was wondering why I could hardly ever pay attention. And they told me. And I was like: 'oh, that's why'.
>
> TS: Was it important to find that out?
>
> Kate: I don't know. No.

For other students, however, the understandings provided by the diagnosis are of importance. For some this provides a much-needed sense of relief from feelings of guilt:

> Well, I realized that [. . .] whenever I got into trouble at school for talking and stuff, it wasn't my fault; it was because I had ADD [. . .]
>
> I couldn't help being distracted and that I wasn't concentrating properly. (Hope)

The diagnosis is also seen to provide an antidote to another deep-seated fear expressed by some students:

> [I] tell people [I've got ADHD] if they ask me what's wrong with me, and if they tell me I'm mad. [I say] 'I'm not mad. I've just got something wrong with me'. It just makes me a bit active sometimes.

As we have already noted, the ADHD diagnosis is seen as particularly stigmatizing, because of its association with extreme and disruptive behaviour. Joan shows how the diagnostic label is less stigmatizing to her than the 'street' label that might be given to her by peers.

Relief from guilt is also coupled, for many students, with a sense of relief at discovering that the diagnosis has led them to a situation in which practical and effective responses to their problems are implemented. For some students the diagnosis itself is of no interest; the value of the diagnosis is its association with what they see as effective treatment:

TS: Was it important to you to find out about ADHD at all?

Kate: Well, not the diagnosis, just the Ritalin. Finding out that I had to take it helped me.

TS: So do you think it was important to find out why you had trouble concentrating in [previous school].

Kate: I don't think it was important. I just think that it was the reason that I was doing it.

Attitudes to treatment

For all of these students the ADHD diagnosis is seen to go hand in hand with the prescription of medication in the form of methylphenidate ('Ritalin'). Therefore, students' spontaneous accounts of the measures taken to help deal with their ADHD symptoms tend to focus predominantly on the nature and effects of the medication.

There is a widely held consensus about the effects of Ritalin as an aid to concentration in the classroom. This is often portrayed as being associated with improved behaviour and work rate and experience of academic success:

When I'm on it [Ritalin] I work harder, and I'm nicer, but when I'm out of school [and not on Ritalin] I'm sometimes silly, or I act stupid, or do things that I wouldn't really do if I was on the Ritalin.

[. . .]

[When I'm on Ritalin] I have more control over what I say [. . .] (Kate)

When I'm taking Ritalin I'm calmer. I can study more and everything. And when I'm not I really can't concentrate or anything. (Stacy, 13)

I can concentrate better on Ritalin, I think like. I get on with my work more, and I don't talk so much. (James)

It makes me – Ritalin and Pemoline things – they make me think first. I can think for myself anyway, but they make me think even better for myself. (Joe)

These quotations reflect the generally positive attitude towards medication expressed by many of the students', welcoming of its effect in enabling them to concentrate more effectively, to be less distractible and to be generally calmer. This generally positive view, however, is only one aspect of a complex pattern of attitudes towards medication and its effects.

A central theme in many of the interviews was the view that the use of medication as treatment for ADHD involved a trade off between formal (educational) and personal goals. On the one hand: the medication was welcomed because it enabled students to succeed in areas where they had previously failed, particularly in the classroom (both socially and academically) and sometimes in the home situation. On the other hand: the price of this success involved personal changes that sometimes led to feelings of discomfort or at least ambivalence. A commonly voiced concern was that Ritalin affected individuals' spontaneity, by calming them down and encouraging them to be quieter and more reflective than they were when they were not taking the medication. Sometimes this trade off was seen as acceptable other times not:

> Sometimes I like it [Ritalin], but sometimes I don't. [. . .] If I do take it when we didn't have school, I wouldn't want to go outside and play with my friends, or, I would just want to stay home by myself and read a book or watch television or something. (Leslie, 14)

Having said this Leslie goes on later in the same interview to describe with great pride how she achieved a very good grade partly, she believes, with the aid of Ritalin:

> [. . .] if I'm on Ritalin, I find it easier to do the work. Or if I don't find it easier I just go up to the teacher for help. And we had to do a report on *The Woman in Black* – the book that we just read – and he helped me on it just a bit. And I was in Ritalin, and I did the whole report by myself, and I didn't ask for anyone's help. And I got an A plus on it, so.

Some students speak of a sense of these effects in terms of their sense of personal identity, often casting their non-Ritalin selves as their authentic selves and the self that is created by the application of Ritalin as a new and different self. Janine is characteristically direct about her preference: 'I like being myself instead of like calm, and everything like that.' Joan echoes these sentiments, providing us with insight into what she sees as the relationship between the medication and problems she experiences in her relationships with others:

> Joan: Well, I'm just being the way I am, and people want me to change. They want me to calm down more. But I do calm down. [pleadingly]

TS: Do you think that you need to calm down?

Joan: Yes. But I still want to be – I still want to have fun.

TS: So, when you calm down, do you feel like you have less fun?

Joan: Yes.

TS: Can you tell me about it: where people have wanted you to calm down?

Joan: Like in the Chinese restaurant. Like if I've had my pills, I don't enjoy – if I've had my pills it makes me too sleepy, and I don't – I do enjoy my food, but I don't eat very much.

[. . .]

[The pills] calm me down, to help me work. They help me calm down, so I don't embarrass my mother.

[. . .]

If I didn't have my tablets [. . .] my mother wouldn't be able to handle me the way that she does.

Joan's account suggests that the main benefits of medication accrue to 'people' other than herself, especially her mother. This view of medication as a means towards making students more socially acceptable is echoed by other students who describe the 'calming' effects of Ritalin (Liam, Jeff), as well as its self-reported effect of making the individual a 'nicer' person (Kate).

These comments portray the use of medication in a very negative light indicating that it is experienced as being used as a control mechanism rather than as a facilitator for other treatments, such as cognitive therapy, social skills training or educational activities. Interestingly many students seem to accept this as a legitimate application for the medication. Two students, however, are less accepting of this. One is Christian, an apparently pro-social student who is keen to succeed in school:

I just don't want to take Ritalin anymore. In my opinion, I never thought that it helped very much. It did help a little bit, but I never thought that it did that much for me. I only take it because if I don't take it they'll chuck me out.

[. . .]

I would probably take it before an exam.

Christian's ambivalence is not matched by Herbert (15), who presents himself as a highly deviant individual, who is both anti-school and a confirmed car thief. He claims to have 'never' heard of attention deficit disorder, and is vehement in his rejection of Ritalin as a treatment:

TS: Do you take tablets?

Herbert: What, Ritalin?

TS: Yeah.

Herbert: No.

TS: Did you ever?

Herbert: No. And I never will either. They muck up my head!

[...]

TS: So, they muck up your head. That would be the bad side. Do you know why people take them? Is there a good side?

Herbert: To calm them down and concentrate on their work. Umm. I don't need that!

TS: Do you think you need help concentrating on your work?

Herbert: No. I can concentrate. As long as there's not a lot of noise. If people can shut up and stop talking, yeah, easy, I can concentrate. But if there's a lot of noise, I won't concentrate. Simple as that. The teachers can't keep the class under control. They don't keep me under control, do they? Simple as that!

It is important to stress that these accounts are not presented as being representative of objective truths about the school these students attend or even about the events they describe. What is being claimed is that what is presented here represents something of these students' authentic thoughts and attitudes. What we can conclude from these latter accounts is that Ritalin is associated with ideas of authority and control for these boys, and that for other students it is seen to serve as a behavioural control function. Having said this, it is also clear that some students welcome the 'calming' and controlling effect of the Ritalin, whereas others reject and resist it.

An important point to note in this section is the almost complete lack of reference by students to interventions other than medication. Though it is true to say that it is common for students to describe the inadequacies of their earlier educational experiences:

Put it this way: a person with ADD – someone with ADHD or ADD would not last five minutes in my [old] school. Because it's all – 'cause they wouldn't know when to go to classes. In my old school it was all very timed – down to the last second – always timed. For instance, [. . .] a lot of people would look at their watches and when their watch said – whenever the time was to stop – they would get up and leave! OK? And that's how it would all work! They all get up at once and leave! [. . .] there was lots of times when the teacher just stopped talking and said: 'that's it'! And then you'd get up and leave. But there was never any bells and buzzers in our school.

Other students describe conflict with staff and the experience of being constantly 'yelled at' (Tom, Kate. Liam). Implicit in their accounts is that they no longer experience these problems, implying that their current educational experience is more conducive to positive involvement and learning. Unfortunately, however, students provide virtually no spontaneous accounts of the measure taken by staff in their current setting.

Conclusion: students' perceptions of ADHD

Every research enterprise has to start somewhere, and this is one of the first systematic study of school students' perceptions of the experience of ADHD to be published in the UK (and, possibly, in the world). The most dangerous (and pointless) thing we could do with the information presented here would be to portray it as being representative of the views of all young people with ADHD. The most useful thing we can do is to take the information presented here for what it is: a set of abstractions drawn from a number of first-hand accounts of individuals who have been reliably diagnosed with ADHD. The fact that these accounts were elicited through the instrument of very loosely structured, non-directive interviews is, we argue, a good reason for having trust in our claim that these are authentic accounts: that is, accounts that represent something of students' genuine thoughts and concerns about the experience of ADHD (see Cooper, 1993c).

The first thing we can conclude from this study is the combined response of these students to the experience of ADHD is highly complex. Almost all of these students see ADHD as a physical and social reality that affects their daily lives and is central to many of these individuals' sense of self. Undoubtedly, as the social psychologist George Herbert Mead (1934) theorized most forcefully, our image of self is influenced to a considerable degree by the image of ourselves that is projected on to us by our 'significant others'. For example, some of the students in this study refer explicitly to the way in which their images of self are influenced by views and perceptions of their parents and others, such as teachers and peers. Nothing in this chapter, therefore, testifies to the biological basis of ADHD. A great deal, however, testifies to the importance of the belief that some social and behavioural characteristics are biologically determined. Many, probably most, of these students see themselves as in some way impaired or damaged. Whether or not there is an objective (possibly biological) reality to these perceptions is immaterial: most of these students operate on the basis of the belief that ADHD is real and that they suffer from it. Furthermore, they experience ADHD as a severely debilitating condition. Within the school ADHD is more stigmatizing than ADD; outside of school ADHD is stigmatizing, as is the medication that is so closely identified with it.

This is not to say that we should dismiss the validity of the ADHD diagnosis for these students, simply because we can detect an element of social construction in its manifestation. It might be the case that the image of an individual is based on an *accurate* (as opposed to fictional) account of his or her actual behaviour. The most important question to ask is: what are the consequences of these beliefs for these students?

Clearly, both the behaviours associated with ADHD and the diagnosis itself are sources of shame for these students: they feel stigmatized. On the other hand, the diagnosis is often welcomed because it provides a rational explanation for their problematic behaviour, and sometimes is associated with relief from guilt about earlier behavioural problems. The diagnosis is also sometimes welcomed because it is seen as a passport to effective treatment in the form of medication. The medication is welcomed by many students because it is experienced as assisting their powers of concentration in the classroom and is in turn associated with educational improvement that some feel would not be possible without the aid of medication. The same students, in some cases, however, express concern about the way in which the medication is perceived to affect their sense of self. This takes the form of the 'real me' being portrayed as the non-medicated self, who, in turn, is sometimes associated with enjoyment and fun. Other students express a negative attitude towards medication and reject or resist it. A common thread uniting many students' (both positive and negative) attitudes towards medication is that it serves a control function. Sometimes the controlling effects of medication are seen by them to serve their personal interests and other times (perhaps mostly) these effects are seen to serve the interests of others (parents, teachers).

A striking feature of these student interviews is the almost universally shared desire to behave in socially acceptable ways and to succeed in school. For the most part the students want to behave in ways that are acceptable to their parents and peers and they want to improve their educational attainment. The ADHD diagnosis and its accompanying medication are seen as means towards these important ends. The negative aspects of these students' accounts, however, are disturbing. Throughout these students' accounts is a sense in which ADHD, its attendant behaviours and medical treatment are associated with a sense of stigma. These students often present themselves as individuals with what Goffman (1968) calls 'spoiled identities'. For these people ADHD is a serious flaw in their personal make up that pervades all aspects of their lives. We suggest that that this is both an unnecessary and unhelpful way of portraying the condition, which has negative effects on students' self-esteem and is, therefore, likely to exacerbate emotional and behavioural problems for some students.

These students present what is essentially a biological determinist account of ADHD, and this is likely to be a function of the ways in which they have been encouraged by adults and professionals to think about the condition. Only one student challenges this view (Herbert) and asserts the importance of environmental factors in relation to concentration problems. Unfortunately, this position is presented from what appears to be an anti-establishment perspective, and is therefore coupled with a rejection of the pro-social and pro-school values and aspirations that other students accept. Clearly, most of these students would benefit from a more balanced view of ADHD, in which the condition is portrayed in terms of the importance of the interaction between psychosocial factors and biological factors. Christian, for example, might well benefit from encouragement to see his distractibility as a problem that is largely the result of the specific demands that schooling places on him and others. By helping him to recognize the ways in which what appears to be negative and unacceptable behaviour in one setting may be desirable and valuable in other setting, damage to his self-esteem might be repaired or avoided. Once schooling is behind him his undoubted specialist talents might come into their own and it will be possible for him to seek working patterns and structures that are more suited to his particular working characteristics. In any event, a recognition of the fact that ADHD is a biopsychosocial phenomenon would be a more accurate account of the condition than the biological determinist account. Such an adjustment of perception might well have a positive effect on these students' self-esteem, as well as their own sense of power and control in relation to the condition. Such understandings might well help students such as these make practical, positive and informed choices about the kinds of settings in which they intend to live or work or study when they leave school.

This chapter has reported on the perceptions, experiences and attitudes of a group of students who are diagnosed with ADHD with particular reference to the condition itself. The outcomes of the study suggest that there are ways in which ADHD can be seen as a positive influence in their lives and ways in which it might be seen as a negative influence. The complexities of these responses indicate the poverty of simplistic responses to ADHD, which seek to either reject ADHD out of hand, or to evangelize the condition as some kind of miracle discovery that will lead to a medical 'cure' for disruptive behaviour. Clearly, this is merely the first step in what should become a major research enterprise that seeks to map the ways in which students construe the experience of having ADHD in different circumstances. The current authors are already engaged in this task and will present further data at a later date.

References

Bowers T (1997) Supporting special needs in the mainstream classroom: children's perceptions of the adult roles. Child Care, Health and Development 23: 217–32.

Bridgeland M (1971) Pioneer Work with Maladjusted Children. London: Staples.

Bruner J, Haste H (1987) Making Sense. London: Cassell.

Cooper P (1993a) Learning from the pupil perspective. British Journal of Special Education 20(4): 129–133.

Cooper P (1993b) Effective Schools for Disaffected Students. London: Routledge.

Cooper P (1993c) Field relations and the problem of authenticity in researching teachers' and students' perceptions of effective teaching and learning. British Educational Research Journal 19(4): 323–38.

Cooper P, McIntyre D (1996) Effective Teaching and Learning: Teachers' and Students' Perspectives. Buckingham: Open University.

Crammond B (1994) ADHD and creativity: Two sides of the same coin? Paper presented at the annual meeting of the American Educational Research Association, New Orleans.

Davie R, Upton G, Varma V (1996) The Voice of the Child. London: Falmer.

DFE (1994) Code of Practice on the Identification and Assessment of Children with Special Educational Needs. London: HMSO.

Goffman E (1968) Stigma. Harmondsworth: Penguin.

Hirst P (1974) Knowledge and the Curriculum. London: Routledge.

Laslett R (1999) Respecting the past, regarding the present. Emotional and Behavioural Difficulties, in press.

Lloyd-Smith M, Dwyfor-Davies J (1995) On the Margins. Stoke-on-Trent: Trentham.

Mead G (1934) Mind, Self and Society. Chicago IL: University of Chicago.

Norwich B (1997) Exploring the perspectives of adolescents with moderate learning difficulties on their special schooling and themselves: stigma and self-perceptions. European Journal of Special Needs Education 12(1): 38–53.

O'Brien T (1996) Challenging behaviour: challenging an intervention. Support for Learning 11(4): 162–4.

Powney J, Watts M (1987) Interviewing in Educational Research. London: Routledge.

Prior P (1997) Peer review of 'The myth of the myth of ADHD: Notes towards a constructive view of ADHD', by Paul Cooper. Education Section Review 21(1): 17–21.

Slee R (1995) Changing Theories and Practices of Discipline. London: Falmer.

Vygotsky L (1987) The Collected Works of LS Vygotsky, edited by R Reiber and A Carton. London: Plenum.

Wakefield J (1992) The concept of mental disorder: on the boundary between biological fact and social values. American Psychologist 47: 373–88.

Index

abdominal pain 72
academic issues 232–4, 239
accidents 3, 15, 177
acetylcholine 97
aconite 130
acupuncture 78, 112–13, 134
addiction 73, 82, 85, 94, 100
adoption 7, 179–80
aerosols 105, 115
Africa 170, 204
aftershave 96, 105
aggression 3, 18, 26, 29, 56, 175, 229
    classroom strategies 214, 218
    complementary therapies 117, 129
    diet 79
    effective learning 140, 152
    medication 63, 73
alcohol 81, 94, 100–1, 103–4
allergies 113, 114, 122, 127
    diet 78, 81, 84–5, 88, 90, 95, 98, 102–4
aloe vera 127
aluminium 86
American Psychiatric Association 3
    DSM 43–4, 187, 193, 194, 198, 205, 234
antecedent, behaviour and consequences (ABC)
    approach 204–5
antibiotics 68, 79, 82, 93, 98, 101. 105, 127
    colourings 95, 98
antidepressants 70
anxiety and anxiety disorder 4, 11, 25, 51, 60, 80

complementary therapies 121, 126, 129
appetite 67, 72
apples 93
argentum nitrum 129
aromatherapy 77, 113–18
    with Bach remedies 117–18, 121
    with homeopathy 130
art 54, 232
arthritis 82, 90, 94, 104
Asperger's syndrome 60, 79, 104
aspirin 88
assessment 12, 26, 43–59, 63, 64–5, 140, 225–6
    classroom strategies 203–7
    teacher's account 178, 179, 180, 181–2
    teamwork 188, 193
asthma 60, 68, 73
    colour therapy 125
    diet 81, 82, 85, 88, 92
atropine 129
attainment and achievement targets 47, 54, 55, 141
attention deficit disorder (ADD) 8, 26, 235–7, 241, 243
    multi-modal approach 56–9, 62
    teacher's account 180–1
attention span 52–3, 54, 79, 103, 125, 152
attention training devices 47–9
Attention Training System (ATS) 49
aura 119, 125
Australia 38, 62, 66–7, 71, 122
autism 10, 44

complementary therapies 125, 132, 135

diet 79, 81, 96, 97, 99, 103

azo–dyes 83, 86, 88, 95

babies 14–16, 170, 177–8

complementary therapies 116–18, 120, 123, 127–8, 131–5

diet 82, 92, 96, 105

Bach flower remedies 105, 118–22

with aromatherapy 117–18, 121

with osteopathy 132

bad language 20, 29, 30, 214

Bailey essences 122

bananas 83, 93, 95, 97, 113

baths 87, 116

bed-wetting 82

behavioural expectations 140, 147, 149, 183, 220

belladonna 129

beta-glucuronidase 102

betonica 127

biopsychosocial approach 7–11, 60, 139–40, 244

teamwork 192, 196

blackcurrant seed oil 88

borage oil (star flower) 88

boredom 15, 29, 44, 80, 156

Bowen therapy 78, 118, 122–4

brain and brain dysfunction 4–5, 6–8, 26, 139

basal ganglia 91

Broca's area 135

complementary therapies 114–15, 119, 124, 127, 129–35

diet 79, 81–3, 85–7, 89, 91–9, 101, 103, 105

frontal lobes 4, 6, 45–6, 81, 91–3, 103

hemispheres 57, 130

hypothalamus 114

medication 60, 68

multi-modal approach 43, 45, 56–7, 60, 68

pia mater 130

teamwork 195, 196, 199

telling the child 195, 199

breast feeding 90, 92, 105

British Medical Association 78

bullying 80, 125

butter 113

cadmium 86, 104

calcium 86, 88

calendula oil 116

camomilla 101

Canada 67, 204, 225, 226

candida 93–4, 102

carbohydrates 86, 89–90

catarrh 82, 94, 122, 130, 135

cat's claw 127

causation 4, 5, 25–6, 223

dietary factors 82–98

perceptions of professionals 187–8, 193, 196–7, 200–1

Centre Academy 43–5, 49, 52–3

cerato 122

chakras 125

chamomile 127

cheese 83, 93, 95, 97, 113

chemicals 86

complementary therapies 115, 116

diet 83, 86, 87, 90, 93, 96, 99, 104

cherry plum 120

chestnut bud 120, 122

chewing gum 101

chicory 120, 122

China 112–13

chocolate 36, 83, 87, 93, 95, 97

chromosomal abnormalities 79, 81

cigarette smoking 196

complementary therapies 115, 122, 131

diet 83, 86–8, 94, 96, 100, 101, 104–5

clary sage 117, 130

class clowning 19, 47, 130, 196

cleaning materials 96

clonidine 70

clothing 17, 21, 31

clumsiness 79, 82, 87, 92

coeliac disease 93, 101

coffee 100, 104

cognitive approach 4–6, 8–10, 158–69, 224–5, 240

cognitive behaviour modification (CBM) 158–68

cognitive behaviour therapy (CBT) 160, 167

cognitive style 153–4, 219

cognitive training (CT) 165, 166

cola drinks 100, 104

colour therapy 124–6

colourings 83, 86, 95, 98, 113
combined subtype 3, 5–6, 44, 187, 193, 227
complementary therapies 76–8, 101, 111–37
complexion 94, 113, 122
computerized transaxial tomography (CT scan) 6, 93
concentration 231–2, 233, 237–9, 241, 243–4
    complementary therapies 122, 127, 129, 130
    diet 91, 92
    effective learning 141, 146, 148, 155
    medication 61–2, 64, 66, 68–9, 73
    mother's story 21, 23, 26
    multi-modal approach 52, 56–8, 61–2, 64, 66, 68–9, 73
    perceptions of professionals 194, 198, 199
conduct disorder 4, 11, 99, 125
    medication 60, 61, 63, 69, 70
confrontation tasks 55, 56
congestion 87, 101, 135
co-ordination problems 60
counselling 23, 51–2, 194, 203
cow's milk 36, 113, 129, 135
    diet 83, 85, 86, 88, 90, 93, 97, 105
crab apple 117
cradle cap 82, 88
cranium 130–1
creativity 153, 154, 234
criminality 4, 126, 241
    diet 81, 99–100, 103, 105
Crohn's disease 82
curriculum 47–8, 171, 203
    effective learning 144, 146, 154, 155
Cylert 67

dandelions 127
dangerousness 230–1
Denmark 91
depression 4, 24–5, 34–5, 170, 181
    complementary therapies 119, 121, 122, 127
    medication 60, 64, 70, 72
    multi-modal approach 56, 60, 64, 70, 72
    parents 11
Dexedrine (dexamphetamine) 67–8, 71, 72

diagnosis 3–4, 12, 54–9, 78–82, 180–3, 197–9, 234–8
    biopsychosocial approach 8–9, 11
    classroom strategies 203, 220
    complementary therapies 112
    dietary factors 76–9, 80–2, 84–5, 100
    effective learning 139
    evidence-based 78–9
    experience of ADHD 33, 35, 223–7, 234–8, 242–4
    mother's story 23, 24, 25–6
    multi-modal approach 43–6, 50, 52–3, 54–9, 61–6, 70, 75
    teacher's account 171–2, 173, 176–9, 180–3
    teamwork 187–8, 192–5, 197–9, 200–1
diaphragm 131, 132
diet 36, 76–110, 193–4
    complementary therapies 112–13, 123, 128, 131, 132
    medication 62, 62, 63, 70
digit span test 54, 55, 57
disorganisation 3, 18, 21, 31, 136, 152
    multi-modal approach 47–8, 52, 53, 54, 56
disruptive behaviour 3, 17, 23, 227–8
    classroom strategies 214–16, 218–20
    complementary therapies 130
    effective learning 141, 144
    experience of ADHD 223, 227–8, 235, 244
    multi-modal approach 49, 51, 54, 56–7, 66
    teacher's account 170, 180, 181–2
distractions and distractibility 18–19, 172, 182
    classroom strategies 205, 208, 212, 213, 215, 218
    cognitive approach 166
    effective learning 145–6, 147, 148, 152, 155
    experience of ADHD 35, 231, 233, 237, 239
    multi-modal approach 46–7, 53, 55, 58, 61, 64, 66, 73
doctors and paediatricians 23, 52–3, 139, 203
    complementary therapies 78, 101, 115, 128, 133
    diet 104

experience of ADHD 36, 38, 225–6
multi-modal approach 44–6, 52–3,
    62–4, 66, 70
teacher's account 177, 178, 179, 182
teamwork 188–90, 192
dopamine 7, 94, 97
drug abuse 94, 100, 131
dysgraphia 55, 56
dyslexia 4, 227, 232
complementary therapies 125, 129,
    132, 134, 136
diet 79, 81, 88, 97, 104
multi-modal approach 44, 56–9, 60,
    64
teacher's account 170, 177
dyspraxia 79, 132

ear problems 81, 82, 87, 135
echinacea 127
eczema 82, 85, 88, 92, 122
Egger, Professor 81, 82, 88, 93, 94
eggs 83
Egypt 114
Einstein, Albert 78, 83
electroencephalography (EEG) 6, 91–3
emotional and behavioural difficulties
    (EBD) 63, 183, 224
employment 34, 38, 100
mother's story 20, 22, 23
English 181, 232–3
classroom strategies 204, 207–11,
    213–14, 216, 219
environmental factors 7, 9–11, 24, 131,
    140, 166
classroom 171, 220
diet 78, 81–2, 88–9, 99, 102, 104
effective learning 138, 139, 140, 152,
    155
experience of ADHD 37, 223, 225,
    244
multi-modal approach 44–6, 49, 52,
    61, 63
teamwork 188–90, 193, 196,
    197–201
enzyme-potentiated desensitization
    (EPD) 85, 100, 102–3
enzymes 85–6, 87–8, 94–5, 97–8, 100,
    102–4
epilepsy 134, 173
die 81, 92, 93
essential fatty acids (EFAs) 87–8

diet 85, 86, 87–8, 94, 98, 101, 105
eucalyptus 101, 121, 130
evening primrose oil 88, 116
exorphins 85

families 3, 7–8
brother's story 28–32
complementary therapies 112–13,
    119, 121, 133, 137
diet 76, 79–82, 86, 94, 101, 103–4
effective learning 139, 150
experience of ADHD 33–8, 229, 231,
    234
mother's story 14–27
multi-modal approach 44, 51–2, 62,
    64, 66, 70, 74–5
teacher's account 170, 173, 176,
    178–9
see also parents; siblings
fathers 11, 36, 37, 64, 122
brother's story 28–9
diet 86, 87, 92, 96
mother's story 16, 21
teacher's account 173, 177, 178
fear 80, 119, 121, 126, 130
feedback 47, 53, 161, 175, 182, 192
classroom strategies 206, 213, 215,
    218
effective learning 143, 147
feet 134–5
Feingold hypothesis 83, 96
finger oscillations 55–6
fingernails with white flecks 87, 92
fish 83, 88, 90
fits 82, 103
see also epilepsy
flavourings 83, 86, 113
flax seed oil 88
food intolerance 82–5
complementary therapies 122, 125,
    127, 135
diet 78, 81, 82–5, 91, 93, 96, 105
France 115
friends 35, 101, 239
brother's story 30, 31–2
mother's story 16, 20–2
multi-modal approach 64, 74
teacher's account 173, 176, 178, 180
Frith, U 188, 193, 196–7, 200–1
fruit and vegetables 83, 90, 92, 93
frustration 53, 65, 125, 173, 228, 232

diet 79, 80
    mother's story 15, 17, 26
further education 19, 30, 34, 37, 236

gambling 30–1
gamma-linolenic acid (GLA) 88
GCSEs 19, 225
gender 3, 79, 208–9, 225, 227, 228
genetics 4, 7, 8–9, 11, 60, 94–6, 139
    diet 89, 91, 94–6, 101, 104
    perceptions of professionals 190,
        193, 196
    see also inheritance
geranium oil 117
Germany 81, 83, 225
gifted children 44, 80
Gimbel, Theo 124, 125
ginkgo biloba 127
glucose 60
glyconutrient deficiency 88–91
glycoproteins 89–90, 94, 99
grapeseed oil 116
Greece 114, 128
group work 62, 172
    classroom strategies 205, 206,
        211–13, 217–18
    effective learning 144–5, 148
growing out of ADHD 4, 63, 99, 193
growth retardation 72, 103, 178
guilt 237, 243
gut factors 93–6, 98–9, 102, 105, 127
gut flora 82, 93–4, 96, 98

Hahnemann 128
hay fever 85, 88
head lice 97–8
headaches 72, 87, 103, 130
healing crisis 134
health authorities 188–91, 200
hearing 45, 46, 55, 57, 58, 144
    complementary therapies 135, 136
    diet 80, 81, 82, 87
heather 120, 122
heavy metal toxicity 81, 86
herbal medicine 126–7
Hippocrates 113, 114, 128
hippus 125
history 204, 207–11, 213, 216, 217, 219
holidays 18
holly 118, 120, 122
homeopathy 118, 121, 127–30

diet 77, 78, 85, 96
homeostasis 89
homework 19, 48, 74, 87, 146, 152,
        228–9
    teacher's account 175–6, 177, 180,
        183
hop grains 127
hormones 89, 102, 104, 114, 115, 131
hornbeam 122
hospital schools 174
hyoscine 129
hyoscyamus 129
Hyperactive Children's Support Group
        (HCSG) 36, 83, 86
hyperactive-impulsive subtype 3, 5–6,
        44, 227, 228
    perceptions of professionals 187,
        193
hyperactivity 3, 8, 43–4, 46, 56–7, 59
    classroom strategies 205, 208–9,
        215–17
    cognitive approaches 158, 164,
        165–6, 168
    complementary therapies 113, 117,
        120, 125, 132, 134–5
    diet 79, 81–4, 86–7, 91–2, 93, 96,
        100, 104
    effective learning 144
    experience of ADHD 36, 223, 227–8,
        232, 234–5
    medication 60–4, 66, 68, 70, 72–3
    mother's story 15–16, 18, 26
    perceptions of professionals 187,
        193, 197
    teacher's account 180–1
hyperkinesis 43, 61, 66, 79, 113, 170
hypnotherapy 136

ibuprofen 88, 105
ignoring undesirable behaviour (I) 206,
        211, 214–25,
        217–18
    effective learning 143, 149
immune system 87, 89, 98, 99, 102, 105,
        127
impatience 5, 15, 26, 152
impatiens 118, 120, 122
impulsiveness and impulsivity 3–5, 35,
        223, 227–31, 234
    classroom strategies 205, 208–9,
        215–16, 217

cognitive approaches 160, 164, 166, 168
diet 79
effective learning139–40, 152, 154
medication 60–4, 68, 70
mother's story 19–22, 26
multi-modal approach 44–7, 49, 51, 54–8, 60–4, 68, 70
perceptions of professionals 187, 193
teacher's account 175
inattentive subtype 3, 5, 187, 193, 227
multi-modal approach 43, 44, 46, 61–2, 64, 74
inheritance 7, 8, 11, 139, 187, 199, 236
see also genetics
instructions 182
cognitive approaches 159–61, 163–4, 166, 168
effective learning 143, 145, 146, 152
see also student instructions (SI)
intellect and intelligence 24, 57, 58, 61
diet 79, 86, 100, 103
intolerance 15, 18–20, 53
iron 86
irritable bowel 81, 82, 93, 94, 104

jasmine 118
jealousy 118, 119, 120
juniper 117

language problems 60, 69, 80, 135–6, 144, 228
complementary therapies 112, 132, 135–6
larch 118, 121
lavender 87, 101, 117, 120
laziness 3, 18, 34, 141–2
lead 86, 101
leaky gut syndrome 94, 95, 96, 98
Learning Assessment Centre 178–9
learning difficulties 4, 44, 191
classroom strategies 203–4
complementary therapies 132, 134
diet 79, 81
effective learning 142–3, 150, 153, 156
medication 60, 61, 66, 69
learning from mistakes 15, 16, 120
lemon balm 127
linseed oil 88

literacy 136, 141, 148, 227, 232
classroom strategies 210, 219
see also reading; spelling; writing
liver function 95, 96, 127
lycopodium 129

macrophages 102
magnesium 86, 88, 96, 101
magnetic resonance imaging (MRI) 6, 91
management 12, 43–59, 64, 65–6, 226
classroom strategies 203–22
teamwork 192, 194, 197–9
mandarin oil 117
mannans 127
marjoram 117, 118
massage 77, 113, 116, 118
maths 54, 55, 57, 181
classroom strategies 204, 207–11, 213–14, 216, 219
mealtimes 17, 21, 29, 54, 92
medication 10, 23, 66–75, 141, 217
classroom strategies 214, 217, 218, 220
cognitive approaches 158, 159, 160, 165–6, 167
complementary therapies 76–9, 81, 88, 93, 100–4, 115, 128, 131
effective learning 138–9, 141
experience of ADHD 36–7, 223, 226, 235, 238–41, 243
multi-modal approach 50, 52–3, 56, 59, 60–75
perceptions of professionals 194–6, 198, 199–201
teacher's account 171–3, 174, 176, 178, 179–83
see also Ritalin
medorrhinum 129
melatonin 92
memory 5, 18, 21, 55, 57, 68, 73
classroom 180, 214
complementary therapies 127, 136
diet 91, 101
effective learning 147
meninges 130–2
methylphenidate 67, 141, 166, 217, 238
dietary factors 76, 94, 98, 103
see also Ritalin
miasms 128–9

microwave cooking 90
migraine 81, 82, 92–4, 97, 104
mild punishment (MP) and reprimands
    206, 211, 213, 217–19
  effective learning 147, 148, 150
  mother's story 19
  teacher's account 183
Miller neutralization technique 85
minerals 86
  diet 85, 86, 87, 101–1, 102
money 21–2, 29, 30–2
monosodium glutamate (MSG) 83
mood swings 68, 92, 97, 122, 130
moro reflex 133
Morrell reflexology 135
mothers 10–11, 14–27, 36
  brother's story 28–9
  complementary therapies 113, 122,
    125
  diet 82, 86–7, 90–1, 94, 96, 101, 105
  multi-modal approach 47, 51, 63
  teacher's account 173–80, 183
motivation 5, 10, 34, 167, 180, 193
  complementary therapies 136
  effective learning 141, 148, 152, 153
  mother's story 19, 20–2, 23, 26
  multi-modal approach 48–9, 54,
    61–2
motor sequencing 56
moxibustion 112, 113
mucus 95, 98, 101, 113
multi-modal approach 43–59, 76, 138,
    182, 200, 218, 225
  medication 60–75
multi-dimensional model 12, 187
multi-disciplinary approach 43, 65, 171,
    187–201
mushrooms 113
music 204, 207–11, 213, 214–17, 219
mustard 122
myrtle 101

neurology and neurobiology 4, 6–9,
    188, 196, 201
neuropsychiatry 192
neuropsychology 9, 44, 45, 54
neurotransmitters 7, 97–9
  diet 87, 89, 94, 95–6, 97–9, 104
New Zealand 122
noradrenalin 97
numeracy 141, 173

see also maths

oak pine 122
obsession 16–17, 60, 70, 117
off-task behaviour 68, 73, 147, 156
  classroom strategies 206–7, 216, 217,
    219
oligo-antigenic 84
on-task behaviour 206–7, 213, 216, 219
oppositional defiant disorder 4, 11, 64,
    68
oppositionality 18, 26, 228–30
  multi-modal approach 51, 60, 61, 64,
    70, 73
  teacher's account 171, 177
oranges 36, 83, 87, 93, 113
organophosphates (OPs) 97–8
orienting response 98
osteopathy 130–2

paracetamol 95, 96, 105
parasites 94, 98, 102
parents 7–8, 10–11, 14–27, 50–2
  cognitive approaches 158, 159, 165
  complementary therapies 117, 123
  diet 79–82, 83–4, 86, 91–3, 96, 101,
    104
  effective learning 141, 155
  experience of ADHD 33, 35–8, 225,
    229, 231, 234–5, 240,
    242–3
  medication 62, 65–70, 74
  multi-modal approach 44–6, 49–54,
    56, 58–9, 62, 65–70,
    74
  teacher's account 170–1, 173, 177–83
  teamwork 191, 194–200
  see also fathers; mothers
pastoral care in schools 155–6
pedagogical strategy (PED) 206, 211,
    214, 217, 218
peers and peer groups 3, 10, 49–50,
    136, 158
  classroom strategies 212, 213, 218
  diet 85
  effective learning 139, 142
  experience of ADHD 36–7, 229, 237,
    242, 243
  mother's story 17, 19, 20–1
  teacher's account 174, 175, 177
pemoline (Cylert) 67, 238

peppermint 121, 130
peptides 85–6, 89, 93–5, 97–9, 127
perfume 83, 86, 87, 96, 105, 115
personality change with medication 72
phenolic compounds 94–6, 97, 98–9
phosphates 83
phosphorus 130
phytotherapy 126–7
play therapy 173
playgroups 18–19
polymorphs 102
positive reinforcement (PR) 206,
    210–12, 215, 217–20
positron electromography (PET) 91
possessiveness 16, 18
pregnancy 196
    complementary therapies 113,
        117–18, 122–4, 131–2
    diet 91, 92, 101, 104–5
preservatives 83, 86, 87
prevalence rates 3
privacy 20
problem-solving 159, 160, 161, 163–4,
    167
prostaglandins 87, 88
psychiatry 38, 174, 180, 192
    medication 62, 63, 70
psychobiological approach 44
psychological, irritable bowel, migraine
        syndrome
        (PIMS) 81, 82
psychology and psychologists 3, 80,
    173, 178, 203, 242
    effective learning 139, 151
    multi-modal approach 44–6, 49,
        52–3
    teamwork 191, 192
psychometric testing 203
psychosocial factors 60, 62, 196, 244
    effective learning 138–9, 140, 141
psychotherapy 173, 180
pulsatilla 130

quantitative electroencephalogram
    (QEEG) 60

reading 54, 57, 58, 232
    classroom strategies 208, 210
    teacher's account 173, 177, 178
rebound effect 72, 73, 172
red wine 95

reflex inhibition 132–4, 135
reflexology 134–5
reframing technique 150–3
repetitive tasks 146, 152, 182
rescue remedy 121, 122
response inhibition 4, 7, 187, 193, 196,
    197
rewards 19, 48–9, 159, 163, 182, 206
    effective learning 145, 147–9, 156
rhinitis 82
Ritalin 64, 67–9, 71–2, 128, 217, 238–41
    diet 76, 99, 103
    effective learning 141
    teacher's account 171, 174, 176, 178,
        181, 183
rollercoaster effect 54
Roman chamomile 101, 117, 118
rose 118
rules 47, 53, 54, 144, 149, 166, 194, 216
Rutter, Michael 63

salicylate 83, 88, 96
sarcasm 148, 149, 151
schools 3–4, 9, 170–84, 203–22
    brother's story 28, 30
    cognitive approaches 158–9, 168
    complementary therapies 112, 122,
        130, 132, 133
    diet 80, 87, 92, 96, 100, 101, 103
    effective learning 138, 140, 141–3,
        153, 154–6
    exclusion 4, 170, 174, 177, 220, 229
    experience of ADHD 34, 35, 224–32,
        234–44
    medication 63–71, 73–4
    mother's story 18–19, 23
    multi-modal approach 44–55, 58–9,
        63–71, 73–4
    teamwork 189–91, 193–4, 197–200
    see also teachers
schizophrenia 84, 92, 126
science and technology 175, 176, 181
scleranthus 122
scotopic sensitivity syndrome 177
scutellaria 127
seating 145–6, 152, 172, 182
    arrangements (SA) 206, 211, 212,
        215, 217–18
secondary schools 19, 203
    teacher's account 170–1, 174, 176,
        180, 183

self-assessment 161
self-control 5, 26, 136, 194–5, 229, 238
   cognitive approaches 158–61, 164,
     166, 168
self-esteem 26, 100, 175, 177, 234, 236,
   244
   complementary therapies 117, 122,
     125, 129
   effective learning 140–1, 145, 147,
     151, 153, 156
   medication 60–1, 64, 68–9, 71, 73–4
   multi-modal approach 48, 50
   teamwork 193, 196, 200
self-evaluation 161, 162, 164, 166
self-healing 77, 111–12, 123, 127, 134
self-instruction 159–60, 161, 163–4,
   166, 168
self-management 165, 167, 168
self-monitoring 161–3, 164–6, 168
self-observation 161, 162, 163
self-reinforcement 159, 160, 161, 163,
   165
self-talk 5, 144, 158, 160, 161, 164
self-worth 224
serotonin 97
Shipley Project 100
siblings 28–32, 33, 79, 170–1
   mother's story 16–23
side effects 71–5, 172, 178
   complementary therapies 115, 128
   medication 66, 67–8, 71–5, 77, 79,
     103
silica 130
single photon emission computerized
   tomography (SPECT)
   scans 60, 91
skin problems 72, 82, 88, 129
sleep 176–8
   complementary therapies 113, 117,
     120, 122, 126–7,
     129, 132
   diet 81, 82, 91–2, 93, 101, 103
   medication 67, 70, 72, 103
smell 114–18
smoking see cigarette smoking
social learning theory 187
socialization and social skills 3, 10, 136,
   178
   cognitive approaches 159, 164–7
   effective learning 139–41, 144–5,
     148, 152

experience of ADHD 225, 235, 239,
   240, 243
   multi-modal approach 49–50, 56,
     60–1, 63–5, 68–9, 73–4
special educational needs 170, 171,
   175, 224–5
special schools 63, 174, 203–22, 225
speech problems 60, 69, 80, 135–6,
   144, 228
   complementary therapies 112, 132,
     135–6
spelling 57, 208, 232
spiritual healing 136
sport and PE 16, 22, 50, 54, 155, 180
statementing 174
steroids 88, 92
Still, George 8, 43, 187
stramonium 129
stress 48, 51, 66, 230
   complementary therapies 115, 117,
     131
   diet 87, 88, 100, 104
   mother's story 15, 17–18, 23, 25–6
student instruction (SI) 206, 211, 213,
   217–19
sugars 36, 113
   diet 83, 85, 88–90, 94, 99, 102, 105
suicide 33, 181
sulphate deficiency 95, 96, 98
sulphur 129
support groups 36, 51, 67, 68

tangerine oil 117
tantrums 175
   complementary therapies 120, 130,
     133
   diet 82, 92
   mother's story 15–19
tap water 83, 101
teachers 8, 10, 19, 170–84
   classroom strategies 203–22
   cognitive approaches 159, 161–8
   complementary therapies 122
   diet 80, 103
   effective learning 141–51, 153–6
   experience of ADHD 36, 224–5, 228,
     230, 235, 239, 241–3
   medication 61, 66–8, 103
   multi-modal approach 45–7, 49–54,
     56–8, 61, 66–8
   teamwork 191, 195, 198, 200

thirst 79, 82, 88
thrush 94
tics 67, 70, 72, 103, 230
time-out 47, 143, 148–9, 183
    classroom strategies 206, 211, 214,
        217, 218
token economies 149, 212, 218
tomatoes 83, 93
toothpaste 101, 130
Tourette's syndrome 72, 79, 103, 132
toxins 6, 81, 86, 125, 127, 134
toys 15, 17, 18
trace elements 85
tuberculinum 129
twin studies 7, 94, 139

United States of America 38, 122, 151,
        158, 170, 225
    classroom strategies 203, 204, 215,
        220
    diet 90–2, 94, 99–101
    medication 62, 66, 67, 71
urticaria 82, 103

vaccination 99, 127
vallerian root 127
verbal fluency 55, 56
vervain 118, 120
vetivert 117
vigilance 45–6, 56, 58
vinca minor 127
vine 122
vision 45, 46, 57, 80, 81
vitamins 86
    diet 77, 85–8, 100–2

walnut 122
water violet 122
wheat 83, 85, 88, 97, 105
willow 120
writing 148, 173, 178–9, 210, 233

ylang ylang 117
yoga 136

zinc 86–8, 92–3, 101, 104, 105